JADE MOUNTAINS & CINNABAR POOLS

知人未易相知實
難情美初交利
乘歲空償生徒心
飽卅必安寧情複亮
含名俱完

弘祖

JADE MOUNTAINS & CINNABAR POOLS

THE HISTORY OF TRAVEL LITERATURE IN IMPERIAL CHINA

JAMES M. HARGETT

A Samuel and Althea Stroum Book

UNIVERSITY OF WASHINGTON PRESS
Seattle

Jade Mountains and Cinnabar Pools was supported by generous grants from the Samuel and Althea Stroum Endowed Book Fund and the Chiang Ching-kuo Foundation for International Scholarly Exchange.

COVER ARTWORK: (*front*) After Tang Yin (Chinese, 1470–1524), *Landscape for Zhao Yipeng.* Hanging scroll; ink and color on silk, 71.1 × 139.7 cm. Purchase, Bequest of Dorothy Graham Bennett. Metropolitan Museum of Art, 67.6.1. (*back*) *Xuanzang on His Journey to the West* (Xuanzang xixing tu 玄奘西行圖), Wikimedia Commons.

FRONTISPIECE: One of the few surviving calligraphy samples written by Xu Xiake (1587–1641), which reproduces a text attributed to Tao Yuanming (or Tao Qian; 365–427) concerning the exemplary friendship bond between two famous figures of antiquity: Bao Shuya (d. 644 BCE) and Guan Zhong (ca. 720–645 BCE). The first line reads: "To come to know someone has never been easy, but to really know someone is truly difficult" (知人未易, 相知實難). Calligraphy sample courtesy of the Xu Xiake Research Society, Jiangyin, Jiangsu, People's Republic of China.

DEDICATION PHOTOGRAPH: Rick (left) and author, Louisville, Kentucky, 2009.

UNIVERSITY OF WASHINGTON PRESS
www.washington.edu/uwpress

LIBRARY OF CONGRESS CATALOGING-IN-PUBLICATION DATA
Names: Hargett, James M. (James Morris), author.
Title: Jade mountains and cinnabar pools : the history of travel literature in imperial China / James M. Hargett.
Description: Seattle, WA : University of Washington Press, [2018] | Includes bibliographical references and index. |
Identifiers: LCCN 2018011972 (print) | LCCN 2018043870 (ebook) | ISBN 9780295744483 (ebook) | ISBN 9780295744469 (hardcover : alk. paper) | ISBN 9780295744476 (pbk. : alk. paper)
Subjects: LCSH: Travel writing—China—History. | Travelers' writings, Chinese—History and criticism
Classification: LCC PL2278.5.T72 (ebook) | LCC PL2278.5.T72 H37 2018 (print) | DDC 895.109/32—dc23
LC record available at https://lccn.loc.gov/2018011972

In memory of
Richard ("Rick") Sterman Hutchison
29 June 1947–6 March 2011

The best man I ever knew;
The best friend I ever had.

既為君子, 又為摯友.

CONTENTS

PREFACE

Traveling—it leaves you speechless, then turns you into a storyteller.

TRADITIONALLY ATTRIBUTED TO MUHAMMAD

IBN BATTUTA (1304–68 OR 69)

This is the first book-length history written in English or any other European language of traditional Chinese travel literature. The chronological breadth is vast, extending from the Six Dynasties period (220–589) to the late Ming dynasty (1368–1644). Although this book is intended primarily for colleagues and students in the field of Chinese literature, I have tried to keep technical sinological matters to a minimum so that specialists working in European and American travel literature and even the general reader might benefit from the results of this investigation.

There are few published critical histories of traditional Chinese literature that cover extended periods of time. The reason for this lacuna revealed itself during the preparation of this book: writing literary history poses daunting challenges. The biggest question of all, of course, is, *How* should one write a literary history? What are the priorities? What should be included and what excluded? How does one structure and organize a literary history? And how exactly do we define what is "literary" and distinguish the good literature from all the rest?

As many scholars before me have observed, there are diverse ways of organizing and talking about that enormous and heterogeneous body of written material we call "literature." Usually, one of two approaches is adopted and almost always with some modification and tweaking involved: either the material is arranged according to form or type ("the novel and its development in England"), which is called "genre study"; or else different genres of literature are discussed in a chronological framework that is usually organized by period(s) ("Victorian Period Literature, 1837–1990"), which is usually referred to as "literary history." This investigation combines both approaches in that it seeks to trace the development of a type of prose literature—travel writing—in China from about the fourth to the early seventeenth centuries. I certainly could have organized my study of ancient Chinese travel literature in other ways. For instance, I could have followed the so-called literary-biography approach and concentrated on key and influential authors, or I could have adopted the "historical-cultural" approach, which seeks to interpret the literary work in its historical and cultural context—to "get inside" the text and the author and the time in which he or she lived. My approach is to consider travel literature as a distinct literary form and then to look at it through different periods of development. The details of this process are outlined and explained in the introduction.

The most essential, characteristic elements of prose travel literature in China emerged during the Six Dynasties. Many of these key features, along with some new ones that came afterward, will be identified in chapter 1 and then traced in the works of subsequent writers in the chapters that follow. What is uniquely fascinating about Chinese travel literature, however, is that many authors, while writing within the general, traditional form and structure of the genre established in the Six Dynasties, changed and adapted it to suit their own personal tastes and needs. Presenting examples of how important and influential authors through the dynasties modified the content of their travel writing provides a systematic framework in which to discuss the material and outline the genre's evolution and development over time. Moreover, highlighting how different authors changed and adapted their travel works at once eliminates the kind of generalization, homogeneity, and vagueness that sometimes weighs heavily on literary history and, on the contrary, highlights the distinctive qualities that define individual masterpieces of the genre. I am aware, of course, that there is a huge body of *shi*—"lyric poetry" dating from the traditional period in China—that deals with travel. I shall severely limit my discussion of such works in this study, however, because the lyrical-expressive modes common in travel poetry are quite different from those found in prose. For this reason, it is my view that verse about journeys in ancient China deserves treatment in a separate study.

Since I view the publication of this book as the capstone of my career as a sinologist, I respectfully acknowledge those mentors who throughout my life have supported and guided me on what has been a most wonderful journey: Albert Berkowitz, Eugene Chen Eoyang (Ouyang Zhen 歐陽楨),

Edward F. Kennelly, Henry Tien-k'un Kuo (Guo Diankun 郭殿坤), Wu-chi Liu (Liu Wuji 柳無忌), Irving Yu-cheng Lo (Luo Yuzheng 羅郁正), Coach Steve Miska, William H. Taft Jr., Eugenia Y. Tu, and Wei-p'ing Wu (Wu Weiping 吳衛平). I owe them all a tremendous debt of gratitude.

Colleagues and friends who have helped with this book project include Jonathan Chaves, Robert E. Harrist Jr., Charles Hartman, Jianye He (He Jianye 何劍葉), Sherry Ho (He Xianlei 何仙蕾), Alister D. Inglis, Lau Nap-Yin (Liu Liyan 柳立言), Li Cho-ying (Li Zhuoying 李卓穎), Luo Manling 羅曼玲, William H. Nienhauser Jr., Ren Xiaomei 任小枚, Deborah Rudolph, Richard E. Strassberg, Julian Ward, Wu Jen-shu (Wu Renshu 巫仁恕), Xu Yongming 徐永明, Robert Yandle, Shu-han Yeh (Ye Shuhan 葉淑涵), and Cong Ellen Zhang (Zhang Cong 張聰).

I am also indebted to the two anonymous readers who reviewed my manuscript for the University of Washington Press, both of whom produced extended, informed, and useful commentary that helped tremendously in my revision work, and to Lorri Hagman and Richard Feit, whose attention to consistency and clarity greatly improved the readability of this book.

Finally, I express warm thanks to the Center for Chinese Studies at the National Central Library in Taiwan, which generously provided me with research support during the spring semester of 2017.

Taipei, Taiwan
15 January 2018

SPECIAL MATTERS AND TECHNICAL TERMS

Translations and Annotations

Except where otherwise noted, all translations from the Chinese are my own. I have made every effort to streamline footnote content, but in many cases, longer and more detailed information is necessary. In the footnote references and bibliography, if a Chinese language work also includes a title in English, I mark the head of that title with an asterisk. Example: "Wan Ming youji wenxue yanjiu" 晚明遊記文學研究 (*Study on travel literature in Late Ming Dynasty).

Chinese Characters

Chinese characters for personal names, places, and other terms are provided in the Glossary-Index. When necessary for discussion of terminology, characters occasionally appear in the text. Traditional (or full-form) characters (*fanti zi* 繁體字) are used.

Romanization

For spelling of Chinese names and terms, I use Hanyu Pinyin. When quoting earlier publications using alternate romanization systems, except for titles of articles and books, I convert the older spelling to Hanyu Pinyin.

Place Names

Traditional and modern place names are given in Hanyu Pinyin. Modern equivalents or approximations are identified on first occurrence.

Date Conversion

Chinese lunar calendar references are converted to Western dates based on the tables in Xue and Ouyang, *A Sino-Western Calendar for Two Thousand Years* (Liangqian nian Zhong-Xi li duizhao biao 兩千年中西曆對照表).

Linear and Area Measures

Chinese linear and area measures vary during the extensive period of literary history covered in this book, so the numbers provided below should be regarded only as approximations.

li 里: approximately one-third of an English mile

chi 尺: a little over one English foot

cun 寸: a Chinese "inch"

bu 步: a "pace" or "step"; sometimes *bu* indicates two steps, or a double-pace

xun 尋: eight *chi*; roughly ten English feet

zhang 丈: ten *chi*; roughly twelve English feet; sometimes translated as "span"

ren 仞: an ancient measure of varying length

mu 畝: an area measure; eight *mu* equaled about one English acre

Special Terms

Changjiang 長江: Since the late Ming (1368–1644) and early Qing (1644–1911) dynasties, Westerners have referred to this great waterway as the Yangtze, a term that is still used extensively outside of China. Originally, Yangzi 揚子 (the Pinyin spelling used today) denoted a ferry crossing near the city of Yangzhou 揚州 in Jiangsu, which Westerners used as a synecdoche for the entire river. In ancient China, it was simply called the Jiang 江, or River. Today in China it is universally referred to as the Changjiang. Throughout this study, I will call it the Great River.

Jiangnan 江南: Literally, "South of the Great River." Jiangnan is a geographical term that generally refers to the area south of the lower reaches of the Great River. This includes the modern city of Shanghai and the provinces of Zhejiang and Jiangsu. Sometimes the southern part of Anhui and the northern section of Jiangxi are also considered to be part of Jiangnan.

Two Jin dynasties: Two separate and distinct Chinese dynasties mentioned often in this study are spelled "Jin" in Hanyu Pinyin (although they are pronounced with different tones and written with different characters): the Jìn 晉 (265–420) and the Jīn 金 (1115–1234). This is potentially confusing, especially to readers unfamiliar with Chinese history, and so I shall make every effort to distinguish them.

Tianxia 天下: Throughout this book, the term Tianxia (literally, "all under heaven") is translated as "the empire." It should be kept in mind, however, that the traditional Chinese conception of "empire" did not envision an aggressive, imperialist political state. Rather, Tianxia is an all-inclusive ideal representing a perfect, legitimate "empire" in which balance and harmony reign supreme in the eyes of both rulers and people.

CHRONOLOGY OF CHINESE DYNASTIC AND HISTORICAL PERIODS

Shang (Yin), *ca.* 1600–1046 BCE

Zhou, 1046–256 BCE

Qin, 221–206 BCE

Han, 206 BCE–220 CE

    Western Han, 206 BCE–25 CE

    Eastern Han, 25–220

Six Dynasties, 220–589

    Three Kingdoms: Wei, 220–265; Shu-Han, 221–263;
       and Wu, 222–280

    Jìn Dynasty, 265–420

      Western Jìn, 265–317

      Eastern Jìn, 317–420

    Southern and Northern Dynasties

      Southern Dynasties

      Liu-Song, 420–479

      Qi, 479–502

      Liang, 502–557

      Chen, 557–589

      Northern Dynasties

      Northern Wei, 386–534

      Eastern Wei, 534–550

      Western Wei, 535–556

      Northern Qi, 550–577

      Northern Zhou, 557–581

Sui, 581–618

Tang, 618–907

Five Dynasties and Ten Kingdoms, 907–960

Liao, 907–1125

Song, 960–1279
    Northern Song, 960–1127
    Southern Song, 1127–1279
Jīn, 1115–1234
Yuan, 1279–1368
Ming, 1368–1644
Qing, 1644–1911
Republic of China, 1912–
People's Republic of China, 1949–

JADE MOUNTAINS & CINNABAR POOLS

INTRODUCTION

Seeing something once is better than hearing about it a hundred times.

"BIOGRAPHY OF ZHAO CHONGGUO"

IF THERE IS ONE CONSTANT THROUGHOUT THE HISTORY OF human activity in the world, it is travel. In many ways, movement across the planet's surface defines human nature. When *Homo sapiens* first left Africa to resettle on the European and Asian continents some seventy thousand years ago, the so-called great migration began. By about 8,000 BCE, every habitable continent on the planet was populated with humans. Over the last several millennia, travel has been undertaken for other purposes, such as adventure, exploration, investigation, and conquest. Many written accounts survive that document these journeys. Homer's epic poem the *Odyssey* (*ca.* eighth century BCE) is often cited as the first masterpiece of "travel literature" in Europe, and Marco Polo's (*ca.* 1254–1324) *Description of the World*, also known as *The Travels of Marco Polo*, is still the most widely read example of travel writing published in any language. Numerous other travel accounts appeared after Marco Polo, including many produced in lands beyond Europe. Among these, one of the best known and most prolific is Muhammad Ibn Battuta's *A Gift to Those Who Contemplate the Wonders of Cities and the Marvels of Traveling* (often simply called *The Travels*), which recounts the Moroccan author's extensive travels throughout North and West Africa, Southern and Eastern Europe, the Middle East, the Indian subcontinent, Central Asia, Southeast Asia, and China. Other familiar examples include such works as the ship logs of Christopher Columbus (1451–1506) and especially Richard Hakluyt's (*ca.* 1552–1616) *The Principal Navigations* (1589; revised and expanded, 1598–1600), both of which helped inspire ocean-crossing voyages for profit and empire building. In East Asia, Matsuo Bashō (1644–94), who ranks as one of the greatest masters of haiku composition, is just one of several writer-travelers who were active during the Tokugawa period (1600–1868) in Japan. And the genre continues to thrive today; numerous authors specialize in producing and publishing books about their experiences while on the road. Among those who are most active, Gao Xingjian (b. 1940), Paul Theroux (b. 1941), Bill Bryson (b. 1951), Kira Salak (b. 1971), and Robert MacFarlane (b. 1976) are probably the most successful in terms of exposure and book sales. Written accounts of travel, then, have been—and continue to be—ubiquitous throughout the world. China is no exception.

TRAVEL LITERATURE IN IMPERIAL CHINA

> Throughout my whole life, I have been fond of sightseeing in famous mountains.
>
> LI BAI, FROM "A SONG OF MOUNT LU SENT TO LU XUZHOU, THE ATTENDANT CENSOR"[1]

Travel literature as a distinct literary form was not studied seriously in China until the 1980s. Initial interest was signaled by the appearance of several anthologies of travel writings dating from the imperial period. One early example is Bei Yuanchen and Ye Youming's *Selections of Travel Accounts from the Successive Eras* (Lidai youji xuan), published in 1980. This and similar anthologies include selections of travel writings arranged chronologically throughout the dynastic eras, to each of which is appended explanatory notes on authors, places, and technical terms for the modern reader. A fifteen-page introduction is also included in Bei and Yuan's collection, but its content is mainly descriptive—who wrote what and when—and it offers little in the way of evaluative or critical remarks about the development of travel literature in China over time.

A question faced by travel literature anthology compilers in China in the 1980s was what name to use to identify the genre. The answer, provided by the editors of the 1979 edition of the authoritative Chinese dictionary *Sea of Words* (Cihai) and adopted by Bei Yuanchen, Ye Youming, and virtually everyone else since, was *youji*, which translates literally as "travel (*you*) accounts (*ji*)." Sometimes this term is expanded to *youji wenxue*, or "travel-account literature." Here is the *Sea of Words* definition of *youji*:

> *Youji*: a literary genre; a type of prose. It employs a lively writing style and vivid description that records and narrates what is seen and heard during a journey about the political life of a certain place, its social life, local conditions and customs, and physical landscape, notable scenery, vestiges of antiquity, and so on. Moreover, it expresses the thoughts and feelings of the author.[2]

The genre label *youji* was not devised by the editors of *Sea of Words*. In fact, like its approximate counterpart in Japanese, *kikōbungaku* (alternately, *kikōbun*), the term was new only in the way in which it was adopted to denote a very old type of prose, which needed a name.[3] Anthology compilers, critics, and readers embraced the term *youji* with great enthusiasm, and today it is probably known by most educated Chinese persons throughout the world.

As it turns out, the Chinese character/word *you* has a fascinating etymology. One of China's oldest dictionaries, *Interpreting Ancient Pictographs, Analyzing Semantic-Phonetic Characters* (Shuowen jiezi, early second century), defines it as follows: "*You* is the streaming of flags and banners" (游旗旌之流也).[4] This gloss suggests a type of movement that is free and without restraint. Hence, *you* often designates a journey undertaken for enjoyment. This is a critical point to keep in mind, because most Chinese travel literature was written to commemorate pleasure excursions. In Modern Chinese, the character/word *you* 游 has largely been replaced with the homonym 遊, the first form now largely reserved for vocabulary related to swimming (for instance, *youyong*, or "to swim"), though modern authors and publications do not always adhere to these distinctions. Also, there are several two-character terms comprised of *you* and another character (or other characters) preceding it that indicate varieties of travel that are not physical but are instead imagined and undertaken with no destination in mind. Examples include *muyou* (eye travels), *shenyou* (spiritual travels), *xinling zhi you* (travels of the mind), *woyou* (recumbent travels; that is, "armchair travels"), and *mengyou* (dream travels). These terms refer to a kind of *imaginary* "roaming" that takes place in a person's mind, and China has a rich tradition of such works.[5] In this study, I focus on actual, physical travels. The reasons for this choice are discussed in chapter 1.

The verb *you* is often contrasted with *xing* 行, which in Classical Chinese usually refers to journeys undertaken out of necessity, such as travel by government officials; and with *lü* 旅, which was originally used to indicate a purposeful journey by more than one person that was "marked by a sense of fear and awe."[6] The overwhelming verb of choice among authors of Chinese travel writing is *you*, though *xing* is used occasionally when describing longer journeys to distant destinations. The term *lü*, despite its everyday use in Modern Chinese in terms such as *lüxing* ("to go on a trip for pleasure"), is employed only sparingly to indicate a journey in Chinese travel writing dating from the imperial period.

Texts that can be classified or grouped together as "travel literature" usually appear in traditional bibliographies, especially in China's dynastic histories, under headings related to history, geography, or biography. There was never a single specific name designation in traditional Chinese bibliographies and anthologies for the type of prose work that is now generally understood as *youji*, or "travel literature," though encyclopedias (*leishu*) on occasion include a category (not a genre) called "miscellaneous accounts" (*zaji*), under which we sometimes find a subcategory identified as "chronicled travels" (*jiyou*). These works are mainly accounts of pleasure excursions to historical sites, attractive party or banquet venues, and especially scenic or landscape destinations.

The word and concept of "landscape," in both its Western and Chinese contexts, has a long history and can yield multiple meanings, depending on how it is used. I understand "landscape" as referring to a physical portion of the earth's surface that can be viewed from a single position or spot, near or distant. In the context of Chinese travel literature, "landscape" (*shanshui*; literally, "mountains and waters") almost always refers to an attractive or aesthetically pleasing portion of land or water (mountains, valleys, rivers, waterfalls, and so on). But unlike Western travel literature, in which viewers usually admire a landscape from a distance (in other words, they are outside of it), many of China's best writer-travelers sought to "move through" and thus "be inside of" their scenic destinations.

CHEN RENYU'S (1212–?) *COMPENDIUM OF TRAVELS* (YOUZHI) AND TRAVEL LITERATURE COLLECTIONS OF THE MING AND QING ERAS

The preface and table of contents of China's first anthology of travel literature, *Compendium of Travels*, compiled by Chen Renyu in 1243,[7] is especially useful because it provides the earliest-known information on how the genre was understood thematically. Like many other collections dating from the imperial period, Chen's anthology comprises individual works (eighty-seven in all) arranged chronologically. Titles in the *Compendium of Travels* span the period from the Jìn dynasty (265–420) to the Southern Song (1127–1279). Here is Chen's preface to the collection:

> In the *guimao* year of the Pure Safekeeping [Chunyou] reign [1243], during the intercalary month in autumn when the scenic aura was at its height, I turned and gazed off at Wujiao,[8] where mountain sheen joins with deep-blue sky. To the left and right, in layer upon layer, appear shapes that seem to summon and invite one another, and so as I stood here for a long time I was overcome with emotion. I happen to have been suffering from a foot ailment and thus cannot go out sightseeing. From time to time alone, I raise my head, offer a toast, and recite "Far-Off Journey" [Yuanyou] and "Summoning a Recluse" [Zhaoyin][9] to express my own contentment. This is because I cherish the beauty of landscapes written about since ancient times, as well as those surpassing sites associated with famous persons, and the pleasure of climbing heights and sightseeing. Although their [that is, authors represented in the *Compendium of Travels*] experiences of, and responses to, the beauty of landscape are not identical, their attitude is one of transcendence. They are unburdened by vulgar attitudes and desire for material objects. My view is that of all the joyful things throughout time, nothing can surpass the delight of sightseeing. Thus, I have made selections from works over the past two thousand years, beginning with ones that sing about the Yi River[10] and ending with the travels to Mount Heng [Hengshan] by Zhang and Zhu.[11] Lofty sentiments and distant charm are assembled and revealed in this collection. If readers partake of its contents daily, the response will be completely favorable, and they will soar aloft, one and all. Alas! There is no one in the world fonder of sightseeing than me! It took fifteen days to compile this collection, and here I provide a preface. Chen Renyu of Tiantai.[12]

What most resonates throughout Chen's preface is his admitted love for "sightseeing" (*youlan*), "the beauty of landscape" (*shanshui zhi mei*), "scenic sites associated with famous persons" (*renwu zhi sheng*), and "the pleasure of climbing heights and sightseeing" (*denglan youtu zhi shi*). He leaves no doubt that the principal focus of travel literature is attractive "scenic sites," including those "associated with famous persons." Chen's textual selections reveal that he is also interested in places associated with historical events. For

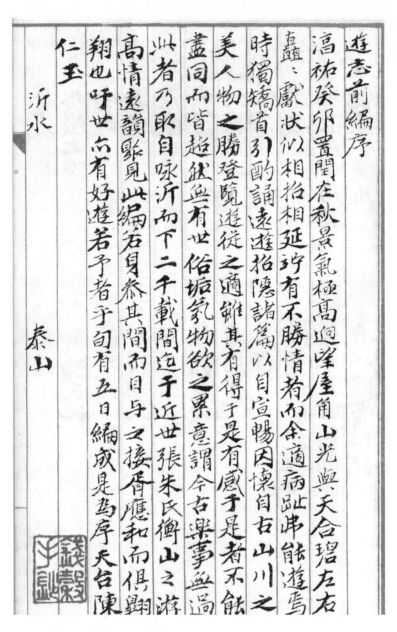

遊志前編序

滈祐癸卯置閏在秋景氣極高迥崖屋角山光與天合碧左右

矗矗獻狀似相掐相延竛有不勝情者而余適病趾串能遊焉

時獨矯首引酌誦遠遊掐隱諸篇以自宣暢因懷自古山川之

美人物之勝登覽遊從之適雖其有得于是有感于是者不能

盡同而皆超然無有世俗埃氛物欲之累意謂今古樂事無遍

州者乃取自詠沂而下二千載間迄于近世張朱氏衡山之游

高情遠韻覯見此編右身泰其間而目与之接昏應和而俱翔

翔也呼世而有好遊若予者于旬有五日編成是為序天台陳

仁玉

沂水　　泰山

1.1. This hand-copied, photo-lithographic version of Chen Renyu's preface to his *Compendium of Travels* is preserved in the 1925 edition of Tao Zongyi's *Compendium of Travels: The Continuation Volume*, published by the noted bibliophile Tao Xiang 陶湘 (1871–1940). The calligraphy is that of the Ming dynasty painter Qian Gu 錢穀 (*ca*. 1508–78). Courtesy of the C. V. Starr East Asian Library, University of California, Berkeley.

instance, he includes Ma Dibo's (first century CE) account of a trip to the site of the *feng* and *shan* sacrifices to heaven and earth, performed by the Han emperor Guangwu (r. 25–57 CE) on Mount Tai (Taishan) in 56 CE.[13] Chen also includes biographies of famous persons, such as the poet Tao Yuanming (or Tao Qian, 365–427), and accounts of famous gardens, such as the historian and politician Sima Guang's (1019–86) "Account of the Garden of Solitary Delight" (Dule yuan ji) in Luoyang. Such works are not related to travel in any direct way, though some relate to authors of well-known travel narratives.[14] Thus, Chen Renyu's view of travel literature was broad and flexible rather than strict and narrow.

Tao Zongyi's (fl. 1360–68) sequel to Chen Renyu's collection, *Compendium of Travels: The Continuation Volume*, includes seventy-eight titles by forty-eight authors, most of whom date from the Song (960–1279) and Yuan (1279–1368) periods. Although there is considerable overlap in the types of works included in both collections—and this is because Tao Zongyi follows Chen Renyu in focusing on works depicting scenic landscapes and historical sites (but not individuals), he does include other types of works, most notably Liu Qi's (1203–50) *Account of an Embassy to the North* (Beishi ji), which describes the ambassadorial mission of Wugusun Zhongduan to the Mongol court of Genghis Khan in 1221. This identification is significant because, as we will see in chapter 3, the embassy account became an important type or subgenre of travel literature during the Song dynasty.

Following Chen Renyu, numerous multi- and individual-author collections of travel literature were compiled and published during the subsequent Ming and Qing periods. It is fascinating to observe that all the general, multi-author collections (*zongji*) include the term *mingshan*, or "famous mountains," in their titles. One prominent example is *Accounts of Sightseeing Trips to Famous Mountains, Ancient and Modern* (Gujin you mingshan ji) in seventeen chapters (*juan*), compiled by He Tang (*jinshi* 1547) and published in 1565. This collection seems to include almost any variety of text that concerns travel for pleasure to famous mountains. Later, in the Qing dynasty (1644–1911), Wu Qiushi revised this and another collection by Wang Shizhen (1526–90) titled *Accounts of Famous Mountains, the Expanded Collection* (Mingshan ji guangbian), removing all the rhapsodies (*fu*), letters, diaries, and descriptive accounts about gardens and for the most part keeping only works that include *ji* in their title and that describe famous scenic mountain sites. A new name was bestowed upon the revised collection, in sixteen chapters: *Travel Accounts about Famous Mountains throughout the Empire* (Tianxia mingshan youji). Wu organizes the 219 selections in his collection geographically by province. I shall have much more to say in chapter 4 about the diverse kinds of travel literature collections published during the Ming and Qing and their importance. For now, suffice it to say that there was no consensus among the editors and compilers of these anthologies, even in the late imperial period, regarding what types of works constituted *youji* and how they should be classified and organized.

THE STUDY OF TRAVEL LITERATURE IN CONTEMPORARY CHINA

Following the appearance of *Selections of Travel Accounts from the Successive Eras* in 1980, dozens of "ancient travel literature" collections were published in China. Most are modeled after Bei Yuanchen and Ye Youming's anthology, and include essentially the same selection of texts. Presumably, then, this is the canon of traditional Chinese travel literature as it is defined in scholarly circles in contemporary China. Regardless of one's views on the relative importance of many of the works in this catalog—and those that are not included but should be—what is especially new and noteworthy is that between 2004 and 2009, no less than three book-length studies of travel literature were published in Chinese: Mei Xinlin and Yu Zhanghua, *History of Travel-Account Literature in China* (Zhongguo youji wenxue shi; 2004); Zhu Yaoting and Gong Bin, editors, *Travel Accounts from China's Ancient Eras* (Zhongguo gudai youji; 2007); and Wang Liqun, *A Study of Landscape Travel Accounts from China's Ancient Eras* (Zhongguo gudai shanshui youji yanjiu; 2008). I have benefited from consulting all three of these studies, and my indebtedness to their authors will be acknowledged in footnote references. However, some of these works have proven to be more useful than others. Wang Liqun's study, for instance, says surprisingly little about the genre during the Song dynasty, which in my view is the watershed period in the development of travel literature in China. The Zhu and Gong volume has likewise not been especially helpful, because its treatment of travel literature considers both prose and poetry. This approach is too broad to yield any focused, critical insights, and the results are limited to generalizations.

By far the most useful among the three studies under discussion is Mei Xinlin and Yu Zhanghua's volume, the only work among the three that bears the word "history" (*shi*) in its title. The value of this work lies in its chronological breadth (from ancient times to the present), its generous presentation of individual texts (many of which heretofore have not received the consideration they deserve), and its attention to subgenres of travel literature beyond those dealing with landscape. The many observations that Mei and Yu make about individual *youji* texts and authors are indeed valuable. Like many literary historians and critics in China, they tend to use general or abstract language to assess literary artistry. For instance, here is what they say about the language used by one prominent Six Dynasties author of landscape prose: "The outstanding achievement of Li Daoyuan in the field of prose benefited from the sustenance he received from the remarkable geographical accounts of earlier eras."[15]

My approach to literary history and criticism is different. In this investigation, I focus on how authors use and manipulate language to achieve an effect or to voice a specific concern. In the case of the statement just quoted from Mei and Yu, I would endeavor to explain how the "benefit" from this "sustenance" (inspiration? influence?) is traceable in the author's language. Mei and Yu do not always follow up in this way, but that is not say that their judgments are inherently wrong. Our approaches are just different. In my own defense, however, I contend that literary merit should be judged by how skillfully an author draws upon, uses, adapts, and sometimes even plays with words to make his voice and concerns heard.

RESEARCH METHODOLOGY

Over the years, I have written about travel literature in China and how it might be understood and defined.[16] Here I propose to fine tune my earlier efforts by addressing this issue in more detail and providing more theoretical support. My guidepost in studying the genre will be an observation made long ago by the literary critic Northrop Frye (1912–91): "The purpose of criticism by genres is not so much to classify as to clarify traditions and affinities, thereby bringing out a large number of literary relationships that would not be noticed as long as there were no context established for them."[17] To paraphrase Frye, then, my approach is to identify what works constitute China's travel literature tradition and its various affinities so as to flesh out the literary relationships among these texts that perhaps would otherwise go unnoticed.

I am aware that because of the influence of post-modernism and post-structuralism on Western literary theory, the traditional approach to genre study[18] has been disparaged and essentially dismissed by numerous literary theorists. Jacques Derrida (1930–2004) and others have made efforts to deconstruct traditional genre theory because, as they see it, the "structuralist approach" is an artificial construct that confines literary study to a fixed set of rules and textual parameters that inhibit understanding. A sounder method, they contend, is a "post-structuralist" one that challenges and tests the traditional genre categories and boundaries favored by the "structuralists," and even considers non-literary phenomena such as cultural norms and reader responses.[19] During the last two decades of the twentieth century, however, genre study regained at least some of its reputation in literary studies and changed its focus. In the words of linguist Lilo Moessner, it is now "conceived of as a dynamic model" rather than a static and fixed one.[20]

The research methodology I employ in this study, informed by a theoretical framework postulated by literary scholars Dirk de Geest and Hendrik van Gorp, is to study the development of *youji* by means of a dynamic or opened-ended conception of genre.[21] The basic assumption of this approach is that some literary genres are "less neatly defined" than others. They argue that such genres consist of a body of texts that "resists efficient classification into any clear-cut matrix of supposedly sufficient and necessary conditions."[22] I favor this line of understanding for two reasons. First, as already mentioned, *youji* literature in China was never governed by a strict and distinctive structural matrix. In other words, Chinese travel literature does not fit well into any static and rigid conception of literary type, and this is mainly because it does not embody any firmly fixed rules governing authorial focus and literary style. The genre does, however, have some general, identifiable traits regarding form and content; these are outlined below. Second, an open-ended approach to *youji* as a literary type or genre will provide more flexibility about what texts constitute travel literature in ancient China, and which selections among those works most served as exemplars to later writers.

The "prototype" theory for literary genre study proposed by de Geest and van Gorp essentially rejects both the traditional "structuralist" and modern "post-structuralist" approaches, and instead "proceeds from a quite different assumption; namely, that not all instances of a particular category of literature are functionally similar or equally representative of their category as a whole."[23] This theoretical framework is especially useful in the study of traditional Chinese travel literature because masters of the genre like Liu Zongyuan (773–819), Fan Chengda (1126–93), and Xu Xiake

(1587–1641) can and did produce *youji* that was different in focus and style but nevertheless still remain representative of the best travel literature written during the imperial period. My primary mode of presentation in this study is to identify exemplar (or prototypical) texts, present them in English translation, and then explicate those texts in such a way as to highlight their contributions toward the development of Chinese travel literature.

KEY ESSENTIALS AND GENERAL OBSERVATIONS

Given the long history of writing about travel in China, it is imperative that I articulate a critical list of essential points that will allow navigation through this large body of material and organization of it into a coherent whole that yields new knowledge. The following reference points will facilitate approaching this material as an open-ended literary genre.

All *youji* literature contains a coherent and indispensable narrative of the *physical experience* of a journey through space toward an identifiable place, written in prose.[24] In some pre-Han dynasty (206 BCE–220 CE) texts in which travel plays a prominent role, such as the *Chronicle of Mu, Son of Heaven* (Mu Tianzi zhuan), the journey is mythical, symbolic, or imaginative. All the works I identify as travel literature, however, concern a real journey, brief or extended, to a geographically verifiable destination. Unlike Western travel literature, with its focus on distant, alien lands, the overwhelming majority of Chinese *youji* describe places inside China, though some prominent examples of the genre, such as the Buddhist monk Xuanzang's (ca. 602–64) *Accounts of the Western Regions during the Great Tang* (Da Tang Xiyu ji), narrate journeys to foreign lands (in Xuanzang's case, India).

Chinese travel literature is written in essay format (that is, a short piece of writing on a single topic) or diary format, and usually is composed as an "account" (*ji*). Most titles of literary travel works in China employ the formulaic title "*you* place-x *ji*," which translates literally as "account (*ji*) of a sightseeing trip (*you*) to place-x." On some occasions, *xing* or *lu* 錄 (not *lü*) is used to describe journeys that were undertaken for reasons other than sightseeing or pleasure. For instance, one important early example of the travel diary, which we will consider in chapter 2, is Li Ao's (d. 838) *Register of Coming South* (Lainan lu).

Youji texts provide descriptive information on the places, phenomena, and conditions observed by the author during a journey. The content of these reports varies, depending on the geographical focus of the narrative and the author's personal interests and tastes. For instance, we might find descriptions of famous landmarks, prominent mountains and rivers, social, political, and religious practices and conditions, local customs and products, and flora and fauna. Authorial observations, comments, and even personal feelings are also present—and this at once distinguishes *youji* from geographical and ethnographic accounts—but Chinese travel literature is written in different registers of language designed to serve widely diverse purposes.[25] Textual examples in the chapters will illustrate the varieties of language employed by some of China's most representative *youji* authors.

"Literary" refers specifically to a variety of descriptive and/or commentarial language that is at once personal and distinguishable from the lists of factual details one finds in geographical monographs, local and regional gazetteers, or the impersonal reporting style common in the Song dynasty and later in anecdotal *biji* (or "notation book") writing. "Personal" in this context involves active engagement between the author (or "self") and the place(s) he visits and describes (sometimes identified in modern Western criticism as "the world" or "the other"). This reverberation between author and place often inspires the writer-traveler to employ an elevated style of language rich in lyrical content and personal association.

Unlike the diverse nature of their counterparts in Europe and the Americas, most travel literature authors in imperial China were members of the so-called scholar-official class (*shidafu*). China scholars in the West also refer to members of this distinguished group as "the literati," "the gentry," or simply "the elite." These men spent their entire youth preparing for China's civil service examinations, which, when passed, usually provided a prestigious, lifelong position in the government bureaucracy. In their capacity as scholar-officials, many of them spent their entire careers traveling to and from official posts in the provinces, and sometimes these assignments took them to remote locations in the Chinese empire. With just a few notable exceptions, virtually all traditional Chinese literature dating from before the later years of the Ming dynasty (1368–1644) was written by *shidafu*. They were not, like their Age of Discovery counterparts in the West, outsiders looking in. The cultural currency they carried was accepted by their readers. For instance, when a traveling Chinese scholar-official observes and describes the local customs of an unfamiliar place, usually he understands them and can interpret those customs for his readers.[26] He can tell readers why something is worth knowing about. The same holds true for reports on places with historical-literary associations. China's best travel writers are highly qualified to guide their readers.

The following general observations are also offered to help the reader navigate through the large body of material and lengthy span of time covered in this investigation.

First, the development of Chinese travel literature was a continuous process that has its origins in the Six Dynasties, its articulation in the Tang, its maturity in the Song, and its florescence in the middle and later years of the Ming. Although several prominent authors in the Qing dynasty—such as Zhang Dai (*ca.* 1597–*ca.* 1679), Gu Yanwu (1613–82), and Yuan Mei (1716–98)—produced *youji* that in some ways reflect the influence of their Song and Ming predecessors, travel writing during the years of Manchu rule reflects many entirely new directions and concerns. The catalyst for these changes was the tremendous physical expansion of the Chinese empire and the corresponding new concern among Qing *youji* authors with non-traditional destinations, especially border regions inhabited by non-Chinese peoples (Tibet, Mongolia, Manchuria, and Taiwan all came under China's control during the Qing) and later—especially in the nineteenth century—foreign lands, including Europe and America.[27] Thus, the content and style of *youji* changed so dramatically during the Qing that the period deserves a separate monograph. It is for this reason, then, that this investigation concludes with the late Ming.

Second, the development of Chinese travel literature through the dynasties was a dynamic process. Changes that took place in the genre's form and content over time were the result of fluid interplay between authors and audiences and between literary milieus and cultural institutions. Identifying and explaining these differences is essential to any history of the genre. This important premise runs counter to most modern scholarship (in Chinese) on *youji*, which, almost without exception, views its development as an essentially static process of "appreciating landscape" that changed little over time.

Third, a major critical concern in this study is how later examples of the genre relate to earlier ones. Fleshing out intertextual connections and affinities can enhance the way we understand *youji* texts. For instance, were Xu Xiake's famous travel journals influenced by earlier writers? If so, how? In fact, unlike Chinese poetry, there seems to be little direct literary borrowing in traditional Chinese prose travel literature, whereby one writer would pattern his work after, or lift famous lines from, a previous author. On the contrary, as pointed out by Xiaofei Tian, Chinese travel literature is "individualized." In other words, the Chinese travel writer did not attempt to present an "objective account of what there is to note, but rather presents the world as seen through the eyes of a historical subject, an individual person."[28] To paraphrase Professor Tian's keen observation, then, Chinese travelers never see—and thus never describe—a place in precisely the same way.

Also, travel literature in China did not develop in a linear manner that evolved from a simple to a more complex form over time. The single key factor that links individual travel works and travelers over time is place and the historical-literary heritage associated with that specific location. For instance, when the Song dynasty writer Lu You (1125–1210) visited the famous Three Sightseers Cavern (Sanyou Dong) in western Hubei in 1170, he was obliged to acknowledge and quote from the works of distinguished literary men who had visited the cave earlier and wrote accounts about it. This included an initial group of three sightseers composed of Bai Juyi (772–846), his brother Bai Xingjian (776–826), and their friend Yuan Zhen (779–831); a second trio that included Su Xun (1009–66) and his two (later famous) sons, Su Shi (1037–1101) and Su Che (1039–1112); and individual visitors, such as the notable writers Ouyang Xiu (1007–72) and Huang Tingjian (1045–1105).[29] In the history of travel writing in China, it is this association between individual texts about a single place (or region), accumulated over time, that mainly links many works in the genre to others.

And fourth, one key aspect of Chinese travel literature is its *visual* quality. Essentially, *youji* authors are creating cinematic-like word pictures of places they essentially want readers to "see" by reading a text.[30] This concept is central to understanding Chinese travel literature. The modern critic Yu Kwang-chung (Yu Guangzhong) has observed that the language of what he calls the "landscape journal" (or Chinese travel literature) is more effective when it is "sensuous" rather than "intellectual," because the "sensory data" provided by the author allows readers "to visualize, to be there, and share the experience." Yu also says that visualization is not enough: the other senses of hearing, smelling, touching, and tasting must be exploited as well.[31] To Yu's insightful comments I would add that an essential quality distinguishes travel literature from other varieties of prose: it narrates movement through space and place.[32] This sense of motion is in many ways the defining quality of Chinese travel literature—what distinguishes it from static depictions of landscape in which scenic details are often enumerated in shopping-list form. The most successful travel-literature writers in China charge their visual and sensual descriptions with motion, which in turn is "experienced" by the reader. This makes the textual landscape come alive, and this helps the reader to experience vicariously the journey itself. But the ultimate value of *youji*, regardless of national origins, is this: accounts based on firsthand observation provide windows through which to see unknown places or to reveal familiar places in a new way; they also tell us much about the author, his values, and his view of the world, which in turn tells us something about the author's society. These are precisely the kinds of "affinities" that Northrop Frye says can result from genre study. My own quest in this book is to find these connections and explain them to the reader.

CHAPTER 1

HARBINGERS IN THE SIX DYNASTIES

Sightseeing at ancient sites did not flourish until the Jin dynasty
(265–420).

ABSTRACTS OF TITLES IN THE GENERAL CATALOG
OF THE COMPLETE BOOKS OF THE IMPERIAL LIBRARY

WHILE ON A MILITARY CAMPAIGN IN 207, THE POWERFUL MILI-
tary strategist and political leader Cao Cao (155–220), also a skilled poet,
wrote the following verse, titled "Strolling Out Xia Gate: A Song" (Bu chu
Xiamen xing):

To the east I look out at Stone Tablet,[1]
So that I might gaze at the deep blue sea beyond.
How gently the waters prance and dance,
While mountain isles stand proudly on high.
Trees grow plentifully, thick in clusters;
The myriad plants are dense and lush.
As the autumn wind whistles and wails,
Gigantic waves leap high into the air.
Sun by day, moon by night,
Seem to arise from their very heart.
The Milky Way, glittering and glorious,
Seems to emerge from their very midst.
How fortunate I am to have witnessed this
    magnificent scene!
I sing this song to voice my heart's content.[2]

In simple and straightforward language, this evocative verse expresses no more or less than the unadorned pleasure of gazing at an ocean vista from a mountain height. There are no allusions, no obtuse expressions, and no references to matters philosophical, religious, or metaphysical. In this sense, it is quite remarkable, and explains why many literary historians have identified Cao's verse as China's "first landscape poem." Whether Cao Cao's poem is truly the first such work in Chinese letters need not concern us. But what we do need to recognize is that literary works like this, in which the author—for no apparent or stated reason—openly and directly expresses aesthetic appreciation of an attractive, outdoor scene, did not appear on any regular basis in China until after the fall of the Han dynasty in 220 CE. The appearance in the Six Dynasties of the earliest manifestations of *youji* writing is directly related to this important development.[3]

The new aesthetic sensibility related to attractive natural settings that appeared after the fall of the Han has been studied in detail by Donald Holzman. In his *Landscape Appreciation in Ancient and Early Medieval China: The Birth of Landscape Poetry*, Holzman argues convincingly that literature written in high antiquity—that is, before the Qin unification in 221 BCE—was intended to praise imperial political institutions and values and especially to express moral sentiments and lessons aimed at finding solutions to the social and political problems of that time. Literature about anything else, he says, was considered inappropriate. Furthermore, like many other scholars, Holzman contends that the birth of landscape or "nature" poetry took place around the fourth century and that this development occurred within the context of a changing Chinese view of the world. This new outlook, he further asserts, included appreciation of appealing landscapes and found expression in lyric poetry (*shi*) in the form of personal aesthetic experience.[4]

While the complex reasons for the appearance of this new Chinese appreciation of scenic landscapes during the Six Dynasties have yet to be fully articulated,[5] there is no doubt that the era produced China's earliest literary texts in which we find admiration of landscape "for itself." And while Holzman's thesis is confined to lyric poetry, the developments he describes also appeared—not coincidentally—in several other types of writing and art forms at about the same time.[6] One important premise upon which this chapter is organized and written is that the content, style, and language of these texts—some of which have been identified by literary historians as China's earliest *youji*—vary greatly and were composed in a number of different literary genres, the most important of which were the rhapsody (*fu*), the letter (*shu*), the preface (*xu*), and the account (*ji*). Other important developments during the Six Dynasties include the appearance of China's first "Buddhist travel account"—Faxian's (*ca.* 337–*ca.* 422) *Accounts of the Buddhist Kingdoms* (Foguo ji)—and Li Daoyuan's *Commentary on the Waterways Treatise* (Shuijing zhu). These harbingers of *youji* writing contributed in diverse ways to the genre's birth and later development.

THE RHAPSODY

> At dusk they return, / But pleasure is hard to forget. /
> For these are the joys of sightseeing, / The delights of eye and ear.
> ZHANG HENG, "SOUTHERN CAPITAL RHAPSODY"[7]

Xie Lingyun (385–433), in the preface to his "Rhapsody on Living in the Mountains" (Shanju fu), declares, "What I now put into *fu* is not the splendor of metropolitan capitals, palaces and watchtowers, pleasure outings and hunts, and music and revelry; rather, I describe such things as the mountain wilds, plants and trees, streams and boulders, and grains and crops."[8] This remark is noteworthy because it draws attention to Han dynasty rhapsodies that include detailed and elaborate descriptions of that era's grandiose capital cities, extravagant royal palaces, and imperial hunting parks (the Chinese word *fu*, or "rhapsody," literally means "to display" or "spread out"). As an example, consider the following excerpt from Sima Xiangru's (179–117 BCE) well-known "Rhapsody on the Imperial Park" (Shanglin fu):

> Sweetwater springs bubble among the cool rooms,
> Free flowing streams pass through the central courtyard.
> Giant boulders line the shores,
> Steeply scarped, leaning and listing,
> Jaggedly jutting, peaked and pinnacled,
> Carved and chiseled, precipitously poised.
> Rose stone, prase, and dark jade;[9]
> And coral grows in clusters.
> Agate gems and large carnelians
> Are striped and streaked like patterned fish scales.

Red jade, mottled and marbled,
Are mixed and mingled among them.
Morning iridescence, rounded and pointed jades,
Mr. He's jewel appears there.[10]

This and many rhapsodies on related topics are included in the *Literary Selections* (Wenxuan), compiled by an imperial prince named Xiao Tong (501–31).[11] Rhapsodies tend to be lengthy compositions with elaborate and extended descriptions (the one quoted above runs over four hundred lines), and the language usually includes hyperbole, presented in the form of extended strings of words or expressions comprised of doublets (that is, two Chinese characters).

A second, noteworthy point about the comment from Xie Lingyun's "Rhapsody on Living in the Mountains" is that he openly rejects extravagant and essentially celebratory subject matter, such as imperial gardens, royal hunts, and the great metropolises of Luoyang and Chang'an.[12] Instead, he prefers to write about rustic scenes comprised of "mountain wilds, plants and trees, streams and boulders, and grains and crops." Many other *fu* authors, beginning in the late Han and continuing into the Six Dynasties, also turned their attention to quotidian matters and even individual experiences.

One activity in this regard that deserves special attention is the journey. In the *Literary Selections*, which incidentally is China's first collection of belles-lettres arranged according to genres, we find three rhapsodies classified as "accounts of travels" (*jixing*) and another three listed in the category of "sightseeing" (*youlan*).[13] What most distinguishes these works (in Chinese, these texts are sometimes collectively called *zhengfu*, or "distant-journey *fu*") is that unlike most other rhapsodies dating from the Han, they were not composed to celebrate imperial rule or to cajole emperors. Rather, they were written by and for the authors themselves, and, with one exception among the six travel *fu* anthologized in the *Literary Selections*,[14] they chronicle real journeys. Moreover, mid- and later Han dynasty travel rhapsodies are written in a much simpler, more personal style—with more emphasis on narration, less hyperbole, and references in real time to real places—than the rhapsodies composed earlier by Sima Xiangru and his contemporaries. Among the best known of such works dating from the Han and Six Dynasties are Liu Xin's (d. 23 CE) "Rhapsody on Fulfilling My Original Intent" (Suichu fu), Pan Yue's (247–300) "Rhapsody on a Distant

Westward Journey" (Xizheng fu), and Lu Ji's (261–303) "Rhapsody on My Thoughts While Traveling" (Xingsi fu).[15] These works describe journeys undertaken by the author. Here is a brief example, culled from Lu Ji's "Rhapsody on My Thoughts While Traveling":

> I turn my back on far-off and faraway Luopu,
> And float along the graceful glide of Yellow Stream.
> Leading on to River Bend by means distant and remote,
> I observe the place where river's flow and current converge.[16]

Now consider the following selection from Pan Yue's "Rhapsody on a Distant Westward Journey." This *fu* is included in the *Wenxuan* under the category "accounts of travel" and describes a trip from Luoyang to Chang'an undertaken in 290:

> I go forth to Anyang,
> And then cross the outer wall of Shan,
> Trek to the confluence of Man and Du,
> Rest at the ruins of Caoyang.
> Oh, how beautiful, how distant,
> This land so ancient![17]

One key element in Lu Ji's and Pan Yue's travel narration is their use of motion verbs.[18] In the selection from Lu Ji's rhapsody, these are *fu* ("float") and *dao* ("leading on"); in the excerpt by Pan Yue, we see "go forth" (or "march"; *cu*), "cross" (*she*), and "trek" (*xing*).

These examples from Han dynasty travel *fu* show that by the late third century, authors like Pan Yue and Liu Ji, when writing about their travels, developed a distinctive narrative style to describe movement through space toward a series of destinations. This style is executed through a sequence of motion or action verbs,[19] usually one in each line, repeated over several successive lines—presented as they relate to a series of place names (in the previous example, Luofu, Yellow Stream, River Bend, and so on). This formulaic sentence structure both relates the physical movement of the traveler and suggests to the reader what the actual journey was like.[20] Moreover, it became a standard feature in almost all subsequent travel writing.

Pan Yue's "Rhapsody on a Distant Westward Journey" is essentially an account of the historical sites through which Pan passed on his way to Chang'an.[21] But Pan offers more in his *fu* than mere mention of these places and their historical associations and significance. As he gazes upon these famous historical sites and reflects upon the memories they evoke, he also adds personal commentary. For instance, in the following lines, written about his movement through lands that were once ruled by the ancient state of Qin, the author laments the cruelty of the infamous warlord Xiang Yu (Xiang Ji, 232–202 BCE):[22]

> I gaze over hills and streams, contemplating the past;
> Disconsolate, in mid-road I pull in the reins.
> How harsh the vicious cruelty of Xiang Yu!
> He buried alive innocent surrendered soldiers,
> Thus rousing the people of Qin to turn unto virtue,
> And resulting in their revival by Lord Liu.[23]

This kind of "reflection on the past" (*huaigu*) is triggered by historical sites, events, and figures as the author "gazes over the hills and streams" of Xin'an. In the works of Pan's contemporaries and later writers, these same sentiments are also aroused by ascending to a high place, such as a tower or mountain, and then gazing into the distance as one reflects on the past. This topos, called *denglin* (literally, "ascend a height and look out"), was employed in the works of numerous later poets and *youji* authors. A well-known early example, penned by the distinguished late Han writer Wang Can (177–217), is included among the "sightseeing" *fu* in the *Literary Selections*. It is titled "Rhapsody on Climbing the Tower" (Denglou fu). Wang Can, like Pan Yue and Lu Ji, both of whom he predates, also favors action verbs in his description of landscape, even when he is standing in place on the summit of a tower:

> I scan the site on which this building rests:
> Truly spacious and open, rare is its peer!
> It hugs the intersecting channel of the clear Zhang,
> Rests upon the long sandbars of the twisting Ju,
> Backs upon a broad stretch of hillock and plain,
> Faces the rich flow of river margin and marsh.

Unfortunately, although Wang Can admits that the beauty of the landscape around the Zhang River is without peer, while gazing from a height into the distance he finds only temporary consolation:

> Though truly beautiful, it is not my home!
> How can I remain here even briefly?[24]

In the remaining lines of his rhapsody, Wang Can's travel narration is completely overwhelmed by melancholy brought on by homesickness.

As for the place of Han travel and sightseeing rhapsodies in the early development of *youji*, it is significant that major writers like Pan Yue, for the first time in Chinese literary history, were writing personal accounts of real journeys in which they voiced private thoughts and concerns that were at least partially inspired by natural landscapes. "Author reaction to scene or place," it will be recalled, is yet another essential component of Chinese travel literature, and we certainly see numerous examples of this practice in the travel *fu* anthologized in the *Literary Selections*. At the same time, however, we should keep in mind that although the travel component of many of these texts certainly references historical sites, events, and persons, these works seem to function primarily as literary vehicles designed to allow authors to display their literary talents and especially to provide an opportunity for them to express intense personal feelings about the sadness of failed careers, unfulfilled ambitions, and sadness aroused by long periods of being away from home and family. In other words, extended description and appreciation of landscape is not a major component of travel and sightseeing rhapsodies; nor is the travel or "ascending a height" element, for that matter. But we certainly cannot fault authors of Han dynasty *fu* for failing to produce a type of writing (that is, *youji*) that did not exist at the time. What *is* important, however, is that influential writers like Wang Can, Pan Yue, and Lu Ji were now writing about real journeys and real places in a literary and lyrical way.

Finally, we should observe that while the many strict rules governing the composition of rhapsodies in the Han period, such as use of alternating prose and rhyme, the presence of rhythmic and metrical elements, parallel sentence structure, extensive strings of binomial compounds or "doublets," alliteration, and ornate rhetoric are eminently appropriate for elaborate language display, they are not ideally suited for travel narration. For this reason, in the Tang dynasty, *youji* authors chose to use a much less restrictive and more informal prose style in their travel writings.

THE LETTER

Note: Bao's composition ["Letter Written to My Younger Sister after Climbing the Bank at Big Thunder Lake"] is superb. In fact, it represents the highest standard among Song dynasty [that is, the Liu-Song dynasty, 420–79 CE] prose compositions, and indeed has no peer!

QIAN ZHONGSHU, *THE LIMITED VIEWS COLLECTION*[25]

Authorial interest in landscape description and travel narration is also manifested in another type of writing popular during the Six Dynasties period: the personal letter (*shu* or *shuxin*). Letter writing was already established as a literary genre by the Han dynasty, and it flourished in China for more than two millennia thereafter. Probably the most celebrated letter in all Chinese epistolary culture is the historian Sima Qian's (*ca.* 145–*ca.* 86 BCE) missive to Ren An (d. *ca.* 91 BCE), in which he explains his decision to live with the shame of castration in order to complete his monumental history of ancient China.[26] Numerous other texts written in the letter form have also survived, and many of these date from the Six Dynasties. Some are preserved in the *Wenxuan* and various histories, biographies, and encyclopedias, but the most extensive source for the study of letters is Yan Kejun's (1762–1843) massive *Complete Prose of High Antiquity, the Three Dynasties, Qin, Han, the Three Kingdoms, and Six Dynasties* (Quan Shanggu Sandai Qin Han Sanguo Liuchao wen).[27]

As in many other cultures, the style and content of letters in ancient China could be formal or informal, depending on the nature of the correspondence and the relationship between the sender and receiver. There were two essential types: official (letters written by government functionaries in the performance of their bureaucratic duties), which were transported via a government-run postal-relay system, first established during the Han dynasty; and personal, which were usually conveyed by couriers. These two varieties of letters reflect a broad menu of styles: some are merely fragments or brief notes; others are lengthy, elaborate dissertations on religion, philosophy, and other matters. The language and literary style used in these missives is equally varied. As for the topical content, personal letters to family and friends most often express homesickness or nostalgia.[28] We also see letters that discuss contemporary literary practices, as well as letters of recommendation to prospective patrons or employers.

Letters sent to family members, friends, or acquaintances, which are often highly personal and sometimes laced with intense emotion, began to flourish in the late Han and continued to be written throughout the Six Dynasties and later periods. "Personal" in this context is not a synonym for "private." We know that many of these communications eventually appeared in anthologies and collections available to the general reader and that some letters were valued, distributed, and collected for their historical importance, literary value, or even praiseworthy calligraphy. Others have been recovered through archeological discoveries.[29] The details of the transmission process are still largely unknown, but since most of the best-known letter authors of the Six Dynasties were major literary figures during their own lifetimes, it seems safe to assume that they were aware that their missives could eventually become public and so paid close attention to the way they expressed themselves, even in such a "personal" communication.

The content of many surviving letters from the Six Dynasties indicates that these are carefully worded texts in which writers made earnest efforts not only to reveal their feelings about separation from friends and family, but also to display their literary talents. Of special interest to us are some surviving letters that combine travel narration, landscape appreciation, and expression of personal sentiments. The landscape component here is yet another literary manifestation of the aesthetic trend toward appreciation of attractive scenery that emerged in the Six Dynasties.

The single most anthologized letter in modern anthologies and collections of *youji* is Bao Zhao's (414?–66) "Letter Written to My Younger Sister after Climbing the Bank at Big Thunder Lake" (Deng Dalei an yu mei shu). Bao Zhao is a major literary figure of the fifth century and is much admired as a skilled poet in the *yuefu*, or Music Bureau ballad, style. Bao's famous letter to his sister chronicles a journey from Nanjing to Jiangxi, where the author traveled to meet his patron and take up a new government post. "Letter Written to My Younger Sister" is important because it is one of the first letters in Chinese literary history to use parallel prose[30] in an extended description of landscape within the context of a journey.[31] But before Bao Zhao even begins to delineate the scenes he witnessed along the road to Jiangxi, he reveals that he is a reluctant traveler and that his pursuit of an official career is the cause of his sadness and homesickness. The following lines relate Bao's thoughts as he reaches Thunder Lake (Leichi) at Big Thunder Garrison (Dalei Shu), a military fortification on the north bank of the Great River (in modern Anhui), and ascends an embankment there:

I have traversed a thousand miles,
Spending over ten days on the journey.
Cruel frost tormented my joints,
Wailing wind sheers off my skin.
Having parted from my family, I became a traveler:
What can I do about it? What can I do?[32]

Bao then begins his landscape description, carefully organizing his letter into sections based on the points of the compass: south, east, north, and west, respectively. When the writer's gaze turns south, his focus shifts to the mountains there. And as he delineates the rugged terrain of those peaks, Bao Zhao employs an epideictic style of parallel prose that is reminiscent of the rhetoric of Han dynasty *fu*:

To the south piled mountains present myriad shapes,
Valiantly competing with one another for height,
Consuming sunset glow and ingesting sunlight,
Jagged and jutting, they alternately claim dominance.
They bestride a long range of hills,
Joined together in one long chain;
They are long enough to girdle the sky,
Spanning the earth as far as the eye can see.[33]

When Bao Zhao alters compass direction, his focus on the landscape changes as well. For instance, his section on the "east" describes plains and wetlands, while the section on the "north" concerns reservoirs and underground streams. In the final and longest segment, on the "west," the author's attention turns to rivers. The landscape imagery in this last section, accompanied by carefully chosen motion verbs, skillfully conveys the experience of heading downriver on a boat. Notice especially how effectively Bao weaves his own deep and personal melancholy into water imagery, creating a water-laden metaphor that represents his tears of sadness:

To the west winding rivers course into the distance,
Long swells are hemmed in by the sky.
In their torrential flow, where will they end?
Spanning far and wide, how can they be exhausted!
From antiquity to the present,

Ship after ship has passed through here.
My thoughts vanish into swells and surges;
My melancholy fills deep pools and ravines.[34]

Bao then shifts attention away from rivers and water, moving back again toward mountains, this time to one of China most famous scenic peaks, Mount Lu:

Looking southwest towards Mount Lu,
I was struck by its remarkable form.
Its base bears down on the river tide,
Its peaks are joined with the Milky Way.
Often gathered above it are clouds and mists,
That are carved into elaborate brocades.[35]

After some additional description, Bao's letter then concludes with the following remarks:

I thought you would want to know my situation,
Thus, I write about what I have seen.
I scrawl this on my journey;
My thoughts are far from complete.[36]

Bao Zhao's letter is justifiably famous. It is a tour de force literary feast in the parallel-prose style; this is probably why the distinguished modern literary scholar Qian Zhongshu praised it (in the epigraph that opened this section of the chapter) in such lofty terms. As was the case with the rhapsody, its primary importance in the early development of *youji* is the extended nature and literary quality of its landscape description. But again, as in *fu* compositions, aesthetic appreciation of the scenery is limited. The reason for this reticence is that another, more serious matter weighs heavily on the author's mind; the pursuit of a government career has forced him to take leave of his family and travel to unfamiliar places. It saddens him greatly, but he is helpless ("What can I do about it? What can I do?").

Another missive often quoted in *youji* anthologies is Wu Jun's (469–520) "Letter to Zhu Yuansi" (Yu Zhu Yuansi shu). Wu came from a humble family background and for a time served the Liang dynasty (502–57) in various minor government positions. He was also a well-known writer and historian, and many readers admire the simple, straightforward, and sometimes even colloquial diction used in his poetry. In a surviving letter sent to his friend Zhu Yuansi, Wu presents an extended, picturesque, and charming word picture of the landscape along the Fuyang River (Fuyang Jiang) in modern Zhejiang:

Wind and mist have both calmed down;
Sky and mountains now match in color.
I follow the current, drifting this way and that,
As it willfully takes me now east, now west.
From Fuyang to Tonglu,
For one hundred-some *li*,
These fantastic mountains and extraordinary rivers
Are unique and unsurpassed throughout the empire.
The rivers are all silvery blue,
With bottoms visible at a thousand *zhang*.
Fish swimming over riverbed pebbles,
I view steadily and without hindrance.
The torrent moves swiftly as an arrow,
While ferocious waves seem to dash at full pace.
Enclosed by banks, lofty mountains
All beget wintertime trees.
Supported by their might, vying to ascend higher,
The mountains rise into the distance.
Contending to be the highest and jutting skyward,
By the hundreds, they form into peaks.
Water from springs surges against the rocks,
Making sounds like "clink and clank."
Beautiful birds call back and forth,
Composing melodies like "chirp and cheep."
The drone of cicadas never ends;
The howl of gibbons never stops.
Hawks swiftly soaring toward the heavens,
Gaze at the peaks as they stop for a rest.
Those who manage government affairs,
If once peeked into these valleys, they would forget to return.[37]
The crisscrossing branches above hide all:
Even in daytime it is still dark.

Only where cover is sparse do we get some light,
And occasionally even see some sunlight.[38]

Observations such as "These fantastic mountains and extraordinary rivers / Are unique and unsurpassed throughout the empire" leave little doubt that Wu truly marveled at the attractive riparian landscape along the Fuyang River.

Wu Jun's letter showcases key elements of *youji* writing that first emerged during the Six Dynasties. The first and most general of these traits is the overall design of Wu's missive, which follows what I shall call the "scenic description–author comment" structure. This syntactic device is related to the "topic commentary on the topic"[39] grammatical construction in Classical and Modern Chinese and in many other languages. Moreover, it has been used in Modern Chinese literary criticism, most notably by Wang Guowei in his *Talks on Ci Poems in the Human World* (Renjian cihua). Wang refers to the "scenic description–author comment" structure as *jing*, or "scene," and *qing*, or "emotion," respectively.[40] This two-part construct functions as a common mode of discourse in many different genres of Chinese literature, especially *shi* and *ci* poetry. It is present in virtually all Chinese travel literature. In fact, it is employed in the rhapsody selections from Wang Can and Pan Yue discussed earlier in this chapter. The "scenic description" component most often relates to the author's movement through a physical environment, such as traveling down a road or taking a boat trip along a river and/or a journey to a destination, such as the summit of a famous mountain. The "author comment" section voices his "reaction" (*qing*) to the scene (*jing*) just described. The author reaction element is often presented in the form of a personal response to the visual qualities of scene.

In Wu Jun's letter, for instance, after describing the beautiful topography along the Fuyang River, his "response" is quite simple: "If only those government officials who shuffle paperwork all day could visit here and witness scenery like this, they would forget all about returning to their desks." Wang Can's response to the beautiful landscape around the Zhang River, however, was very different: "Though truly beautiful, it is not my home! / How can I remain here even briefly?" One of the most appealing aspects of the "author comment" component of *youji* is that authors always differ in the nature, content, and emotional intensity of their reactions to scene.

Another important aspect of Wu Jun's scenic description is that it is essentially comprised of mountain- and river-related vocabulary. This idea of using an alternating, binary structure of mountain (*shan*) and water (*shui*) imagery is central to the idea of "landscape" (*shanshui*) in traditional China and is usually credited to Xie Lingyun. Its purpose is to bring an immediate sense a balance and symmetry to descriptions of place. According to Wendy Swartz, Xie used this technique in his poetry "in order to impress upon his audience the densely layered composition of the natural landscape."[41] The overwhelming majority of *youji* texts dating from the traditional period in China similarly include description of scenic mountain and water/river environments.

One additional point about Wu Jun's letter: unlike the rhapsody authors discussed earlier in this chapter, Wu Jun says virtually nothing about himself, nor does he provide any details about his itinerary. In fact, he does not even mention his final travel destination. His only concern is to convey—in writing—the beauty of the Fuyang River environment to his friend Zhu Yuansi. Wu's commentary seems aimed mainly at praising the beauty of Fuyang and Tonglu, though his observations about officials who "manage the affairs of the world" could certainly be regarded as social-political commentary.

Beginning in the Han dynasty and continuing thereafter, non-poetic literary genres like the letter were often written in a style that has since come to be known as parallel prose (*pianwen* or *pianti wen*). Keeping in mind that there are different types of parallel prose and that these developed and changed over time, we can identify three hallmark qualities of this form: close attention to parallel verbal structure, consistency in the number of Chinese characters employed in each line, and emphasis on tonal patterns (a development that appeared in the late fifth and early sixth centuries, after the so-called Wei-Jin period).[42] As an example, compare the literal rendition of this line from Wu Jun's letter:

蟬則千轉不窮,
chan-ze-qian-zhuan-bu-qiong
cicadas | then | by the thousands | buzz | do not | end
[The drone of cicadas never ends]

with the one that follows it:

猿則百叫無絕。
yuan-ze-bai-jiao-wu-jue

gibbons | then | by the hundreds | howl | never | stop
[The howl of gibbons never stops]

Notice how nouns in one line parallel or match the position of those in the next (cicadas > gibbons), as do numbers (thousands > hundreds), verbs (buzz > howl; end > stop), and so on.[43] Although attacked by many later critics as an "artificial" literary form with formal, prosodic attributes that tend to stifle creativity, in the hands of a skilled writer, extended descriptions of attractive scenes written in the symmetrically balanced style of parallel prose can at times be quite evocative and appealing. However, later *youji* authors will find the verbal demands of parallel prose, like those of the rhapsody, too restrictive and will thus turn to a looser or more informal type of prose.

Wu Jun's letter, on the other hand, unabashedly proclaims a deep appreciation of the scenic mountains and rivers of Zhejiang. Such aesthetic appreciation of landscape in prose is an important concern in *youji*. What is most noteworthy about "Letter to Zhu Yuansi" and several similar works, all of which date from the fifth and sixth centuries, is that they all essentially follow the "scenic description–author comment" structure employed in Wu Jun's text.[44] Later travel writers, especially those composing in the popular "sightseeing account" form in the Northern Song period (960–1127), and others who favored the "vignette" (*xiaopin*) style during the late Ming, will adopt the same topic-comment structure. One reason for the preference for this format is that it is ideal for shorter *youji* compositions of a few hundred Chinese characters. And brevity was desired because these accounts were often written to be inscribed on stele, or flat rocky surfaces.

THE PREFACE

> Descriptions of landscape in prefaces to poems during the two Jin
> and Southern Dynasties not only contribute to accounts written
> about sightseeing destinations, but also have their own achievement
> in the history of landscape description.
>
> WANG LIQUN, *A STUDY OF LANDSCAPE TRAVEL*
> *ACCOUNTS FROM CHINA'S ANCIENT ERAS*[45]

Like the rhapsody and letter forms, prefaces (*xu* or *qianxu*) occupy a prominent place in the early development of *youji*. In ancient China, prefaces were often written for collections of historical documents, literary works, and other varieties of compendia and individual texts. They were also produced to accompany collections of poems, either by single or multiple authors. The best-known preface in Chinese literary history is Wang Xizhi's (fourth century) "Preface to the Lanting Poems" (Lanting shi xu), which describes a springtime outing enjoyed by Wang and some friends in 353.[46] Many poems were composed at the gathering, and these were later compiled into a single volume. Although the contents of the poetry preface can vary greatly, most—Wang Xizhi's famous text among them—sought to provide context to readers regarding the authors of the poems, who wrote which poems in the collection, the circumstances of composition, the place where the writing took place, and the physical features of the host locale.

Three prefaces to verse collections that survive from the Six Dynasties, which describe journeys to scenic locations, deserve close attention. These are Shi Chong's (249–300) "Preface to the Gold Valley Poems" (Jingu shi xu), Tao Yuanming's "Preface to the Poem about a Sightseeing Trip to Slanted Creek" (You Xiechuan shi xu), and Huiyuan's (334–416) "Preface to the Poems about a Sightseeing Trip to Stone Gate by the Lay Buddhists from Mount Lu" (Lushan zhu daoren you Shimen shi xu). These works deserve scrutiny because unlike the rhapsodies and letters considered earlier in this chapter, they describe travel to scenic destinations and how the authors responded emotionally—sometimes even religiously—to the sights they viewed.

Shi Chong was a government official, preeminent writer, and wealthy magnate who owned a large estate near Luoyang called Gold Valley (Jingu). He once hosted a lavish banquet there in honor of a military official named Wang Xu (dates unknown), who was passing through Luoyang on his way to Chang'an. Shi Chong invited thirty friends to attend the farewell festivities. Much poetry was produced on the occasion, and Shi wrote a preface to commemorate the event. Here is a part of his preface:

> Together with all the honorable guests I accompanied General Wang
> Xu into the valley. Day and night, we were sightseeing and feasting, fre-
> quently changing our seats.[47] Some climbed heights to look down; some
> sat in rows along the riverbank. From time to time musicians with zithers
> and zitherns, reed organs and bamboo zithers, accompanied us in the
> carriages and performed together as we moved down the road. When
> we stopped, the musicians were commanded to take turns with players of
> the percussion and wind instruments. At this point, each of us composed

a poem to express our innermost feelings. Those unable to do so were punished by having to drink three dippers of wine. There were feelings expressed about the brevity of human destiny and fears about when the leaves will wither [that is, the passage of time]. Thus, I have listed the titles, names, and ages of those present and have copied out and appended their poems. I wonder if connoisseurs of later generations will ever look at them?[48]

Shi Chong's preface is not written in parallel prose but in a more informal prose style that later became known as *sanwen*, or "relaxed prose" (there are several four-character lines in Shi's preface, but these are not written in grammatically parallel form).[49] This practice was unusual in the late third century and was followed by a trend away from parallel prose in the descriptions of landscape. Note that the "scenic description–author commentary" structure is also present in this text, but Shi Chong adds details about who participated in the outing, the carriage tour he arranged for his guests, the various sightseeing activities they engaged in, and even the names, ages, and office titles of those present (not translated). Finally, readers will certainly have noticed that Shi's "commentary," where the author informs us that he and his guests, perhaps inspired by the beauty of his valley estate and several dippers of wine, expressed feelings about human mortality and the irrevocable passage of time. Such sentiments are quite common in Six Dynasties literature, most notably in Wang Xizhi's "Lanting" preface.

The next work we will examine is Tao Yuanming's "Preface to the Poem about a Sightseeing Trip to Slanted Creek." Slanted Creek is located at the southern foot of Hanyang Peak (Hanyang Feng), on the northern side of Mount Lu:

Fifth day, first month, of the *xinchou* year.[50] The weather was clear and pleasant; the scenic view was quiet and lovely. Together with two or three neighbors I went on a sightseeing trip to Slanted Creek. We looked down at its long flow, and then gazed out at Tiered Citadel.[51] As bream and carp leapt out of the water, their scales shone in the twilight; as river gulls rode gentle winds, their wings flapped in flight. As for that South Mountain, its name has certainly been celebrated for a long time, so there is no need for me to praise it any further.[52] Now, as for Tiered Citadel, alone it towers aloft, with nothing around it—a solitary elegance centered on the riverbank. I imagine Numinous Mountain far away, with its charm and

1.1. Hua Yan 華喦 (1682?–1756).
Painting of the Gold Valley Garden
(Jingu yuan tuzhou 金谷園圖軸).
178.7 × 94.4 cm. Courtesy of the
Shanghai Museum.

admirable name.[53] But enjoying Tiered Citadel's presence was not enough,
and so we dashed off some poems. Saddened by the passage of days and
months, grieved by the impermanence of our years, each of us wrote down
our age and native village so that we might commemorate our time together
on this day.[54]

The form and content of Tao Yuanming's account of his trip to Slanted
Creek resembles Shi Chong's preface in several ways. First, despite the presence of several lines comprised of four Chinese characters, Tao's prose is
written in the *sanwen*, or "relaxed" prose style. The "scenic description–
author comment" structure is also present, and, like Shi Chong, Tao Yuanming provides several background details about the trip, including the year
in which it took place, the identity of those people who accompanied him

(including their ages and native villages), details about the scenery and weather at Mount Lu, and special praise for the landscape features of Tiered Citadel. And finally, as in Shi Chong's preface, the attractive scene at Slanted Creek notwithstanding, ultimately Tao and his companions react to that scene by dashing off some poems that lament the passage of time and the impermanence of life.

The third and most important preface, also concerning Mount Lu, is titled "Preface to the Poems about a Sightseeing Trip to Stone Gate by the Lay Buddhists from Mount Lu." Authorship of this work is sometimes attributed to the venerable Buddhist monk Huiyuan, who, with another monk named Huiyong (332–414), established a religious center on Mount Lu in the late fourth century. "Stone Gate" (Shimen) is the name of towering twin rocky walls between which flows an attractive stream:

> Shi [or "I," presumably referring to Huiyuan himself], the Dharma Master, in the second month of spring in the fourth year of the Eminent Stability [Longan] reign period [400 CE], had been singing of the hills and streams of Mount Lu, and so I went sightseeing there with my tin staff in hand. At the time, friends and novices with similar tastes—more than thirty of them—all dusted off their robes and trekked out with me at dawn, previously chagrined but now in heightened spirits.[55] Although the forests and ravines were secluded and remote, we nonetheless opened a path and trudged further on to advance. Although we scaled perilous heights and treaded over boulders, the pleasure of it all put us at ease.
>
> Upon reaching the gorge, we took hold of trees and grabbed at creepers, passing dangerous spots until we finally reached a cliff. With gibbon-like arms we clambered, dragging one another upward. Only then were we able to advance to the summit. Thereupon, I leaned against a crag at a place of good vantage, and carefully observed the scene below. Only then did I come to know the beauty of the Seven Precipices [that is, Mount Lu] and the collected wonders found there. The twin pylons at Stone Gate Gorge face the peaks to their front; layered crags cast reflections to their rear. Ridges and hills, circuitous and meandering around the pylons, form a screen. Noble crags, laid out all around, create a universe. Within it are images of stone terraces, stone ponds, and palatial lodges. The physical features one encounters here are totally delightful. Clear springs run separately then come together to flow forth; the profound depths of the Celestial Pond are mirror-like in their clarity. Patterned stones emit

a luster, brilliant as if a beautiful face had been unveiled. The tamarisks, pines, and redolent grasses dazzle the eyes with their luxuriance. They make a divine beauty which, for its part, is now complete. On this day, numerous feelings hastened our delight, and we gazed and scanned to no end.[56]

The author of the "Stone Gate" preface was a skillful wordsmith, especially adept at weaving together distinct types of language and imagery, sometimes more oriented toward beautiful landscape depiction, at other times more concerned with philosophical and religious matters. At one point in the preface, the author imagines the arrival of a *yuren*, or "feathered one," which is another name for a Daoist immortal. Now, although we certainly can find lines in the preface that reflect the influence of the parallel-prose style ("Patterned stones emit a luster, brilliant as if a beautiful face had been unveiled" is just one example), most of Huiyuan's preface is written in relaxed prose. Moreover, because detailed narration of a journey necessarily requires language that indicates sequential action or movement, with the increased presence of action and motion verbs here we thus see more frequent use of sequential terms such as "and then" / "thereupon" (*yushi*), "then / only then" (*nai*); temporal expressions such as "after arriving, then..." (*jizhi, ze...*); and causatives like "because of this" (*yinci*). This is yet another indication—also evident in the prefaces by Shi Chong and Tao Yuanming—that some Six Dynasties authors, when describing sightseeing trips to attractive locations, preferred to write in a more relaxed or "free" style of prose.

Huiyuan's preface is part of the *denglin* tradition described earlier, whereby an author in the company of friends ascends a height to gain an aerial view of a scenic location and reacts in some way—usually emotionally—to the perspective. Here, however, Huiyuan provides a detailed description of the ascent, using action and motion verbs in his description of the climb (opening a path, struggling to advance, scaling heights, treading over boulders, and so on). This register of language punctuates the physical difficulties he and his companions had to endure to reach Stone Gate. Although the latter portion of the preface, and especially the poem that follows it, reference matters pertaining to how religious enlightenment can be attained through contact with a pristine, remote, and ethereal mountain landscape ("As the sky opened and closed, it seemed to reveal a numinous spirit beyond human comprehension.... How could the spiritual meaning

1.2. Shen Zhou 沈周 (1427–1509). *Mount Lu on High* 廬山高 (Lushan gao; 1467). Hanging scroll, ink and colors on paper, 193.8 × 98.1 cm. The Collection of the National Palace Museum, Taipei.

of all this be limited to just mountains and streams?"), more important here is the fact that Huiyuan's preface is the earliest text that in every respect conforms to our definition of *youji*, making it our first prototype of Chinese travel literature. That is to say, his preface includes a detailed narration of a real journey undertaken essentially for pleasure purposes ("I went sightseeing."); a sustained and lively description of an identifiable landscape appreciated for its natural beauty ("The physical features one encounters here are totally delightful."), which is followed by a generous amount of author reaction that was inspired by that scene; identification of the (probable) author and his traveling companions ("friends and novices"); the date of composition (400 CE); and the circumstances under which the excursion was made ("I had been singing of the hills and streams of Mount Lu, and so I went sightseeing there with . . . friends and novices with similar tastes.").

Although Huiyuan's preface is our earliest *youji* prototype, this does not indicate any sort of literary trend or "birth" of travel literature in ancient China. While various Six Dynasties authors narrate journeys and express appreciation of, and reaction to, scenic landscapes, they did so in different literary genres and in diverse registers of language.

THE ACCOUNT

The rise of Buddhism created a major incentive for people to travel far and wide, and as a result, religious seekers journeyed to Central and Southeastern Asia alongside imperial expedition teams and traders.

XIAOFEI TIAN, *VISIONARY JOURNEYS: TRAVEL WRITINGS FROM EARLY MEDIEVAL AND NINETEENTH-CENTURY CHINA*[57]

Among all the various genres of writing that are crucial to our understanding of the rise of travel literature discussed in this chapter, the most important is the *ji*, or "account." This is because by the Tang dynasty, *ji* had become the preferred literary form for several varieties of prose; that is, works in the same form but with different content and written for different purposes. Literary historians sometimes call such works "subgenres." One of these Tang forms of the account was *youji*, which modern literary historians sometimes also call *shanshui youji*, or "landscape travel accounts."

The *Shuowen jiezi* dictionary provides the following definition: "*Ji* means 'to elucidate'" (記, 疏也.).[58] Some editions of the dictionary give the "definition word" in this formulation as *shu* 疋 rather than *shu* 疏. Duan Yucai (1735–1815), the Qing dynasty philologist and commentator on the *Shuowen jiezi*, explains further: "The two characters *shu* 疋 and *ji* 記 are derived characters (*zhuanzhu*).[59] As for *shu* 疋, in current orthography it is written 疏. It means 'to distinguish and elucidate something and then make a written account of it.'"[60] During the Han dynasty, *ji* as a verb meaning "to make or maintain a written account" was used in the titles of many well-known texts. Familiar examples include the ancient work *Accounts of Rites* (Liji; there is also a chapter in this text titled "Accounts on Education," or Xueji); the "Accounts on the Scrutiny of Crafts" *(Kaogong ji)* chapter in the *Rites of Zhou* (Zhouli); and of course, Sima Qian's *Historical Records* (Shiji).[61] With just a few exceptions, *ji* was used in the titles of these and other Han texts to mean "accounts of." Usually, the reference of *ji* in such titles is to sagely words, deeds, or practices associated in some way with the Confucian canon or, in the case of Sima Qian, history (*shi*) that was worth recording. *Ji* was also used in some government office titles during the Han and thereafter. One well-known example is *jishi* 記室, or account keeper, whose job was to maintain records of the emperor's words and actions, as well as major events of the day. But at no time during the Han dynasty was *ji* ever used as a name for any genre of prose writing.

One of the most significant works regarding genre classification during the Six Dynasties is the *Literary Selections*. Xiao Tong's anthology is especially important in this regard because genre classification in China has always been closely related to the compilation of literary collections and the classification headings used therein. Among the many classification headings of prose styles provided in the *Literary Selections*, none are labeled *ji*. When Xiao Tong compiled his anthology in the early sixth century, the *ji* had not yet developed into an independent prose genre.[62] Perhaps even more significant, the major prose forms that are identified by name in the *Literary Selections*, some examples of which include the *lun* (treatise), preface, letter, memorial (*biao*), and proclamation (*xi*),[63] were generally written in parallel prose. Works with *ji* in their title, such as the *Liji* (*Accounts of Rites*) and *Shiji*, however, were not associated with the parallel-prose style of writing but instead with works whose purpose it was "to keep a factual account" of noteworthy events related to history, ancient rites, and so on. This idea of "keeping a factual record or account" (*ji*) of a journey in narrative form later became *the* dominant structural characteristic of Chinese travel literature. Such practice, however, did not become widespread until the Northern Song dynasty (960–1127). In fact, the very first literary anthology to recognize *ji* as an independent prose genre is the *Choice Blossoms from the Garden of Literature* (Wenyuan yinghua), which was compiled under imperial orders and completed in 986. It was later revised several times. Of the one thousand chapters in this collection, thirty-seven are devoted to *ji* compositions.[64]

During the Jìn (265–420) and Liu-Song periods, more and more works began to appear with the word *ji* included in their title.[65] Many of these texts concern a geographically specific location, so literary historians and compilers of anthologies often designate them *diji*, or "accounts of places."[66] Well-known examples include *Miscellaneous Accounts from the Western Capital* (Xijing zaji; compiled *ca.* 500), much of which describes events and people in Chang'an during the Former Han dynasty (206 BCE–25 CE); *Accounts of the Buddhist Monastic Complexes of Luoyang* (Luoyang qielan ji; sixth century),[67] which essentially is a memoir heavy with description of places, events, and people, written largely in parallel prose; and Tao Yuan-ming's familiar "Account of the Peach Blossom Spring."[68] Another good example, though much less well known, is Yuan Shansong's (d. 401) *Accounts of the Mountains and Streams of Yidu* (Yidu shanchuan ji).[69] Here is a brief selection from Yuan's description of the famous Three Gorges (Sanxia) along the Great River:

> I often heard about the swift flow of water in the gorges, and both written and oral accounts warn of vertigo. No one has ever praised the beauty of its landscape. Having clambered into this region on foot, I was delighted to discover that hearing about something is not as good as seeing it in person. As for the layered cliffs and lovely peaks, extraordinary forms and odd shapes, these are indeed hard to describe in words. Forests desolate and dreary, thick and lush, rest upon the rosy mists of dawn. I gazed upward and peered downward, and the more I got used to the scene, the more attractive it became. I lingered on, staying for two additional nights, and unconsciously forgot all about returning home. What I have seen here is something unknown to me before. Thus, I am delighted to have found such extraordinary sights. If this landscape has a soul, it should be surprised to find a true confidant like me after so many countless years of neglect.[70]

Like the landscape description in Huiyuan's preface, which was written at about the same time, here we find a good example of just how genuine appreciation of landscape in south China found expression in prose during the fourth and fifth centuries. Yuan's *ji* also reveals two additional developments in description of landscape: it illustrates that in the hands of skilled writers like Shi Chong, Tao Yuanming, Huiyuan, and Yuan Shansong, relaxed prose could be used effectively to describe an attractive physical environment. And even though most literary historians would probably classify Yuan's text as a *diji*, the author voices a strong personal presence in the work (as did Huiyuan): Yuan himself "clambered" to the gorges where he "discovered" a place of great physical beauty that had been neglected for a long time. Other *diji* dating from around the same time, such as Sheng Hongzhi's (fl. early fifth century) often-cited "Account of Jingzhou" (Jingzhou ji), provide good description, especially of local topography, notable persons, and products, but seem more like early forms of the local gazetteer because their texts lack authorial voice. And although Yuan Shansong's *Accounts of the Mountains and Streams of Yidu* does not include narration of a journey, the author's extended description of the Three Gorges and his lyrical response makes this one of the most important "mountain and river" prose accounts of the Six Dynasties. The prefaces by Tao Yuanming and Huiyuan, along with Yuan Shansong's *Accounts*, all appear around the beginning of the fifth century, which strengthens the argument suggested earlier that several major authors, when describing sightseeing and landscape in a lyrical way, chose to write in relaxed rather than parallel prose. As for Yuan Songshan's *ji*, its lack of journey narration notwithstanding, surviving remnants of the text strongly suggest that it closely approximates our definition of *youji* and thus must be regarded as one of the earliest-known examples of the genre.

The contemporary scholar He Li has done research on the ninety-two pre-Tang dynasty *ji* texts preserved in *The Complete Prose of High Antiquity*. Some fascinating results emerge. Eighty of these works—87 percent—are related to religion in some way, and among those, seventy-nine are directly related to Buddhism. He Li organizes these seventy-nine Buddhist-related texts into three broad categories: translations, usually from Sanskrit (forty-three); miscellaneous *ji* (fourteen); and *ji* on statues of images (twenty-two).[71] Categorizing the twelve texts that are *not* related to religion is difficult for several reasons. In some cases, later editors added the word *ji* to titles. In other cases, only the title survives, so we cannot be sure about the original content. Also, some important works, such as Yuan Shansong's *Accounts of the Mountains and Streams of Yidu*, are not included in *The*

Complete Prose of High Antiquity, presumably because only parts of the original text survive. Some of these texts are not really "accounts" of anything, but for unknown reasons carry *ji* in their titles. Finally, and most important, one of the eighty texts listed among the titles that are related to religion—the Buddhist monk Faxian's *Accounts of the Buddhist Kingdoms*—is related in an important way to the development of travel literature.

Our main concern is to determine which of these works carried *ji* in their original title and if any chronicle trips or excursions to scenic sites or historical locations. Only a handful of such works survive. These include Ma Dibo's "Account of the Feng and Shan Ritual Observances" (Fengshan yi ji), Wang Xizhi's *Accounts of Sightseeing Trips to the Four Commanderies* (You sijun ji), Tao Yuanming's "Account of the Peach Blossom Spring," and two titles by Huiyuan: "Account of Mount Lu" (Lushan ji) and "Account of a Sightseeing Trip to the Mountains" (Youshan ji). Unfortunately, only a few lines of the Wang Xizhi text and Huiyuan's "Account of a Trip to the Mountains" survive. As for Tao Yuanming's tale about discovering the Peach Blossom Spring, for reasons stated earlier (notably, its imaginary content), I have decided to not include this title in our discussion. Of the remaining works mentioned here, Ma Dibo's account of a journey to the summit of Mount Tai in 56 CE merits close attention.

Ma Dibo's report has been shown to contain narrative features "associated with the later travel account,"[72] the most important of which is that "Account of the Feng and Shan Ritual Observances" is the earliest surviving text of a real journey told in the first person. Also noteworthy is the almost matter-of-fact language style that Ma Dibo uses to narrate his journey, and that he provides precise distances in Chinese miles, identifies places by name along his itinerary, and explains the reasons for their name:

On this morning [17 March] we ascended the mountain on horseback.
Frequently, where the road grew steep and precipitous, we dismounted
and led our horses on foot. Sometimes we walked and sometimes we rode,
roughly in equal amounts. We arrived at the Midway Temple where we
left our horses, a distance of seven miles from flat ground. . . . We went
another two and a half miles straight upward. The path was convoluted,
winding its way around, so it is called Circle Path.[73]

Among the various *diji* texts mentioned earlier, Huiyuan's "Account of Mount Lu" is the most important. This is because of the keen attention he devotes to individual sites on the mountain and their names. Also important is the early history of Mount Lu and historical figures who once visited there:

> Mount Lu is in Xunyang Commandery, Jiang County. To the south it adjoins Palace Pavilion Lake; to the north it faces the Nine Rivers.[74] South of the Nine Rivers the Great River becomes the Minor River. The mountain is thirty-some *li* from the Minor River. On the left, it harbors Pengli Marsh; on the right, it sits beside Passage Stream. Mount Lu attracts the flow of several rivers and then nestles against where they merge. The *Treatise on Mountains and Seas* [Shanhai jing] says, "The source of the Lu River is Mount of the Three Sons of Heaven Metropolis [San Tianzi Du]. It enters the Great River west of Peng Marsh." Mount of the Three Sons of Heaven Metropolis is also called Mount of the Son of Heaven's Barrier [Tianzi Zhang], which is Peng Marsh. Mount Lu is west of it, and long ago Pengli Marsh was regarded as its border. There was one Master Kuangxu from the Yin and Zhou periods. When he escaped from the world and became a recluse, he hid out by living on Mount Lu. Some say that Kuangyu [that is, Kuangxu] learned the Way from an immortal and then went traveling to its peaks, where he tugged away at the mountain's peaks and tors. He built a lodge next to a peak. Thus, the mountain was so named because people of later generations felt that the site of his lodge was once the hermitage of an immortal.[75]

Although brief, this selection contains several features that later became stock topoi in *youji* writing. First, Huiyuan pays great attention to Mount Lu's precise location as it relates to the surrounding topography. Note that he gives the distance to the mountain from the Minor River in *li*. He is also concerned about the source of the Lu River, and he quotes a line from the *Treatise on Mountains and Seas* and then adds a note of his own: "Mount of the Three Sons of Heaven Metropolis is also called Mount of the Son of Heaven's Barrier, which is Peng Marsh." Finally, Huiyuan references Kuangxu, an immortal associated with the mountain, who supposedly "found the Way" on Mount Lu during the Zhou dynasty. He does so to explain the origin and meaning of the word Lu in the name "Mount Lu": Lu literally means "hermitage," and since Kuangxu was thought to have once built a hermitage (*lu*) on the mountain, it was so named. Later in Chinese literary history, when *youji* authors visited famous landmarks like Mount Lu, they will similarly pay close attention to names, locations, and distances, as well as the history of the place and famous visitors who may have stopped there in the past. Quotations from authoritative sources are also quite common, for these can emend or support descriptive information about the place in question.

Another text worthy of attention is Xie Lingyun's *Notes on Sightseeing Trips to Famous Mountains* (You mingshan zhi). Unfortunately, only the preface to Xie's text and thirty-some entries are extant, many in fragment form, and these have survived only because they were copied into some Tang and Song dynasty encyclopedias, such as *Accounts of Elementary Studies* (Chuxue ji), *Classified Collections of Arts and Letters* (Yiwen leiju), *Imperial Scannings of the Great Peace Era* (Taiping yulan), and others.[76] The modern editor and commentator on Xie Lingyun's *Works*, Gu Shaobo, has collected the preface and extant entries, reprinted them, and added some useful explanatory notes.[77] Gu's geographical arrangement of the entries indicates that the contents of *You mingshan zhi* concern specific "famous mountains" in four commanderies: Yongjia (the general area around modern Wenzhou, Zhejiang); Dongyang (modern Jinhua, Zhejiang); Guiji (the area in and around modern Shaoxing, Zhejiang); and Linchuan (the general area west of modern Fuzhou, Jiangxi). Based on the contents of Xie's entries, Gu Shaobo estimates that *Notes*—based on personal visits and observations by Xie Lingyun—was written over a ten-year period, from 422 until 432.[78] Here is a portion of the preface:

> Now, as for food and clothing, these are what support human life; as for mountains and rivers, these are what accord with human nature [*xing*]. Nowadays, bound up as we are with the toils of supporting ourselves, we simply crowd out the dispositions that accord with our human nature. Worldly discussions for the most part say that joy and satisfaction are based in owning fancy estates [*huatang*; literally, "flowery halls"], while those who pillow on cliffs and rinse their mouths in streams are said to lack great ambition. Thus, they hold on to their withered state in the world. I say this is not the way to go.[79]

Here, as he does time and again in his poetry, Xie expresses an affinity with "mountains and waters" that runs counter to prevailing contemporary views regarding ambition and success, joy and satisfaction. Xie Lingyun did not fit in with the politics of his time, and instead preferred to "pillow on cliffs and rinse his mouth in streams."

No doubt many of the extant entries of *Notes on Sightseeing Trips to Famous Mountains* are longer in their original form, but still enough text survives to draw some conclusions about the nature of the work and its purpose. Here are four surviving entries:

> After entering Camphor Tree Creek [Nanxi] and proceeding 130 *li*, there is Stone Chamber Mountain [Shishi Shan].[80] To the north, it faces Clear Spring [Qingquan], stands seven *zhang* high, spans thirteen *zhang* across, and extends for sixty *bu*. The area can seat a thousand people. In shape, it resembles a tortoise shell; the color of the stone is yellowish-white. If you rap on the stone, it sounds like a drum. The stone wall that follows along the mountain is twelve *zhang* high. The ancients have passed down that this is Stone Chamber Corridor [Shishi Bulang]. Among the herbs at Stone Chamber is a generous lot of yellow essence [*huangjing*].[81]

> There is a large lake on the summit of Spring Mountain [Quanshan].[82] In the lake is a solitary island peak, standing alone, where beehives are visible. In the *Han History* [*Hanshi*], Zhu Maichen [d. 116 BCE] sends up a memorial saying, . . . "With just one person guarding the island peak, a thousand men could not take it."[83] . . . Spring Mountain has lots of tree peonies [*mudan*].

> The taste of oysters [*li*] in New Creek [Xinxi][84] is especially sweet, and some are even sweeter than those at Purple Creek [Zixi].

> If you ascend the path from River Prospect Tower [Linjiang Lou][85] and go south for two-some *li*, on the left you gaze off at the lake, and to your right is the Great River.[86]

Kang-I Sun Chang has proclaimed Xie Lingyun the "originator of 'travel literature' in China,"[87] and this identification appears to be based, at least in part, on the surviving entries of the *Notes on Sightseeing Trips to Famous Mountains*.[88] While Xie's text certainly falls into the category of *diji* (note that there is no author reaction present in the surviving entries of the text), this work does indeed have a place in the early history of *youji*. Its importance becomes apparent as soon as one understands that the word *zhi* in the title means "notes" or "jottings," specifically as they relate to geographical observations.

The descriptive and informational nature of Xie's language in the *Notes*, which is completely different from the delicately crafted structure and lyrical/expressive idiom in his landscape (or "nature") poetry and in most of the texts so far discussed in this chapter, is designed specifically for readers unfamiliar with these "famous mountains" in the south, especially future travelers to these sites. Both the subject matter of Xie's entries (which includes mainly locations, distances, and dimensions; shapes and colors of physical objects such as stones; quotations from authoritative sources such as the dynastic histories; and unique local products such as oysters, special herbs, and tree peonies) and the formulaic language constructions Xie uses to provide guidance, directions, and information on these matters ("after entering/reaching place-x, if you proceed for a certain number of *li*, you then reach different place-y; in shape, unknown object-x resembles familiar object-y; local product-x is delicious, and even tastes better than the same product in such-and-such famous place"), later became standard conventions in travel writing.

Faxian, whose name literally means "illustrious of the Dharma," has the distinction of being the first Chinese pilgrim known to have successfully traveled overland through Central Asia to India, visit holy places of Buddhism there, and then return home alive to tell about it. Accompanied by some fellow monks, Faxian left China in 399. The purpose of his trip was to seek out the precepts and regulations (*jielü*) of Buddhism, which Faxian says were in a "fragmentary and deficient" (*canque*) condition in China. His itinerary took him westward through several well-known oasis cities, such as the Buddhist centers at Dunhuang and Khotan (Yudian; modern Hetian), through the Gobi and Taklamakan Deserts, and over several major mountain ranges, including the Hindu Kush and the Pamirs. After spending several years visiting Buddhist holy sites and other places in India and gathering "precepts and regulations" (that is, sacred Buddhist texts and scriptures), Faxian returned home to China by sea via Ceylon (modern Sri Lanka) in 414. The *ji* account of his travel experiences through Central Asia and in India was written after his return home.[89]

The author's main focus in the *Accounts of the Buddhist Kingdoms* (Foguo ji) is to describe Buddhist practices in foreign lands, especially India, with particular attention devoted to religious ceremonies, holy sites, and Buddhist legends.[90] Faxian's primary target audience was certainly readers in China with an interest in Buddhism, especially members of the monastic community, though no doubt others read about his "journey through hell to paradise and back"[91] with great interest and curiosity. That Faxian would decide to write his travel account in the *ji* form is not surprising, for his stated purpose in writing the *Foguo ji* was to "report his experiences on bamboo and silk (that is, in writing) so that worthy readers might share in what he heard about and saw."[92] And since firsthand reports of foreign lands were practically nonexistent before Faxian composed the *Accounts of the Buddhist Kingdoms* (with just a few exceptions), the importance of Faxian's account as a religious and historical document cannot be overstated.

First, let us look at how Faxian describes the topography observed during the initial stages of his journey. The physical landscape encountered during the long, arduous, and dangerous journey to India was essentially composed of deserts, mountains, and rivers. Here is part of Faxian's account of the Gobi Desert, which he calls the "River of Sand" (Shahe):

> There are many evil spirits and scorching winds in the River of Sand. Those who encounter them perish without exception. There are neither birds flying above nor beasts ambling below. Gazing all around as far as the eye can see, if you desire to seek out a place to get across, no one will have any idea how to proceed. The only road markers are the dried bones of dead men.[93]

This passage is quoted often, and for good reason. Not only is it highly dramatic, it also seems designed to serve as an admonition to future pilgrims who might consider making the overland trip to India ("If you are not careful, your bones may end up here as well!"). But our main interest is the narrative style and register of language employed by Faxian. Throughout most of the *Accounts of the Buddhist Kingdoms*, he employs a narrative that is unadorned with literary effects. On the contrary, the language he uses is a very straightforward type of Classical Chinese peppered with an occasional colloquial term or expression. A longer example of Faxian's travel-narrative style describes the terrifying mountains that tower above the Indus River along the frontier of India:

> We followed along the mountain range toward the southwest, traveling for fifteen days. The path was difficult and rocky; the steep bank was frightening and sheer. The mountain is simply a rocky wall standing erect for a thousand *ren*. When you look downward, the eyes become blurry; when you desire to advance and tread onward, there is nothing to support

your feet. There is a waterway here called the Indus River. Men of antiquity chiseled through rock to open a path, and deployed ladders between the rocky ledges altogether numbering seven hundred. After traversing the ladders, you are then tracking along a suspension bridge of ropes that crosses the river. The distance between the two shores of the river is about eighty *bu*. According to the accounts of the multilingual interpreters,[94] neither Zhang Qian [d. 113 BCE] nor Gan Ying of the Han ever got this far in their travels.[95]

Again we see Faxian's straightforward reportorial manner of travel narration. There are three essential elements to this style. First, direction ("toward the southwest") and distance markers, both temporal ("fifteen days") and physical ("seven-hundred" ladders, "eighty" *bu*, and so on), present a set of details that establish a physical context for the travel narration. The second element, a small collection of selective adjectives, describe the environment at hand. In this case, it is a frightening place, where the path is "difficult and rocky" and the cliff sides are 'frightening and sheer," where your eyes get "dizzy" when you look down and if you move forward, there is no foothold. The third and most essential component is a series of motion verbs ("follow along," "travel," "tread onward," "open a path," "track along," "cross the river") that "carry" or "move" the traveler and the reader through the perilous heights above the Indus River.

Different from his style of travel narration is the language he uses when describing a physical structure, as in this example:

> Seven or eight *li* to the west of the city there is a monastic community, which is called King's New Monastery. It took eighty years to build and three reign periods passed before it was completed. It is about twenty-five *zhang* in height and is adorned with engraved writings and elegant inlay in gold and silver covered on top with a combination of all precious gems. Behind the pagoda, a Buddha Hall has been built, which is majestic and imposing, marvelous and outstanding. Its beams and pillars, door leaves, and windows, are all covered with gold leaf. The separately built monk's quarters are also imposing and striking, orderly and decorated. There are no words to describe them.[96]

There are numerous passages in the *Accounts of the Buddhist Kingdoms* that resemble Faxian's report on the King's New Monastery. While the underlying organizational feature of the text is the travel itinerary format, descriptive passages like this—concerning one noteworthy place—are found throughout the text. These are designed with the reader in mind, which means providing location information ("seven or eight *li* to the west of the city"), a generous amount of detail (in this case, the adjective-heavy description concerning the history of, and especially the magnificent architecture seen at, the King's New Monastery), and the author's commentary at the coda of the passage (this element can vary from little or no commentary to more extended author reaction, though the latter style is uncommon[97]).

There seems to be no doubt that Faxian modeled this descriptive technique for places after the prose style used by Sima Qian in the chapter on the Han envoy Zhang Qian's journey to the Western Regions in his *Historical Accounts*.[98] This language style is unmistakable. Here is a brief example, in which Sima Qian quotes from Zhang Qian's original report. The state of Dayuan (or Ferghana) was located west of the Tarim Basin, in what today is Uzbekistan:

Dayuan lies southwest of the territory of the Xiongnu, some ten thousand *li* directly west of China. The people are settled on the land, plow the fields, and grow rice and wheat. They also make wine from grapes. The region has many fine horses that sweat blood; their forbearers are supposed to have been foaled from heavenly horses. The people live in houses in fortified cities, there being some seventy or more cities of assorted sizes in the region. The population numbers several hundred thousand. The people fight with bows and spears and can shoot from horseback. Dayuan is bordered on the north by Kangju, on the west by the kingdom of the Indo-Scythians [Yuezhi], on the southwest by Daxia [Bactria], on the northeast by the land of the Wusun, and on the east by Wumi [Keriya] and Yutian [Khotan].[99]

Zhang Qian's description of Ferghana reads like an intelligence report. And for good reason: it was designed to provide information about the location of China's neighbors to the west, as well as their natural resources, fortifications, and population. Essentially, what Faxian did was to take the reportorial style and adopt it to his own itinerary and purposes, which were essentially religious. While Zhang Qian and Faxian's readers both shared an interest in reading about distant and exotic lands far to the west of China, they probably had other motives or concerns about the content. Most relevant to our discussion here is that the clear purpose of his writing style is reportorial; in other words, providing information to readers and future travelers, be they Han military commanders sent on a punitive mission to Ferghana (which happened later) or future pilgrims traveling through Central Asia to India. China's most famous Buddhist pilgrim, the Tang dynasty monk Xuanzang, spent sixteen years on an overland pilgrimage and visit to India. The famous account of that journey, titled *Accounts of the Western Regions during the Great Tang*, which will be discussed in chapter 2, is modeled directly on Faxian's prose style.

COMMENTARY ON THE WATERWAYS TREATISE

> The value of the *Shui jing zhu* as a literary work lies in its numerous descriptions of places and scenery. Modern scholars consider it as the precursor of the *you ji* or "travel note."
>
> DAVID R. KNECHTGES AND TAIPING CHANG, *ANCIENT AND EARLY MEDIEVAL CHINESE LITERATURE: A REFERENCE GUIDE, PART 3 & 4*[100]

One of the most important and influential works related to geography and dating from the period under discussion is *Commentary on the Waterways Treatise* (Shuijing zhu), compiled by Li Daoyuan (*ca.* 469–527), a scholar-official who served the Northern Wei dynasty (386–534). Li's work is a commentary on a Han dynasty (third century?) work concerning rivers and titled the *Waterways Treatise* (Shuijing). Li's commentary differs from all other works discussed in this chapter in one significant respect: it is much longer. In all, the text comprises forty chapters. This makes it more than twenty times longer than the original work to which it is intended to serve as a commentary. More importantly, it is one of, if not *the*, most complete and authoritative geographical "guidebooks" on China's rivers and historical monuments ever compiled. It is no surprise, then, that the *Commentary* has had a significant impact on the development of travel writing in China.

The following observations on the Three Gorges illustrate Li Daoyuan's contributions to *youji* writing. First, let us look at the kind of language the author uses to introduce a landmark (in this case, the Three Gorges), how he places that site in the overall topography of the region, and the kind of language he uses to introduce a place to readers.

> The river moves further east, passing through Broad Creek Gorge [Guangxi Xia].[101] This, in fact, is the head of the Three Gorges. It measures thirty *li* in length. With collapsed cliff side rocks and trees closely nestled together, its topography is virtually interlocked.[102]

In this example, and in practically every other section of the *Commentary*, we find formulaic language that relates to movement through landscape. The expression "The river moves further east" is repeated throughout the *Commentary* as a literary device to push the author's narration eastward along the Great River. As in some of the other texts discussed earlier in this chapter, distances between places are given in *li*, which helps readers get some sense of the lay of the land.

After introducing a place, Li Daoyuan next provides a brief description of the landscape—often in four-character phrases, indicating influence of the parallel-prose style, which is intended to serve as a brief introduction to the visual characteristics of the scene:

> Atop the mountain on the north bank is the Divine Chasm [Shenyuan]. North of the chasm is the White Salt Embankment [Baiyan Ya], probably standing over a thousand *zhang* high, and looking down on the Divine Chasm. Locals, observing that the embankment is lofty and white, have thus so-named it. During times of drought, the locals burn trees on top of the bank and then push the ashes and cinders from the trees down into the chasm. It then immediately begins to rain. Chang Qu [*ca.* 265–*ca.* 316] says, "In the town[103] there is a mountainous marsh with a water spirit. In times of drought, if locals beat drums and pray for rain, the reward will certainly then be favorable and benevolent [that is, it will rain]." This relates to the remark "Responding to the beat of a drum, it started to rain" in the "Rhapsody on the Shu Capital."[104]

Li Daoyuan was a devoted historian, and so in the *Commentary*, he quotes from over four hundred historical, geographical, and other sources, many of which are now lost, to confirm or sometimes question his own reports or those of others. He also quotes from numerous literary sources including poems and rhapsodies, as well as hundreds of stele inscriptions. As an example, in the passage just presented, he cites two authoritative sources—one geographical and the other literary—to confirm the successful rainmaking activities in Yong'an: Chang Qu's early fourth-century

Chronicle of the Land South of Mount Hua and Zuo Si's (*ca.* 250–305) "Rhapsody on the Shu Capital."

Local flora and fauna also receive much attention in the *Commentary*, as in this report about gibbons (*yuanhou*) in Qutang Gorge:

> There are many gibbons in this gorge. They do not reside anywhere along the north bank, and they are not just absented in one area there [in other words, they are found nowhere along the north bank of the river]. Some people have caught gibbons and then released them on the north bank mountain. Henceforth, no sounds were ever heard from them again. Is it possible that, as in the case of the ferret-badger, when gibbons crossed the Wen [or Min River] they never remained on the north bank of Qutang Gorge [Qutang Xia]?[105]

Gibbons once thrived along the banks of the Three Gorges, and, not surprisingly, their plaintive cries attracted the attention of many ancient poets. Here, however, Li Daoyuan's concern is the distribution of the primate along the Great River in Qutang Gorge; specifically, why the ape lived only along the southern bank. Li does not know the reason for this, and thus he can only speculate that perhaps, like the ferret-badger, when it migrated south from Sichuan and crossed the Min River, it settled on the southern rather than northern bank of the Great River. It is a testament to Li Daoyuan's scholarly integrity that he limits his commentary to speculation (the Chinese character *jiang* 將 in the last line of this passage means "it is possible"), as he did not have an authoritative source to cite that would have resolved the issue.

Finally, we come to that feature that most distinguishes Li Daoyuan's prose: the literary quality of his extended descriptions of place, which is evident in this often-quoted passage from his description of the Three Gorges:

> The two banks along the seven-hundred *li* stretch of the Three Gorges link with the mountains on both banks, without the slightest opening in between. Tiered crags and layered walls hide the sky and block out the sun: unless it is high noon or midnight, you will never see sunshine or moonlight. With the arrival of summer, the river's waterline rises to the hills, and travel is obstructed and cut off in both directions. Sometimes, when the king [that is, the emperor] mandates the swift dissemination of

1.3. Qutang Gorge today. Photo by Gary Larson. www.flickr.com/photos/chinesegary
/1149831543/in/set-72157601503576704.

a proclamation, there are occasions when the court dispatches it by boat
from White Emperor City. By sunset it reaches Jiangling, having covered
twelve hundred *li* in one day. Even if one were to mount a swift horse and
ride with the wind, it would not be considered faster than this. In the sea-
sons of spring and winter, white torrents rush into green pools, where
swirling clear ripples cast their reflections. Sheer stacks beget many
unusual cypress trees; suspended springs and cascading waterfalls fly and
scour among them. Such purity, abundance, loftiness, and luxuriance—
truly this has much gusto and appeal![106]

The literary qualities of Li Daoyuan's language in this passage, which
is representative of his extended descriptions of landscape, are prominent.
The foci of his attention, at the most basic level, are mountains and waters.
He seems mainly concerned with emphasizing the lofty, sheer cliffs in the
gorges and the ever-changing swift and sometimes dangerous flow of the
Great River, which he accomplishes by presenting a series of carefully chosen images. For instance, the cliffs are so high that there is not "the slightest

opening in between" them; in fact, unless it is "high noon or midnight," the river traveler will never see "sunshine or moonlight." As for the river, it flows faster than a "swift horse riding with the wind," and an imperial messenger—with the aid of the swift current—could travel twelve hundred *li* (roughly, four hundred miles) in a single day. This sort of description, along with additional motion-laden images that punctuate the massive amount of water moving through the gorges (rushing torrents, flying waterfalls, and so on) and the intense physical beauty of the gorges themselves, with their "unusual cypress trees" growing out of cracks in "sheer stacks," logically leads to the exclamation that ends the passage: "Such purity, abundance, loftiness, and luxuriance—truly this has much gusto and appeal!"

Mei Xinlin and Yu Zhanghua raise two important points about Li Daoyuan's *Commentary* that deserve repeating. They argue that the text represents two key turning points in the formative development period of *youji*: first, the prose style that Li Daoyuan employs in his extended descriptions represents a move away from the fact-oriented reportorial language seen in many geographical accounts dating from the Six Dynasties; and second, in his *Commentary* he writes in a register of language that is distinctly literary rather than geographical in style.[107] These literary descriptions, written for the most part in relaxed prose,[108] are presented within an overall structure of a moving itinerary,[109] but Li Daoyuan, like Faxian before him, usually remains in the background, unless he is moved emotionally to make a comment or correct an error in an earlier text. What Li has thereby brought forth in the *Commentary* is a new variety of extended landscape-and-monument (or famous-place) description, one that is written mostly in a register of free prose that is more literary in style than geographical in orientation and that is organized around an itinerary designed to take the reader through space (that is, in a generally eastward direction down the Great River) to various places of scenic beauty or historical interest along way.

Once the text reaches one of the places selected by the author, the focus can then turn to any number of local topics, such as notable landmarks, gravesites of famous people, unique or unusual flora and fauna, and local customs and products. Since author reaction in the *Commentary* is limited, it does not merit prototype status. This, however, does not diminish its importance. Although long regarded essentially as a "geography of ancient China," the literary qualities of Li Daoyuan's relaxed prose style, along with his keen interest in local sites and notable monuments, were new among

authors writing about place in the Six Dynasties. Later *youji* writers, especially those recounting their experiences while traveling by boat, will follow
this same style.

ADDENDUM

It is certain that most of the literary texts composed during the Six Dynasties, when writing activity was quite vigorous, are lost. Thus, what survives
today is probably only a small portion of what was once a prosperous
textual storehouse. Moreover, what critical remarks we have about literature
and genre development that survive from the period are also limited to
just a handful of works, such as the *Literary Selections, Literary Mind and
the Carving of Dragons,* and a few other titles. It is this fraction of extant
material that literary critics and historians often assume to be representative
of the age. This is a false premise, because we do not know for sure if what
has survived constitutes a representative selection. Nor do we know if the
texts that have been passed down to us are faithful to the language of the
original work. This is because textual tampering and interpolation are common in the Chinese literary tradition, especially among works initially
transmitted in hand-copied, manuscript form.[110] Thus, one could make a
convincing argument that many works survive from the Six Dynasties not
because of their intrinsic literary worth but, in many instances, because of
the prominence of the author. An example of one such case is Xie Lingyun's
Notes on Sightseeing Trips to Famous Mountains. But these surviving materials are all we have to work with. The readings and conclusions that literary
historians draw from these materials can be useful and informative and can
help us flush out what Northrop Frye described as "a large number of literary relationships that would not be noticed as long as there were no context
established for them."[111] But we must never forget that our conclusions
necessarily embody some limitations.

If we follow an open-ended conception of genre, then works like Huiyuan's "Preface," Yuan Shansong's *Accounts of the Mountains and Streams
of Yidu,* and Li Daoyuan's *Commentary* more closely align with my definition of *youji,* while others, such as Pan Yue's travel rhapsody and Bao Zhao's
"Letter," accord much less so. Still others, such as the prefaces of Shi Chong
and Tao Yuanming, along with Faxian's account of his trip to India, are
what have been called "borderline cases."[112] These works can (and have
been) considered as early forms of *youji,* though the only "prototype" of the

genre that emerged in the Six Dynasties is Huiyuan's "Preface." At the same time, the various other literary works discussed in this chapter could also be regarded as a kind of "proto-*youji*"[113]—that is, early versions of the form that, to lesser or greater degrees, embody various traits that will coalesce in the works of later "prototype" authors. Subsequent writers, beginning with Yuan Jie (719–72) and then later with Liu Zongyuan, will selectively adopt various features and styles from Huiyuan's "Preface" and these proto-*youji* texts. Sometimes, later writers who are more creative will alternately employ or even invent new literary features and devices to suit their own personal tastes and expressive needs.

One final and critical point: as for the new aesthetic appreciation of landscape that appeared in the Six Dynasties, it seems quite likely that this development would never have happened when it did if it had not been for the fall of the Jìn dynasty in the early fourth century. When Luoyang, the capital of the Jìn, was overrun and ransacked by non-Chinese Xiongnu forces in 311, many government officials, along with members of several powerful families, fled south as refugees to the general area around the Great River Delta. It was precisely this population migration that introduced transplanted northerners—and later, their descendants—to the scenic vistas in Jiangnan. Before the population exodus to south China that began in the early fourth century, few writers in the north ever composed literary works about travels to beautiful, verdant mountain environments or scenic river areas, and this is precisely because such places are rare in the heartland of north China, where the topography is generally rugged and bland in color (loess in the Yellow River Valley colors virtually everything there a distinctive shade of yellow-brown). But those who could flee south after the fall of Luoyang and who chose to resettle in Jiangnan found the beautiful "mountains and waters" scenery that Xie Lingyun, Li Daoyuan, and many others would later extol in their writings.

CHAPTER 2

ARTICULATION IN THE TANG

Climb the mountains and get their good tidings. Nature's peace will
flow into you as sunshine flows into trees. The winds will blow their
own freshness into you, and the storms their energy, while cares will
drop away from you like the leaves of Autumn.

JOHN MUIR, *OUR NATIONAL PARKS*

SEVERAL DEVELOPMENTS IN TRAVEL LITERATURE TOOK PLACE
during the Tang dynasty, two of which are especially important: first, the
ji, or "account," evolved into an independent genre of prose writing; and
second, in the works of two late eighth and early ninth century authors—
Yuan Jie and Liu Zongyuan—the *ji* form further developed into a new type
of descriptive prose about place, sometimes in English called the "landscape
essay" or "landscape journal," which includes both literary language and
lyrical expression. Practically every modern literary historian and critic of
Chinese travel literature singles out Liu Zongyuan as the "creator" (*chuang-
zao zhe*) of *youji* in ancient China. At the same time, they also stress the key
role of a style of writing that emerged in the late eighth and early ninth
centuries called *guwen*, or "ancient-style prose," and its influence on Liu
Zongyuan's famous masterpiece of landscape essays, the "Eight Accounts
of Yong County."

THE ACCOUNT (*JI*) AS AN INDEPENDENT PROSE GENRE

To confirm that the *ji* became an independent form of literary prose writing during the Tang, one need only browse through the *Choice Blossoms
from the Garden of Literature* and *Complete Tang Prose*, the two primary

repositories of extant Tang dynasty prose. For our purposes, the *Choice Blossoms* anthology is the most important because it is the first major collection of Chinese letters to list *ji* as an independent prose genre. In all, thirty-seven chapters out of one thousand are devoted to "accounts." The way chief compiler Li Fang (925–96) and his fellow editors organized and arranged these texts suggests how they conceptualized *ji* as a prose form in the late tenth century. With just a few exceptions, the classification scheme for accounts in the *Choice Blossoms* is keyed to writings about buildings (and *not* landscapes), beginning with palaces (*gongdian*) and then divided into subcategories such as office buildings (*tingbi*; literally, "office walls") in the Department of State Affairs (Shangshu Sheng) and Hanlin Academy (Hanlin Yuan). Most *ji* anthologized in the *Choice Blossoms from the Garden of Literature*, however, concern more modest structures, such as pavilions (*ting*), galleries (*ge*), towers (*lou*), halls (*tang*), city walls (*cheng*), waterways and canals (*hequ*), memorial temples (*cimiao*), Buddhist cloisters (*yuan*), and Daoist abbeys (*guan*). In most cases, these works were composed to create a commemorative account that would provide information on the person responsible for building the structure and the thought process by which a suitable name for it was devised. Among surviving Tang dynasty *ji* texts concerning structures, those on pavilions are by far the most numerous.[1]

Typically, when the construction or restoration of a pavilion was completed, a *ji* would be commissioned to celebrate the occasion in writing. The text of the account, which almost always includes a date, was then inscribed on a rock, wall, or stele—again to serve a dedicatory purpose (this also helps explain why most *ji* run only a few hundred characters in length) and inform future visitors about the history of the structure and its patron-builder.[2] If the structure was new or if for some reason it needed a new name, the author of the *ji* would often propose one.[3] Whenever possible, a well-known writer would be commissioned to compose the *ji*, although on some occasions, owner-builders would pen their own *ji*.

Most Tang dynasty *ji* composed before Liu Zongyuan do not include a travel component. Thus, when it came time for the editors of the *Choice Blossoms* collection to find an appropriate place for Liu's famous "Eight Accounts of Yongzhou," which mainly concern individual *landscapes* rather than structures, they placed them into a subcategory of account designated as *yanyou*. This term, which literally means "banquet outings," refers to pleasure excursions undertaken for social purposes where food and drink were served to guests; the term was taken directly from the title of Liu Zongyuan's first Yongzhou essay, titled "On First Finding West Mountain: Account of a Pleasure Outing" (Shi de Xishan yanyou ji).[4] Li Fang and his fellow editors also mention in a note that they were not sure how to classify the Tang author's Yongzhou essays because they are all "confused and mixed up" (*congza*),[5] which indicates that even in the late tenth century, prose works with travel components did not easily correspond to the *ji* form as it was understood at the time.

Nevertheless, some *ji* works of the Tang dynasty are important in the history of Chinese travel literature precisely because of the innovative ways in which authors such as Yuan Jie and especially Liu Zongyuan use literary language to describe place. More specifically, in the late eighth and early ninth centuries, there emerged novel approaches to writing about place and sightseeing that would have a noteworthy influence on later *youji* authors,[6] especially Liu Zongyuan, who was the most mature and influential practitioner of this style of writing.

XUANZANG AND HIS *ACCOUNTS OF THE WESTERN REGIONS DURING THE GREAT TANG*

> Those [ancient travelers] who contented themselves with short trips to scenic spots could stay completely within the realm of *wen* [belle lettres] and write short pieces on the beauty of mountains and rivers; they were not subject to the exigencies of historiography. Those who traveled to foreign lands and had to report had no choice but to adopt the stance of the historian.
>
> PEI-YI WU, *THE CONFUCIAN'S PROGRESS: AUTOBIOGRAPHICAL WRITINGS IN TRADITIONAL CHINA*[7]

Following Faxian's *Accounts of the Buddhist Kingdoms*, the next important surviving written account of a pilgrimage to India undertaken by a Chinese monk is that of Xuanzang. This work, titled *Accounts of the Western Regions during the Great Tang*, is important for three reasons. First, it is the longest and most detailed among the handful of surviving Buddhist travel accounts. Second, Xuanzang's text is written in a style of the *ji* form that is related to chronicling and describing places unfamiliar to the reader. And third, it is one of the very few extant texts dating from the traditional period in China that provides a detailed account of a real journey to a foreign land.[8]

2.1. *Xuanzang on His Journey to the West* (Xuanzang xixing tu 玄奘西行圖). Wikimedia Commons, Public Domain, https://commons.wikimedia.org/wiki/File:Xuanzang_w.jpg.

Xuanzang's trip to India was long and difficult. He left China in 629 and did not return until 645.[9] The main purpose of the journey was to secure texts that would resolve sectarian disputes and contradictions in the holy books of Buddhism—mainly, those circulating in China—and to obtain a complete Sanskrit copy of an encyclopedic work now known as the *Yogācārabhūmi-śāstra* (Treatise on the foundations of the yoga masters; Chinese title, *Yujia shidi lun*). The Tang emperor Taizong (r. 626–49) recognized the geopolitical value of Xuanzang's knowledge of foreign lands and asked the famous pilgrim to compile a written account of his travels that would include detailed description of the climate, customs, products, rulers, and especially the political geography of the lands in the "Western Regions." Xuanzang, of course, complied with the emperor's behest. It took him about a year to write the *Accounts of the Western Regions*. The book, in twelve chapters, was completed in the fall of 646.[10]

That Xuanzang would choose the *ji* form over other genre possibilities, such as the biography (*zhuan*),[11] comes as no surprise, especially since a precedent for using the *ji* form to pen accounts of foreign lands was established by Faxian centuries earlier. More important, however, is that since the *Accounts of the Western Regions* was written at the request of the emperor, Xuanzang certainly regarded it primarily as a work of political and historical geography, with substantial ethnographic content and not—strictly speaking—as a religious text. It made sense, then, for him to use the *ji* genre, because there were numerous descriptive works written about real places (many of them foreign) during the Han and Six Dynasties that used *ji* in their title.[12] Some of these accounts, including *Accounts of the Buddhist Kingdoms*, were loosely modeled after chapters about foreign lands included first in the *Historical Records* and later in the *Documents on the Han* (Hanshu) and *Documents on the Later Han* (Hou Hanshu). I refer here especially to chapter 123 in the *Historical Records*, in which Sima Qian essentially retells the story of the Han general and envoy Zhang Qian's extensive travels and experiences in Ferghana, Wusun, Sogdiana (Yancai), and other places in the "Western Regions."[13] We also find descriptions of the people of these lands, such as the Xiongnu and Indo-Scythians, as well as information on cities, military fortifications, distances between kingdoms, population figures, arms, "horses that sweat blood" (*ma han xue*),[14] and unique local products, such as alfalfa (*muxu*) and grape wine (*putao jiu*).[15]

Sima Qian's account was based on information personally gathered by Zhang Qian during his various missions to Central Asia.[16] The *Accounts of the Western Regions* follows this same reportorial format. Xuanzang, like Faxian before him, usually remains in the background and writes in a largely impersonal style that focuses on providing information about places. Xuanzang's text also recounts many stories from scriptures and legend associated with Buddhism, and it describes major incidents from the life of the historical Buddha, especially as they relate to famous relics, shrines, and holy sites. But the overriding purpose of the text is secular; in other words, to provide accurate and precise descriptions and itinerary information, such as distances between places, the circumference of kingdoms measured in *li*, and so on. The result was a definitive work on the geography and civilizations of western China, Central Asia, and India. Such detail is found nowhere in earlier surviving geographical accounts, and this perhaps had more to do with Xuanzang's own ideals and concerns about writing comprehensively and accurately than it did with the Emperor Taizong's military intelligence needs.[17] That Xuanzang collected "a mass of papers consisting partly of accounts of his own experiences and impersonal accounts of various kingdoms in India and elsewhere"[18] proves that even during the journey itself, he was assembling documents that would help him "verify the facts and seek the truth" (*shishi qiushi*)[19] about his pilgrimage to India. And this concern for accuracy and precision in description of place most certainly draws directly on Sima Qian's historiographic style in *Shiji* 123. Notice what Xuanzang himself says in a "footnote" following the twelfth and concluding chapter of the *Accounts of the Western Regions*:

> The purpose of this book is to advance a list of the mountains and rivers in the Western Regions, investigate borders and regions, to detail the truculent and flexible customs of various kingdoms, and to compare climates as they relate to local topography. Circumstances are never constant, so my choices and selections about what to include vary. It was difficult to trace the ultimate origin of everything, but I never resort to veneration or hyperbole. Wherever my travels took me, I jotted down an outline in summary form, mentioning what I heard and saw, and maintained an account of the adoration of and submission to [Buddhism in the lands I visited]. . . . Considering the formation of the empire and unity in the world, how could I boast of passing through post-stations for ten thousand *li* when I am just a solitary envoy in a single carriage![20]

The detail in the *Accounts of the Western Regions*, especially numbers related to distances in *li*, reveals that Xuanzang kept detailed notes during his journey, not merely "outlines in summary form."

The Tang pilgrim's attention to detail is also evident in the following passage, taken from the account of his passing through the kingdom of Bālukā (Balujia guo):[21]

> I proceeded from this kingdom for more than three hundred *li* to the northwest, crossed a rocky desert, and reached Ice Mountain. This is the northern plain of the Pamirs Range, from where most rivers flow eastward. In its mountain valleys snow piles up and remains frozen even in spring and summer. Although from time to time some of it melts away, in no time at all it freezes over again. The road I followed was dangerous

and difficult; the frigid wind was blustery and severe. There are many "ferocious dragons" in these parts and one should never approach them.[22] Travelers who take this route cannot wear reddish-brown clothing, nor carry gourds or shout.[23] If there is the slightest violation of these taboos, disaster and misfortune will occur right before your eyes. Violent winds will suddenly gale, with sand flying about and pebbles raining down. Those encountering this catastrophe will perish, or at the very least it will be difficult for them to escape with their lives.[24]

This passage, which is representative of many of Xuanzang's entries in the *Accounts of the Western Regions*, reveals him to be a meticulous observer, a writer who could express himself clearly and accurately. The translations from Sanskrit into Chinese he executed after his return to the Tang capital at Chang'an also manifest this same concern for precision. And in the *Accounts*, the Tang monk took great care when transliterating foreign place names and rendering Buddhist religious terms into Chinese.[25] It is not surprising, then, that Xuanzang would pay great attention to detail in his descriptions of place.

The following passage provides a good example of how Xuanzang enumerates details about a place, in this case the ancient Kingdom of Samarkand:

The Kingdom of Samarkand is sixteen or seventeen hundred *li* in circuit, long from east to west and narrow from south to north. The kingdom's great capital city is twenty-some *li* in circuit. It is extremely well protected and well fortified, with a large resident population. Precious goods from the different directions are mostly gathered in this kingdom. The soil is fertile; all kinds of crops are cultivated. Trees in the forests are lush and rich; flowers and fruits are teeming and profuse. Samarkand produces many fine horses. The deft skills of its craftsmen are the best among the various kingdoms. The climate is mild and temperate; the people in their observation of customs are strict and harsh. In general, this is just one among the various kingdoms of *hu* tribes.[26] Their conduct and manner, and dignity and decorum toward other kingdoms, depends on whether those kingdoms are far away or near. Their king is gallant and brave, and neighboring kingdoms follow his orders. His military forces are strong and abundant and include many Čākar warriors. The people of Čākar are by nature brave and courageous, fearless of death, and without rivals in combat.[27]

The *Accounts of the Western Regions* altogether contains descriptions of more than one hundred different kingdoms, walled-cities, and areas, and most of these entries are strikingly similar in how they describe place and present information on topography, defense, roads and communication, local customs and products, weather, culture, and politics. Xuanzang crafted and organized the *Accounts* into a series of entries on different kingdoms, presented consecutively according to their distance from China and India.[28] This format has its origin in *Shiji* 123. Given the large amount of information provided in the *Accounts*, on one level the text functions as a geographical schematic from which a map of the Western Regions— including the Indian subcontinent—could easily be drawn. Of course, Faxian, Xuanzang, and other Buddhist pilgrims who traveled west were all quite familiar with earlier Chinese exploration of the Western regions— especially the accounts that appear in the *Historical Records, Documents on the Han*, and *Documents on the Later Han*. In chapter 2 we saw one occasion where Faxian directly mentions Zhang Qian, boasting that he had reached a place far from China that the Han envoy had not. The Buddhist travel accounts, then, should be considered a part of the written tradition associated with ancient travelers like Zhang Qian, some of whom mixed miracles and mythic tales with natural phenomena and accounts of foreign lands. But the Buddhist travelers, and especially Xuanzang, make distinctions between myth and reality, personal observation and hearsay, and fact and fable. And no doubt, the Buddhist conception of the universe influenced the geographical orientation of the pilgrims and how they saw and described the world.[29] Nevertheless, throughout the *Accounts*, Xuanzang remains an observer and commentator and rarely refers to himself directly. His style is intentionally detached and impersonal; again, this was because his main concern was to provide accurate and detailed description and information.

One final and key point: most of the Samarkand passage just cited and portions of the selections from the *Accounts* quoted earlier are composed of lines of four characters. No rhyme scheme is employed, and verbal parallelism is used in only four lines ("Trees in the forests are lush and rich; flowers and fruits are teeming and profuse"; and "The climate is mild and temperate; the [people in their observation of] customs are strict and harsh."). The remaining lines are written in a straightforward and unadorned descriptive style that seems to approximate vernacular prose. That is not to say, however, that Xuanzang's text is not without drama and descriptions of the bizarre.

Nor does it lack lyrical moments and emotionally charged language. But what is most worthy of attention here is that Xuanzang's description of place is consistently written in a kind of prose that is essentially comprised of two general language styles. The first of these is informational-based language. Typically, this element appears in the opening lines of an entry ("The Kingdom of Samarkand is sixteen or seventeen hundred *li* in circuit, long from east to west and narrow from south to north. The kingdom's great capital city is twenty-some *li* in circuit. It is extremely well protected and well fortified with a large population."). Most important here is the content concerning facts, numbers, and distances.

The second element is descriptive-based language. This portion of Xuanzang's text is usually written in consecutive lines of four characters each. He uses this language technique throughout the *Accounts of the Western Regions*, and clearly it is a convention utilized to describe place. The ultimate source of this style is difficult to pinpoint; it is not used by Sima Qian in the *Historical Records* and appears only occasionally in earlier works, such as the *Accounts of the Buddhist Monastic Complexes of Luoyang* and *Commentary on the Waterways Treatise*. Xuanzang, however, is the first author to employ this technique consistently throughout a *ji* text. As we will see below, a few centuries later, Yuan Jie and Liu Zongyuan will also use similar "quartets" (that is, strings of four Chinese characters) in their descriptions of landscape, but they will develop them far beyond Xuanzang's simpler, more straightforward description into a variety of language one might even call "prose-poetry."

LI BAI'S "PREFACE TO THE POEM 'BOATING ON COURT GENTLEMAN LAKE IN MIAN COUNTY'"

No significant development took place in travel literature during the period from the founding of the Tang dynasty in the early seventh century until the era usually designated as the "High Tang" or "Flourishing Tang" (Shengtang; roughly, the first half of the eighth century). During this period, the rhapsody and especially the poetry preface continued to be employed as literary vehicles for writing about sightseeing experiences and attractive outdoor venues. For instance, several notable early Tang writers, such as Wang Bo, Yang Jiong (650–95?), and Luo Binwang (seventh century), have all left numerous prefaces to poems in which details of trips to scenic landscapes are provided.[30] One especially well-known and often-cited example is Wang Bo's "Preface to the Poems Composed at a Farewell Feast upon Climbing the Prince Teng Gallery in Hong Municipality on an Autumn Day" (Qiuri deng Hongfu Teng Wang Ge jianbie xu).[31] The majority of such works, including Wang Bo's preface, are written in parallel prose and thus can be viewed as a continuation of the style popular in the Six Dynasties period. At the same time, however, some prefaces related to sightseeing written during the so-called Mid-Tang period (Zhongtang; roughly, 750 to about 850) seem to suggest interest in a writing style with antecedents in the works of Yuan Shansong, Huiyuan, and Li Daoyuan during the Six Dynasties; that is, movement away from the dominance of parallel prose toward a more relaxed prose form. An often overlooked but nevertheless important example is the preface to Li Bai's poem "Boating on Court Gentleman Lake in Mian County" (Fan Mianzhou Langguan hu), written in 758 while the Tang poet was traveling to Yelang (in modern Guizhou):

> Eighth month, autumn, Supernal Prime [Qianyuan]] year (758): while on my way to take up an exile post in Yelang, I ran into my old friend Zhang Wei [*jinshi* 743], the Secretariat Court Gentleman, who was on an official mission to Xiakou [modern Hankou in Hubei; during the Tang also known as Ezhou]. We drank together with Master Du, the metropolitan governor, and Master Wang, the magistrate of Hanyang, on South Lake in River City, and celebrated the restoration of peace in the empire.[32] Just when the nighttime moon in the lake water seemed silky white, its clear radiance could have been plucked. Master Zhang found a place of extraordinary scenic beauty, where the views all around were surpassing. He then turned to me and said, "Since ancient times, there have been many worthy and prominent visitors to this lake. But they treaded upon this lovely scene without leaving any records[33] and so the lake remains unknown. Now, perhaps you can tender a fine name for me, so it will be passed down and never be forgotten?" I thereupon raised a cup of wine, poured it into the water, and named it "Court Gentleman Lake." This name also has a precedent in Chariot-Archer Slope in Zhengpu.[34] Among the men of letters in attendance, Fu Yi and Cen Jing considered my choice of name to be a wise one. Thereupon, Zhang Wei commanded us to compose poems and make a written account of the events that transpired, which would then be engraved on a rock beside the lake. Thus, it will wear away only when Big Divide Hill wears away.[35]

The main purpose of Li Bai's preface is to explain to readers the details of when, why, and how he selected a new name for a body of water that hitherto had been known simply as "South Lake." The new name, "Court Gentleman," is a reference to Li Bai's old friend Zhang Wei, who held the office "secretariat court gentleman." Li Bai has shortened this office title to *langguan*, or "court gentleman."

Now while the act and process of naming structures such as pavilions and scenic features is especially important in *ji* works dating from the Tang, the language style used in Li Bai's preface uses no parallel prose or strings of quartets. Instead, he writes in a form of relaxed prose that is informational- and reportorial-focused. He is "reporting" to readers on a social activity by providing "information" on the date of the outing, who participated, the attractive nighttime scene on the lake, Zhang Wei's request for a new name for the lake that "will never be forgotten," and how and why the name was selected. Finally, to make a long-lasting account of the events (*jishi*) that transpired, it was decided that Li Bai's preface explaining all these details would be engraved on a rock beside the lake.

These features of language style and content will become popular later with many Song dynasty authors, especially those writing about their sightseeing experiences in short works describing outings to scenic or historical locations. However, this style of prose—used specifically in this case to describe a social gathering organized around a pleasure trip to an attractive landscape environment—was *not* common in the early and mid-Tang periods. Only a few examples survive. More will appear later in the Tang. But in the Northern Song (960–1127), sightseeing will become *the* main theme in travel writing.

A related development dating from the mid-eighth century is the appearance, for the first time in Chinese literary history, of prose texts that employ the formula "*You* place-x *ji*" in their title. The first Tang dynasty occurrence of this convention seems to be Da Xixun's (d. 758) "Account of a Sightseeing Trip on the Ji Canal" (You Jidu ji).[36] Another example from the Mid-Tang period is Lu Yu's (733–804) "Account of a Sightseeing Trip to Benevolent Mountain Monastery (You Huishan si ji).[37] Again, this formulaic title structure was not common in Tang prose texts describing sightseeing activities; this would not happen until the late tenth century. But afterward and continuing throughout the remainder of the imperial era, the overwhelming majority of *youji* authors will employ this formula, or a close variation, in their titles. Later *ji* authors wrote about sightseeing in ways that distinctly resemble the form, content, and language just observed in Li Bai's "Boating on Court Gentleman Lake in Mian County" preface.

YUAN JIE (719–72)

> Cishan [or Yuan Jie] indulged himself in landscape and truly blazed a trail that heralded Zihou [or Liu Zongyuan]. His writings are profound and subtle, admirable and impeccable. He indeed was able to create scenes endowed with appeal.
>
> WU RULUN 1840–1903[38]

A major poet and prose stylist of the mid-eighth century, Yuan Jie is best known for the literary works he composed during his tenure as chief administrative officer (*cishi*) of Dao county (Daozhou; modern Dao *xian*, Hunan), in the far south of China, an area long celebrated in Chinese literature for its pristine and dramatic scenery. Two of Yuan's prose compositions, "Account of the Winter Pavilion" (Hanting ji) and "Account of Rightside Creek" (Youxi ji), both written in Dao county, are anthologized in practically every published collection of Chinese travel literature and have been translated and studied by several scholars.[39] Literary historians and critics universally praise these texts as outstanding examples of "mature" or "relatively mature" Tang dynasty *youji*.[40] Yuan Jie's landscape essays are indeed important in the history and development of Chinese travel literature, but the precise reasons for their significance deserve commentary. Although most literary historians regard Yuan Jie's *youji* compositions as precursors (in Modern Chinese, *qianzou*) of a style of travel essay writing that they say reached full maturity in Liu Zongyuan's "Eight Accounts of Yong County," this view needs some adjustment. And Yuan Jie deserves more credit for his key role as an early proponent of a looser *guwen* prose style, which influenced the composition of the *ji* form in both the "Eight Accounts" and the writings of numerous subsequent *youji* authors.

We begin with "Account of the Winter Pavilion," written in Dao county in 766:

> During the *bingwu* year of the Eternal Majesty [Yongtai] reign [766], while on an inspection tour of the towns under my administration, I

arrived at Jianghua town. The grand master, Qu Lingwen,[41] inquired of me, asking, "South of town the rocks and waters shine upon each other, and are most lovely when gazed upon. Tradition has it that the landscape there could not be climbed and thus spied from a distance. I then dispatched some people to find it. They discovered a cave and went inside, and therein erected plank walkways in the dangerous spots to allow passage through it. Only then was I able to have a thatched pavilion erected upon the rocks. When the pavilion was completed, by means of stairs and railings, it seemingly stood suspended in midair. Overlooking the long river below,[42] balcony railings supported the tips of the clouds, while the pavilion reached up to the very tops of the mountains. At dawn and dusk, when winds blow fair, mists and clouds reveal extraordinary hues; the verdant green stone wall around the pavilion tints and reflects water and trees. I wanted to give this pavilion a name but did not know how to describe it. Dare I implore you to name it so it might become known to future generations?" Thereupon, while we rested at the pavilion and discussed the matter, I said, "Today, as we climbed up here in the period of Severe Heat,[43] it seemed as though the season was about to turn to winter. In this land of scorching and steaming heat, here where it is clear and cool we may take our repose. It seems fitting, then, to name it "Winter Pavilion." And so, I composed this account on behalf of the Winter Pavilion and had it engraved in stone behind the pavilion.[44]

Yuan Jie's text is remarkably similar in structure and content to Li Bai's preface to the poem "Boating on Court Gentleman Lake in Mian County." Li Bai was on his way to Yelang in 758; Yuan Jie was on an inspection tour in 766. Both begin by providing dates and background information. Next comes identification and description—presented in strings of mostly four-character quartets—of a local scenic spot (for Li Bai it was South Lake; for Yuan Jie, the thatched pavilion built by Qu Lingwen and the attractive view it provided). Moreover, both authors serve as "guests" of local officials at these sites, and both are asked by their host to coin names.

Concern about names and the act of naming is prominent in *ji* compositions dating from the Tang and thereafter. Some of these works concern known scenic areas, such as South Lake, while others describe remote, previously unexplored or inaccessible areas, such as the rocky location of Yuan Jie's "Account of the Winter Pavilion." Xiaoshan Yang makes a useful distinction between these two types of Tang landscape essays: the former he designates "social"; the latter he calls "personal" (more on this distinction below). At the host's behest, the guest then proposes a name for the site, which, of course, is accepted and, as in Li Bai's case, is even praised as a "wise choice" by the other guests in attendance. And finally, it is announced that the *ji*, or account, would be inscribed in stone to commemorate the occasion and ensure that future generations know about it.

With this structure, content, and prose style in mind, we now turn to Yuan Jie's "Account of Rightside Creek." This work is undated,[45] but dating in this case is not essential.

> At one-hundred-some *bu* west of the walled seat of Dao county there is a small creek, which flows south several tens of *bu* to join with Ying Creek. Its waters lap against the two shores, where everywhere are fantastic rocks, leaning and sinking, coiling and twisting, in forms that cannot be described. Its clear current bashes against the rocks, splashes back, and projects onward in its flow. Remarkable trees and unusual bamboos hang shadows that shelter one another. If this creek were situated in mountainous wilds, it would be a fitting retreat at which retired persons or reclusive scholars could sightsee. If it were situated in human realms, it could serve as a surpassing scenic spot in some metropolitan district, the sylvan pavilion of those seeking quietude. And yet, ever since this county was established, no one has appreciated and admired it. As I shilly-shallied along the banks of the creek, I felt despondent because of this neglect. Hence, I had the weeds dredged and cleared from the creek, so I could build a pavilion and cottage there. Pine and cassia trees were planted, among which were mixed fragrant grasses to enhance the scene's physical attractiveness. Since the creek is located to the right of the county seat, I have thus named it "Rightside Creek." I have had this name engraved on a rock to make it known to future visitors.[46]

This text is an example of what Xiaoshan Yang calls a "personal" landscape essay. There is no "local host" present; there is no familiar scenic site like South Lake. The only person present is the author, and the only landscape feature described is an essentially unknown creek just west of the wall that surrounds the Dao county seat. Note that in this work, after Yuan Jie identifies the location of the creek and describes the attractive scenery surrounding it in strings of "quartets," he moves directly to what might be called "author reaction." This format reflects the "topic comment" topos described earlier. What is significant is the personal nature of Yuan's reaction and the emotional intensity by which it is expressed. Of course, some background information is provided about the site and creek, but the focus here is not on the landscape but instead on the author's emotional reaction to it. In fact, he tells readers straight away that he is despondent because the untouched area around the creek, though quite beautiful, has been hidden away in the remote reaches of the Chinese empire and so has remained neglected. At the same time, Yuan Jie also remarks that if the creek's attractive features were known in the world, it would be much appreciated. Critics have viewed the author's despondency in this text as autobiographical. In other words, Yuan Jie's talents as a government administrator are untapped and thereby unappreciated because he has been posted to a remote, miasmic region in south China, far away from the capital where he should be serving the emperor. This is a convincing argument, but more important for our purposes is that Yuan Jie, in "Account of Rightside Creek," infuses the account form with a level and intensity of emotional content that is conspicuously absent in earlier *ji* writing, which emphasized providing information about and description of places. This new direction in *ji* writing will find further expression in Liu Zongyuan's "Eight Accounts."

Regarding structure, the writings of Li Bai and Yuan Jie discussed so far reflect what William H. Nienhauser Jr.—in reference to Liu Zongyuan's landscape essays—identifies as the "quadripartite structure."[47] This construct includes the following four components: (1) an introduction or preface, often dated, that introduces the physical setting of the essay, such as a local lake or a creek outside the town wall; (2) description—sometimes detailed—of the scenic focus of the piece, which often stresses the beautiful view it provides ("South of town the rocks and waters shine upon each other and are most lovely when gazed upon."); (3) author reaction to the landscape, the degree and nature of which varies, at times expressing aesthetic admiration, at times expressing valediction or even moral concerns[48]; and (4) a closing section, which often explains the process by which a name was selected for the site, gives the names of the guests in attendance, and provides related information. Quite often, as we saw in the examples from Li Bai's and Yuan Jie's writings above, the closing lines announce that the text of the *ji* would be inscribed on a rock or wall to commemorate the occasion and make sure that future generations of visitors know about it. This practice is most common in "social" landscape essays.

Another composition dating from his years in Dao county, also a *ji*, titled "Account of the Incomparable Pavilion" (Shuting ji), also exhibits Yuan Jie's talent as a prose master, especially as it relates to *youji*:

> In the *guimao* year [763] Ma Xiang of Fufeng *managed* Wuchang. The *principles* on which he acted were clarity, trust, strictness, decisiveness, compassion, and fairness. Thus, his administration succeeded in no time at all. Indeed! If one is clear but not trustworthy, strict but not decisive, compassionate but not fair, then even if he desires to *regulate* himself, in the end he will fail to *control* himself, not to mention others! The master [Ma Xiang] could make others [that is, the people he governed] *orderly*, allowing himself to have much leisure. He invited me over for a visit, but I fear the heat. So he also built a pavilion for enjoying coolness. The pavilion overlooked the Great River. In addition, it is located on a mountain, where remarkable trees shelter one another and where usually there is a refreshing breeze. I scouted about and took in the broad views, never tiring of the distances. I observed that the master's talent was *incomparable*, and that his administration was *incomparable* and deeds *incomparable*. Because of this, the pavilion is *incomparable* as well. Thus, I designate that it be called "*Incomparable* Pavilion." Stone was cut, on which my account was engraved. I hope that future visitors will not be puzzled in any way.[49]

This essay, I would argue, follows the same four-part organizational structure seen in "Account of Rightside Creek," but with the introduction extended disproportionately to praise the various "incomparable" qualities of Ma Xiang and his pavilion. Xiaoshan Yang calls this "moral discourse,"[50] but it might also be seen simply as an available rhetorical option used by Yuan Jie to flatter Ma Xiang, who presumably commissioned Yuan Jie to compose the *ji* in the first place. The extended introduction, however, has resulted in a shorter-than-usual description of the scene, though here Yuan Jie once again executes his scenic description in four-character strings of quartets, specifically the line "The pavilion overlooked the Great River . . . never tiring of the distances."

The length of the introduction and brevity of the description notwithstanding, this is the first dedicatory *ji* of the Tang in which there is a dominant *literary* component that moves beyond the customary quartets;

specifically, the skillful way in which Yuan Jie praises Ma Xiang. Yuan initially organizes and voices his praise around the character/word *li* 理. He uses *li* on five separate occasions, each of which seems to suggest a slightly different nuance of meaning. My five different translations of *li*, in italics, reflect these distinctions.[51] This level of literary craftsmanship is not evident in any *ji* text that predates Yuan Jie. There is additional wordplay in "Account of the Incomparable Pavilion" on the word *shu* 殊, which Yuan Jie seems to apply in the consistent sense of "incomparable," referring to both Master Ma Xiang and his exemplary administration.[52]

In "Account of the Incomparable Pavilion," the *ji* form has moved beyond simple description in four-character phrases, presented in the dedicatory-commemorative context described earlier. Now, for the first time in Chinese literary history, we have commemorative *ji* about a structure and place in which literary language and technique play a leading role. Yuan Jie's skill as a wordsmith is revealed in how he deploys language, especially in "Account of the Incomparable Pavilion," to achieve an effect, in this case to sing the praises of Ma Xiang and his handsome pavilion. The result is that *ji* texts are no longer exclusively social in their purpose and predictable in their content. Now we have literary *ji*.

Finally, although the influence of the parallel prose style is apparent in Yuan's quartet-style language used to delineate scene, there is no sustained parallel verbal structure in any of the texts we have considered. Nor is Yuan Jie's descriptive language bound by any tonal or grammatical rules. When read aloud, however, lines of equal length in Chinese most certainly can produce a verse-like cadence. One might even be justified in calling such language a loose form of prose-poetry, because it can serve to heighten the effects of scenic imagery and even the level of lyrical intensity (this technique will be discussed further in the next section on Liu Zongyuan). Without a doubt, Yuan Jie's prose-poetry is written in a language style that is distinctly different from parallel prose employed in such works as *Accounts of the Buddhist Monasteries of Luoyang* and the matter-of-fact, reportorial language in Xuanzang's *Accounts of the Western Regions*. It is not clear if Yuan Jie has borrowed this descriptive technique from an earlier author or devised it himself (under the influence of parallel prose) to serve the needs of his *ji*. Whatever the case, we can be reasonably sure that he was one of the first Tang authors— if not *the* first Tang author—to exploit this descriptive technique in a *ji* text of literary merit, and in Yuan Jie's accounts, there are certainly indications that the *ji* form, as it relates to description of place, is now, at least in the hands of one author—Yuan Jie—being nudged in a new direction.

LIU ZONGYUAN (772–819)

> Yong county is in the southernmost part of Chu. Conditions there are like those in Yue. Whenever I felt depressed, I would go out exploring, but when I went out exploring, I became even more terrified. When I ventured out into the wilds, there would be venomous snakes and huge wasps. As I looked up for wasps and glanced down for snakes, just taking a short step would leave me exhausted. Each time I approached water, I would fear the bombardier beetles and chiggers, which would stealthily spray poison when angered. Once the spray hits a person's form or shadow, they would then break out in abscessed sores.
>
> LIU ZONGYUAN, "LETTER TO LI JIAN,
> THE HANLIN ACADEMICIAN"[53]

Liu Zongyuan has traditionally been honored as one of the "Eight Great Prose Masters of the Tang and Song" (Tang Song bada sanwen jia). Author-group formulations like this are common in Chinese literary history (the "Seven Sages of the Bamboo Grove," "Four Eminent Writers of the Early Tang," and so on), but they are not especially useful from a critical point of view. Still, it is noteworthy that among the eight prose writers included in this distinguished octet, only two are from the Tang period: Han Yu (768–824) and Liu Zongyuan. Now while the epithet "great prose master" is certainly based on Han and Liu's considerable talent as authors, the two friends are also often heralded together as innovators at writing *guwen*, or ancient-style prose. Their joint effort to promote *guwen* was an attempt to replace the highly affected style of parallel prose, still popular in the mid-Tang period, with a more relaxed or looser form of *sanwen*. It is important to understand, however, that Han Yu and Liu Zongyuan were not attempting to copy or duplicate some long-lost literary form from ancient times. Rather, their aim was to promote a return to the Confucian moral-didactic purpose of literature "based on the ancient (pre-Qin and Han) ideals of clarity, preciseness, and utility."[54] Many literary historians regard Liu Zongyuan's "Eight Accounts" as *guwen* because they reveal many of the same rhetorical devices and didactic intent inherent in other writings by

Liu and Han Yu written in the ancient style. It is essential to keep in mind, however, that the so-called *guwen* promoted by Han Yu and Liu Zongyuan was a multi-faceted prose form and that the "Eight Accounts" are just one example of this style.[55] Our main interest is how and why this form of prose became important in the history and development of *youji*.

Liu Zongyuan's political career mirrors that of many other Tang dynasty government officials. After earning his *jinshi*, or "advanced scholar," degree in 793, Liu embarked on a career in public service. While still a young government official serving in the capital at Chang'an, he had already achieved some notoriety because of the skill with which he could compose government documents. No doubt, his career was on a fast track to success and fame. Unfortunately, the political faction in the capital with which Liu had aligned fell from power in 805. The result for Liu Zongyuan—and other members of the so-called reform clique with which he was associated—was political exile. Liu was dispatched to a place called Yong county in the far south, only about one hundred miles from Dao county in southern Hunan, where Yuan Jie had earlier served an official. He remained there for a decade. Liu was briefly recalled to the capital in 815 but was almost immediately reassigned to yet another aboriginal region even further south, called Liu county (Liuzhou; in modern Guangxi). He died there in 819, without having ever known that a general amnesty had been proclaimed in the capital that would have allowed him to return to Chang'an.

Liu's fall from political grace troubled him greatly, and feelings of moral and political alienation reverberate in many of the literary works he composed in the south. In fact, in the very opening line of the first of Liu's "Eight Accounts," he openly admits, "I have resided in this county ever since becoming a disgraced person and have lived in a constant state of fear."[56] It is no coincidence that Liu Zongyuan begins his "Eight Accounts" with these words, for after his removal from the capital, the disgrace and embarrassment of political exile defined his life and view of the world. Banishment to southwestern Hunan was certainly regarded as a death sentence, for in the early ninth century, it was one of the most remote and perilous outposts of the Tang empire. The greatest danger was malaria, which claimed the lives of more than a few Tang exiles.[57]

What is fascinating is that by the time Liu Zongyuan composed the first of his "Eight Accounts" in 809, something of a personal transformation had already taken place: he now started to notice and write about some of the "wondrous scenic qualities" (*guaite*) observed in and around Yong county, especially nearby West Mountain (Xishan) and the scenic area thereabouts. In "Account of Rocky Rivulet" (Shiqu ji), for instance, he employs adjectives such as *qi* ("remarkable"), *yi* ("unusual"), *guai* ("wondrous"), and *meili* ("gorgeously lovely") to describe the appealing scenery along the rivulet.[58] And in the second of his "Eight Accounts," referring to a viewing terrace above a pond he had acquired and refurbished, Liu Zongyuan even dares to use the word *le*, or "happy": "What else but my building efforts here could make me happy to live with barbarians and forget about longing for my native land?"[59]

To understand Liu Zongyuan's literary artistry in the "Eight Accounts," it is essential to be aware of a dynamic that is almost always present in his Yongzhou landscape essays. I refer to a sort of a tension between the disgrace and embarrassment of his forced residency in a malaria-infested land inhabited by "barbarians" (*yi*) on the one hand, and the occasional pleasant digression he found exploring the native, scenic beauty of Yongzhou and the surrounding area on the other hand. The relationship between these diverse elements or opposites provides a form and establishes a unity in the "Eight Accounts," and this is an essential quality of his Yongzhou landscape essays. But just so we are clear: the backwater of Hunan was certainly no "temporary heaven" to Liu Zongyuan. In fact, on several occasions in his Yongzhou writings he refers to himself as a "prisoner" (*qiu*) there.[60] But the attractive physical landscape did provide him with at least a temporary comfort zone, one to which he could repair—almost always with friends who were fellow exiles—and find some temporary solace or, as He Peixiong puts it, "to find diversion from his own depression" (*paiqian ziji de kumen*).[61] Liu Zongyuan's "Eight Accounts" are not revealing symptoms of what Richard E. Strassberg calls the "exilic syndrome"—situations where writers banished to distant, alien lands seek to redefine themselves in their writings in order to demonstrate their "rehabilitation" and thereby justify their return to public service.[62] Rather, "Eight Accounts" is a good example of how a highly skilled writer consciously or unconsciously develops a survival strategy to deal with severe adversity.[63] In Liu's case, the key feature of that strategy involved exploring, discovering, and then writing about attractive landscapes. And his reactions to and commentary on these scenic descriptions provided him with a convenient literary opportunity for direct or indirect self-expression.

The "Eight Accounts of Yong County"[64] are important not only as individual works of significant literary merit, but also because they have served as models for prose description of landscape ever since the Song dynasty. Among the best and perhaps most representative of the Yongzhou essays is the third, written in 809, titled "Account of Little Hillock West of Flat-Iron Pool" (Gumu Tan xi Xiaoqiu ji):

Eight days after discovering West Mountain, I traced along a path northwest of the mountain pass for two hundred *bu*, and next found Flat-Iron Pool. Twenty-five *bu* west of the pool, where its waters rush and deepen, a fish weir has been built. At the edge of the weir there is a hillock where grow bamboo and trees. The rocks that suddenly spring up, lying prone and looking proud, bearing earth as they protrude, and vying to form fantastic shapes, are practically beyond count. Those that descend, toppling downward in layer upon layer, resemble livestock drinking at a creek; those that ascend, poised to charge upward in pointed ranks, resemble bears clambering up a mountain.

The hillock is smaller than a *mu*, and one could fence it in and possess it. I made inquiries of its owner, who said, "This is the abandoned property of the Tang family. They put it up for sale, but it has not been sold." I made inquiries about its price, and he said, "Just four hundred cash." Since I was fond of the place, I bought it. Li Shenyuan and Yuan Keji accompanied me on the outing, and all of us were greatly delighted at this unexpected good fortune. Then gathering tools, we rooted up the weeds and mowed away the grasses, cut away the inferior trees, and built a roaring fire and burned them. *The choice trees then stood out, the attractive bamboos were disclosed, and the marvelous rocks were displayed.* When you gaze afar from within their midst, the heights of the mountains, the drifts of the clouds, the courses of the streams, and the roaming and rambling of birds and beasts all gaily present their skills and proffer their talents to offer their services below this hillock. When we set out our pillows and mat, and then lay down, the clear and cool shapes were *in accord with* our eyes, the far-distant void *merged with* our spirits, and the profound quietude *blended with* our minds. So, within a period of ten days I had discovered two extraordinary sites.[65] Even the landscape connoisseurs of antiquity were probably never able to accomplish such a feat.

Indeed! If you took the surprising beauty of this hillock and removed it to Feng, Hao, Hu, or Du,[66] then those gentlemen who prize sightseeing would vie to buy it, each day offering a thousand more gold, yet be even more unable to obtain it. Abandoned now in this county, farmers and fishermen pass by it and yet disdain it. It could be bought for four hundred cash, yet for many consecutive years it could not be sold. And now Shenyuan, Keji, and I alone enjoy it. Could this be the result of good luck? I have written my account in stone, to convey congratulations to this hillock on its good fortune.[67]

There are some immediately noticeable similarities between this work and Yuan Jie's "Account of Rightside Creek,"[68] and this is not the result of literary coincidence. Most notably, Liu Zongyuan is actively emulating the quadripartite organizational structure employed by Yuan Jie in "Account of Rightside Creek," although there is clear amplification in Liu's text of the scenic description and authorial commentary sections. Liu Zongyuan's literary portrait of the area around Flat-Iron Pool is quite detailed, and, like Yuan Jie, he includes a string of descriptive lines but prefers, instead, grammatically parallel lines (adjective-noun-verb) of three Chinese characters rather than four: "*The choice trees then stood out, the attractive bamboos were disclosed, and the marvelous rocks were displayed.*" And again, like Yuan Jie, there is also extended description of landscape written in parallel lines keyed to repeating a single character/word, in this case *mou* 謀 ("When we set out our pillows and mat, and then lay down, the clear and cool shapes were *in accord with* our eyes, the far-distant void *merged with* our spirits, and the profound quietude *blended with* our minds."). As should now be apparent, verbal parallelism can vary in length—with short phrases, couplets, or even entire passages—and content—using synonyms, antonyms, and other variations and combinations. Parallelism is an essential feature of *guwen*, and its function is clear: balanced opposites provide form and unity to a literary work comprised of diverse components.[69] Liu Zongyuan exploits this feature to the fullest in his "Eight Accounts."

Despite these various similarities, there are also some significant differences in the way Yuan Jie and Liu Zongyuan use language to delineate landscape. In the account just considered, one passage stands out in this regard:

The rocks that suddenly *spring up, lying prone* and *looking proud, bearing earth* as they *protrude* and *vying* to *form* fantastic shapes, are practically beyond count. Those that *descend, toppling downward* in layer upon layer, resemble livestock *drinking* at a creek; those that *ascend, poised to charge upward* in pointed ranks, resemble bears *clambering up* a mountain.

What in its natural state is essentially a motionless, fixed cluster of rocks is here, by use of motion verbs and simile (created by the character/word *ruo* 若, meaning "resemble"), transformed into a vivid landscape charged with *motion*. Notice how the boulders on the hillock are "springing up" and "looking proud" as they "protrude" and "compete" to "form fantastic shapes," while others "topple downward" in layers, resembling "livestock" getting a drink at a creek. Still others "ascend" and are "poised to charge" up the hillock in "pointed ranks," like "bears clambering up a mountain." I know of no previous author writing in the *ji* form who produced such vibrant description of landscape. It is precisely this expressive quality that led Mei Xinlin and Yu Zhanghua to refer to Liu Zongyuan's "Eight Accounts" as "*youji* masterpieces from a poet" (*shiren youji de jiezuo*).[70] Although the Chinese phrase does not translate well into English, Mei and Yu's meaning is clear: the language in this and similar passages in the Yong-zhou essays is infused with a level of lyricism that in some ways resembles poetry, especially when read aloud. Liu Zongyuan draws upon and exploits prose-poetry language often in his landscape essays.

Another fascinating linguistic feature that we see in the "Eight Accounts" is Liu Zongyuan's use of a rhetorical device called "linked text" or "stringed pearls" (*lianwen* or *lianzhu*; in Western rhetoric, this technique is called "anadiplosis" or "doubling"), whereby the last word in a line is repeated as the first word of the following line. A good example appears in the first of the "Eight Accounts":

> There was no hidden spring or fantastic rock that, no matter how
> far away, we failed to *reach*. After *reaching* it, we then pushed aside the
> weeds and sat down. We tipped our jugs until we were *drunk*. *Drunk*, we
> then used each other as pillows to *sleep*. *Asleep*, we then dreamed.[71]

In the conclusion of this same account, Liu employs anadiplosis again, but this time with *you*, or "sightseeing": "My mind is numb, my form is released, and I mysteriously merged with the myriad transformations. Only then did I know that I have not yet begun my *sightseeing* and, as a result, my *sightseeing* [activities] began."[72] Doubling is an especially useful rhetorical device in landscape essays because it creates a repetitive pattern that brings emphasis to the author's narration of the sightseeing experience. At the same time, when read aloud it produces an unmistakable verse-like cadence. These examples mark the first use of anadiplosis in a *ji* about place in Chinese letters.

Yet another distinguishing feature of Liu's talent as a *guwen* stylist is his use and manipulation of simile. Simile is a common feature in all genres of Chinese literature, especially poetry, mainly because as a rhetorical device it provides a convenient and compact way by which to draw an analogy. Simile is especially useful in the context of landscape description because it can help authors create an image-based word picture that in turn helps readers visualize the unfamiliar scene being described. Liu Zongyuan's description about the boulders on the hill near Flat-Iron Pool that "resemble livestock drinking at a creek" and others that "resemble bears clambering up a mountain" is especially evocative in this regard. Describing a place in *language* whose most striking quality is *visual* is extremely difficult to do well, and this is certainly one important criterion by which the "more successful" travel literature authors can be distinguished from those who are "less successful." Liu Zongyuan was a master of this technique.

The fourth of Liu Zongyuan's "Eight Accounts" is titled "Account of Reaching Little Stone Pool West of Little Hillock" (Zhi Xiao qiu xi Xiaoshi Tan ji). Note the author's repeated use of motion and action verbs (in italics), especially in his landscape description:

> *Walking* westward one hundred *bu* from Little Hillock, from across
> a clump of bamboo I heard an aqueous sound that seemed to tinkle
> like jade pendants. My heart delighted at this. I *cut away* the bamboos
> to *make a path*, and below beheld a little pool, the water of which was
> especially clear and bracing. Its bottom was made completely of rock.
> Near its banks, rocks from the depths *unfolded upward* and *lay exposed*,
> *forming* islets, *forming* cays, *forming* bluffs, and *forming* cliffs. Azure
> trees and halcyon creepers *screened* and *entwined*, *wavered* and *touched*;
> in irregular patterns, they *fanned* and *brushed*. There were perhaps a
> hundred-some fish in the pool, all of which seemed *suspended* in empti-
> ness. Sunbeams *descended* into the lucid water; fish *cast* their shadows
> upon the rocks, content and motionless. Then, suddenly they *darted*
> into the distance. Their *goings* and *comings* were swift and sudden, as
> if they were sharing their delight with the traveler. Gazing southwest-
> ward from the pool, the river *bends* like the Dipper, *winding* a snake
> path that is detectable when in view and when hidden from sight. The

conformations of its banks are like dog teeth—*zigging* and *zagging*. Its source cannot be known.[73]

Liu Zongyuan's skillful deployment of verbs adds a cinematic-like quality to his landscape description, which almost seems to invite the reader to partake in the author's experience and adventure. Note that in this selection from the "Eight Accounts," Liu is physically moving through the landscape. As the scene unfolds before the "traveler's" eye (the "traveler" mentioned here is Liu Zongyuan himself), a combination of verbs and use of simile again work together to bring an animated quality to the author's narration. This dynamic approach to landscape depiction contrasts markedly with the more "static" accounts—that is, instances where the author views and describes the landscape from essentially one fixed angle.

With one notable exception—Huiyuan's "Preface"—virtually all the texts considered so far in chapter 1 and in this chapter (that is, before Liu Zongyuan), including Yuan Jie's various commemorative-dedicatory accounts, fall in varying degrees into the category of static description of landscape. Of course, there is nothing at all bad or inferior with this approach. Indeed, as we have seen, in the hands of skilled writers such as Yuan Shansong and Li Daoyuan, it can produce charming and evocative descriptions. The point here is that Liu Zongyuan in his "Eight Accounts" employs literary language in accounts about sightseeing in a new way, emphasizing the physical movement of the author and, by extension, the reader through a landscape rather than describing it from an inert position. Narration of actual passage across space helps produce dynamic description of movement; this is because the author's viewpoints are constantly changing, which in turn not only adds a sense of motion to Liu Zongyuan's descriptions of place but creates a feeling of spontaneity as well.

While Liu Zongyuan's landscape descriptions certainly showcase the writer's literary artistry, his author reactions are equally fascinating because of their variety. Moreover, even though not all the accounts are dated, except for "You Huangxi ji" (or the so-called ninth account), we know that they are arranged in Liu's collected works in a general chronological order, even perhaps in the precise order in which they were written.[74] Thus, the ordering gives some idea of how the author's responses to landscape may have developed and changed over a period of about four years, from 809 to 813.

Central to Liu Zongyuan's personal responses to the scenic landscape in and around Yongzhou is the idea that it is worthy of praise in writing so that others may come to know about it and perhaps even experience these places vicariously through his essays. In the "Eight Accounts," Liu specifically identifies his primary, reading audience: *haoyou zhe*, or "those fond of sightseeing," and *haoshi zhe*, which in this context means something like "landscape connoisseurs."[75] Since no early-ninth-century scholar-official in north China would ever consider going traveling or sightseeing in the tropics of the far south unless he were posted there or dispatched under order of exile, it is certain that the primary audience for the "Eight Accounts" was future political exiles from the north who one day might find themselves in the climes of southwestern Hunan. Xiaoshan Yang's distinction between social and personal landscape essays is especially useful in the context of our discussion here because Liu Zongyuan's practice of writing about unknown scenic areas he discovered in and around Yongzhou to inform future "landscape connoisseurs" about their beauty and location would later became a common theme among *youji* authors who wrote about places that were less well-known to readers. China's most renowned travel writer, Xu Xiake, is probably the most famous follower of this practice.

As for other forms of author response, they vary. This is because the "Eight Accounts" were written over a period of about four years. For instance, in "Account of Rocky Ravine" (Shijian ji), there is no authorial response at all, but as we saw earlier in the first account, Liu Zongyuan draws an obvious analogy between the fantastic but unappreciated landscapes of Yong county and his own predicament as a neglected exile ("If you took the surprising beauty of this hillock and removed it to Feng, Hao, Hu, or Du . . ."). This is the most central and unique feature of his "Eight Accounts" and those written during his later exile in Liuzhou: Liu Zongyuan correlates his own dire predicament with the natural setting around Yong county, and he does so because it allows him to express the isolation, frustration, embarrassment, shame, rejection, resentment, and all the other emotions related to disgrace and political exile. This idea of expressing personal feelings through analogy to the natural and human worlds is common in Tang dynasty *guwen* prose, and it is this quality that sets it apart from earlier descriptive accounts of attractive scenery, such as those in Li Daoyuan's *Commentary on the Waterways Treatise*.[76]

Perhaps not surprisingly, Liu Zongyuan reserves his most extensive and teleological personal commentary until the close of the eighth account. "Fashioner-Creator" (Zaohua Zhe) is a supernatural entity that is responsible for "fashioning" and "creating" all the "myriad creatures" (*wanwu*) of the world, both animate (including humans) and inanimate. As pointed out by Edward H. Schafer long ago, "it was the traveler to distant places who had his eyes and mind opened to the works of the creator, as a stay-at-home never could".[77]

> Alas! For some time now I have doubted the existence or not of the "Fashioner-Creator." But upon reaching here, I have come to believe even more that he truly exists. But I also find it strange that he would not make this place in the Central Plains [that is, in the heartland of north China], and instead situate it among barbarians. For hundreds and thousands of years, it has not been able to showcase it talents, and for this reason its labor has been a complete waste. If a god can act in such an inappropriate manner, does this mean that he does not exist after all? Some say, "Its purpose is to console worthy men disgraced in exile here"; others say, "The potency of its life force does not produce great men but only produces such natural things as landscapes. Thus, to the south of Chu [that is, southern Hunan] there are few outstanding people but many attractive rocks." I do not believe either of the two explanations.[78]

It seems fitting that here, in the closing section of what has traditionally been regarded as the last of his "Eight Accounts," Liu Zongyuan would attempt to come to terms with his life of exile in south China. Not surprisingly, he again expresses his feelings by drawing an analogy between the natural and human worlds to ask a direct question: if there really is a "Fashioner-Creator" with a conscious mind, then why would he create such a beautiful physical environment in a land populated by "barbarians," where few could truly appreciate it? The indirect reference to Liu Zongyuan's own predicament is unmistakable: if the "Fashioner-Creator" produced a talented and dedicated public servant like Liu, then why would he be sent to a place where his skills to serve the emperor could not be utilized? Liu Zongyuan suggests two possible answers; then he rejects them both. Note that Liu explicitly discounts the "consolation" argument I made earlier, but this could indicate that his attitude in 812 (when this piece was written) may have changed since 809, when he began writing the "Accounts." In any case, the Yongzhou landscape essays collectively reveal that the sublime scenery in the south provided a diversion (sightseeing) and at least some temporary relief from his frustrations as a political exile, although it did not liberate him in any way from the anguish and humiliation of political exile.

As far as the history and development of travel literature in China is concerned, the "Eight Accounts" in general, and especially the "Account of Little Hillock West of Flat-Iron Pool," are significant for three important reasons. First, there is a travel-sightseeing component (*you*) in all of Liu's landscape essays, though this is indicated in the title of only one of these texts (the first one; if we count "You Huangxi ji," which traditionally has not been considered as one of the "Eight Accounts," then travel is indicated in two of them). Admittedly, travel does not play a key role in any of these compositions, for the excursions only cover short distances. Nevertheless, we have brief narrations of journeys undertaken ostensibly for pleasure (note that in the first of the Yongzhou essays, *two* trips are described: Liu Zongyuan's initial "discovery" hike and the follow-up outing undertaken with his two friends). The kind of traveling Liu Zongyuan is engaging in here is clearly *you*, or "sightseeing for pleasure" (he mentions that "gentlemen who prize sightseeing would vie to buy" the land around Flat-Iron Pool). There is no doubt that Liu Zongyuan's Yongzhou landscape essays, with their emphasis on *you*, served as a direct inspiration for the "sightseeing accounts" of the Song, which almost always bear the title "*You* place-x *ji*" and chronicle brief excursions to pleasure spots.

A second point is that unlike Yuan Jie, in "Account of Little Hillock West of Flat-Iron Pool" and others among the "Eight Accounts," Liu Zongyuan includes himself and his two friends in the narration ("We rooted up the weeds and mowed away the grasses, cut away the inferior trees, and built a roaring fire and burned them."). He is an active participant in the scene and the experience described, and at times he even colors the landscape with personal feelings and emotions or colors his feelings and emotions with landscape ("The clear and cool shapes were in *accord with* our eyes, the far-distant void *merged with* our spirits, and the profound quietude *blended with* our minds" is a good example of this).[79] Again, Yuan Jie and Liu Zongyuan are the first authors in the history of Chinese travel literature to compose sightseeing-landscape *ji* in which emotion is drawn from scene. The importance and influence of this innovation cannot be overstated. The *ji* form is now changing from highly descriptive depictions of attractive structures and landscapes to a type of literary text in which landscape description and lyrical expression each play complementary roles and, at times, even merge.

Finally, the "political dislocation" component in the Yongzhou accounts, which is also detectable in some of Yuan Jie's writings,[80] does not play any significant role in the development of later travel literature in China, for virtually no later *youji* authors used landscape features as metaphors or symbols of political neglect or personal suffering. Liu Zongyuan's most important and influential innovation was his expansion of lyrical intensity in the authorial commentary section of a *ji*. Essentially, this meant that rather than describing landscape as an outside observer, as Yuan Jie did earlier, a precedent has now been established whereby authors can make their observations from inside it: "My mind is numb, my form is released, and I mysteriously merged with the myriad transformations. Only then did I know that I have not yet begun my sightseeing journey, and that my sightseeing journey here was my first."[81] Clearly, for Liu Zongyuan, *you* involved both physical excursions and mental journeys.[82] We need not explore the dimensions of the latter variety, for they do not play any significant role in subsequent prose travel literature. But use of metaphorical language does play a substantial role in Song travel literature, and Liu Zongyuan was the one author most responsible for establishing this precedent. This is precisely the reason why the Yongzhou landscape essays collectively rank as an essential prototype in the history of Chinese travel literature.

CHINA'S FIRST TRAVEL DIARY

Li Ao (d. 838) was a scholar-official of the mid-Tang period and a contemporary of Liu Zongyuan. Both were closely associated with Han Yu, and both shared the experience of exile to south China. Although Li Ao is known mainly as a synthesizer of Confucian and Buddhist thought, he was also a key advocate and supporter of *guwen* prose.[83] Li Ao deserves our close attention because he wrote China's first travel diary, *Register of Coming South* (Lainan lu).[84]

In 809, Li Ao and his family set off on a journey from Luoyang (in Henan) to Guangzhou (in Guangdong) in the far south. Li had gotten himself into some political trouble and was demoted and exiled as a result. This was a very long trip and took about sixth months to complete. Following are some sample, representative entries. Note that each entry is dated:

> Tenth Month in the Third Year of the Prime Accord [Yuanhe] reign [808]:
> I, Li Ao, upon receiving orders . . . on *jichou* day of the justified month in
> the fourth year of the Prime Accord [31 January 809], departed with my
> wife and children from our dwelling in the Manifest Goodness Residence
> [Jingshan Di] and boarded a boat in the transport channel.

Yiwei day [6 February]: Departed from the Eastern Metropolis [Dongdu; that is, Luoyang]. Han Tuizhi [Han Yu] and Shi Junchuan [Shi Hong] rented a boat to see me off.

Wuxu day [9 February]: I was sick with a cold . . .

Dinghai day [30 March]: Our government junk developed a crack, water seeped in, and the boat was ruined.

Wuzi day [31 March]: Reached Hang county.

Jichou day [1 April]: Proceeded to the hills of Martial Wood, which in fact are home to the Spirit's Retreat and India Monasteries [Lingyin, Tianzhu Si].

Bingshen day [8 April]: Passed Seven Mile Rapids [Qili Tan] and reached Mu county.

Jiazi day [6 May]: My daughter, named so-and-so, was born.

Bingzi day [17 July]: Reached the burial vault of the Master of Shixing [Shixing Gong; that is, Zhang Jiuling].[85]

Guiwei day [24 July]: Reached Guang county.

Following this last line, which is the final entry in Li Ao's diary, he provides an "appendix" listing the distances between various stops on his itinerary. Here are some examples:

The distance from the Eastern Capital [Dongjing, or Luoyang] to Guang county, by means of the waterways through Qu and Xin counties, is 7,600 *li*; through Shangyuan and the Western Jiang [Xijiang] it is 7,130 *li*. From Luo Stream [Luochuan], down the Yellow River to Bianliang [or Kaifeng] and through the Huai to Huaiyin town, it is 1,830 *li* downstream. From Huaiyin to Lake Shaobo [Shaobo Hu] it is 350 *li*, upstream. . . . From Hang county to Constant Mountain is 695 *li*, upstream. How numerous are the frightening rapids there! If hawsers are used to tug the boat, you may proceed onward. From Constant Mountain to Yushan town it is 800 *li*, a land route. This is referred to as Jade Mountain Pass [Yushan Ling].[86]

These sample entries reveal that Li Ao's diary is essentially designed to provide information concerning his travel itinerary, such as the date of his departure from Luoyang, the friends who saw him off, the dates when he reached various major counties on his itinerary, a leak in his government-provided junk, the birth of a daughter, a brief sightseeing trip in scenic Hangzhou, a visit to the grave of a famous Tang dynasty poet Zhang Jiuling, and the date when he reached his final destination (24 July 809). Similarly, the distance information provided in his "appendix" seems earmarked mainly for government officials who one day might also be traveling to the hinterland of south China. No doubt, future exiles—who always traveled under strict government orders regarding when they needed to reach their new post in the area "South of the Ranges" (Lingnan)—could (and did) find Li Ao's itinerary information on distances, place names, key landmarks, available land and water routes, and river travel (upstream vs. downstream) extremely useful.

Strictly speaking, because it has no literary component, *Register of Coming South* does not fall within the generic borders we have adopted for *youji*. *Register of Coming South* is written for utilitarian purposes; that is, to help other government officials traveling south. What is important about Li Ao's diary, however, is that he was the first Chinese writer to use a diary format to describe a journey. No doubt the reason he employed this form was because using a dated-entries format was an efficient and convenient way of organizing an account of a lengthy trip and keeping track of the key places passed along the way (most travel accounts that predate the ninth century are much shorter and local in nature, so there was no need for a diary format). Later writers who composed lengthy travel diaries, most notably Lu You, Fan Chengda, and Xu Xiake, all adopted this same diary format and include an opening section in which they explain the background and circumstances of their journey, who accompanied them, their destination, and so on.

ADDENDUM

The form and content innovations initiated by Yuan Jie and Li Zongyuan transformed the account into a style of writing that could never have been written in parallel prose. Liu Zongyuan's "Eight Accounts," by their design to chronicle sightseeing excursions, needed to embody a sense of freedom, flow, and movement that parallel prose could never have accommodated.

This idea of "movement through space" is the central, defining motif in all travel literature and serves as the one quality that most distinguishes it from other forms of belles lettres written in prose. The innovative writing style crafted by Yuan and Liu is not so much a "rejection" of parallel prose in favor of *guwen* as it is an adaptation of the *ji* to new, literary demands in the eighth and ninth centuries. No earlier literary style existed for the kind of landscape description and authorial commentary/lyricism that Yuan Jie and Liu Zongyuan needed, so they took an existing form (*ji*) and adapted it to their own needs. Liu's essays are especially important in the process, for he was the first author to add a sightseeing component to a literary *ji*, thereby creating an essential prototype of Chinese travel literature. But there are only eight (or nine) of his Yongzhou essays and just a few from his later posting in Liu county in Guangxi. Moreover, no Tang authors who wrote *ji* after Liu Zongyuan followed the precise literary style in his "Eight Accounts." Thus, *youji* as a literary genre during the Tang dynasty was limited to some selected works by the handful of authors discussed in this chapter.

CHAPTER 3

MATURITY IN THE SONG

Previously, when I was in Guilin, I counted silently to myself that in
the span of nine years I had seen the mid-autumn harvest moon in
nine separate places. The distance between them is perhaps ten
thousand *li*.

FAN CHENGDA, *ACCOUNT OF A BOAT TRIP TO WU*

DUE TO THE PRINTING, PUBLICATION, AND PRESERVATION OF
Song textual materials in individual author collections (*bieji*), notation
books (*biji*), and collectania (*congshu*), a large corpus of Song *youji* survives
today. This body of material represents a watershed period in the history
and development of travel literature in imperial China. Scholar-officials
between the tenth and thirteenth centuries regularly composed *youji* during their trips to and from bureaucratic job postings in the provinces or
while they were stationed at a given administrative location. Their usual
destinations were either scenic areas, such as a famous mountain, or historical sites, such as the ruins of an ancient palace or temple. What immediately
distinguishes Song authors from their predecessors is that their trips were
almost always regarded as a form of leisure activity, to be undertaken in the
company of friends and/or family members. Moreover, with the popularity
of composing *youji* during the Song came generic changes in both form and
content.

The three broad categories of Song dynasty travel writing are the sightseeing account, the river diary, and the embassy or ambassadorial account.[1]
This framework provides a useful approach by which to distinguish the
major form and content variations in Song travel writing, as well as a convenient means by which one can approach a generous catalog of generically

similar textual material. The Song period is especially significant in the history of the genre because the "sightseeing account" and the "river diary"—and later variations of those two forms—became the standard formats for most subsequent *youji* composition. Moreover, these prototypes will go on to serve as models for numerous later travel writers. The embassy accounts describing Song ambassadorial missions to foreign states along China's northern border are also important, mainly because of their longer, travel-diary format.

HISTORICAL CONTEXT

Many historians have studied and written about the major shifts that took place in Chinese society after the collapse of the Tang dynasty in 907, the fractured period of the Five Dynasties in the north and the Ten Kingdoms in the south that followed, and the consolidation and order that came with the founding of the Song in 960. Among the many fundamental changes that resulted from this transition, two are almost always mentioned first: the collapse of the old Tang aristocracy and its power and dominance in government; and the rise of a new brand of social and political elites in the Song at both the local and national levels. The primary pathway to power for these new elites was success in the civil-service examinations. Three other developments accompanying the Tang-Song transition that have also received much attention are the increase of China's population from approximately fifty million in the Tang to about one hundred million in the twelfth and thirteenth centuries,[2] the development of large metropolitan cities, and unprecedented growth in trade and commerce.[3]

Especially relevant is the growth of the civil-service examination system under the Song and the resulting expansion of the government bureaucracy, which have been well documented.[4] More officials serving in an expanded bureaucracy that governed a large empire meant that most of them spent the bulk of their careers serving in regional posts away from the capital, relocating to new assignments on average once every three years. Thus, for most of these public servants, geographical mobility was a routine part of their government service. This relates to two additional and important points: first, "movement" is a key concept for observing and comprehending Song society; and second, travel literature offers unique insights into understanding Song culture, society, and literati not available in other sources. Until quite recently, the travels of Song *shidafu* have served essentially as background to other dimensions of their lives. But thanks to recent scholarship, this orientation has been challenged.[5] Study of *youji* can enhance our knowledge and understanding of movement and its importance in the lives of Song literati.

The travel of government officials around China, however, was not something new in the Song. This practice can be traced as far back as the Spring and Autumn and Warring States periods (*ca.* 771–*ca.* 475 and 475–221 BCE, respectively), when thinker-philosophers like Confucius (551–479 BCE) traveled extensively in search of political patrons for their ideas on how to govern society. This practice continued during the Han period, when members of the ruling class, like Sima Qian, in pursuit of scholarly and bureaucratic careers, spent time touring the empire to undertake firsthand investigation of historical sites and ancient monuments. Others, like the military official Zhang Qian, even journeyed beyond China's borders to gather intelligence on potential military threats to the Han dynasty. And during the Six Dynasties, aspiring government officials like Bao Zhao were sometimes compelled to undertake lengthy, difficult trips to places far from home to secure a bureaucratic post. Tang dynasty officials were also routinely moved to and from office postings. Sometimes, as in the case of Yuan Jie, it was because of routine changes in office assignment. At other times, as in the cases of Liu Zongyuan and Li Ao, it was the result of political troubles. What was different about the Song was the unprecedented number of officials serving in the bureaucracy, the corresponding frequency of their movement throughout the empire, and the elevated place that travel occupied in the lives of the literati. Of course, "non-literati" travelers such as merchants, military personnel, seasonal laborers, and religious pilgrims also plied the roads and waterways of Song China.[6] And "tourism" may have even played a role in the development of the Song economy.[7] Our focus, however, is the written travel records of government officials. This is because the overwhelming majority of *youji* that survive from the Song were written by these servants of the emperor. Beginning in the eleventh century, sightseeing and composition of *youji* became a prominent element of literati culture. Typically, if a government official's travels to a new office took him near a scenic spot or historically significant location, he would undertake a sightseeing excursion there, accompanied by friends, family members, or local hosts.[8] And almost always, the occasion would be commemorated with the composition of poems, a prose *youji* account, or both. Thus, an important result of the many travels undertaken by Song *shidafu* was literary production.

SIGHTSEEING ACCOUNTS

By far the most extensively written form of Song dynasty travel literature is the "sightseeing account." During the second half of the twelfth century, when Fan Chengda saw the mid-autumn harvest moon in nine separate locations over the course of nine years, there were approximately four thousand civil-service officials of the administrative grade serving in the Song bureaucracy.[9] As they traveled to and from bureaucratic postings, many wrote sightseeing accounts about attractive natural landmarks or some physical remnant of ancient culture they stopped to visit along the way. And like their earlier, eighth-century analogs, prose texts written to celebrate such occasions are usually titled "*You* place-x *ji*," or "Account of a Sightseeing Trip to place-x." These works chronicle activities at one site over a brief period, usually a day or two. Sightseeing accounts are the shortest of Song *youji*, rarely running more than a few hundred Chinese characters in length.

What explains the proliferation of writing about sightseeing during the Song? Officials in the Song bureaucracy were subject to systematic government personnel policies that reallocated civil servants on a regular basis—meaning that more literati were traveling—and overland and river travel was more convenient in the Song than in any previous period of Chinese history.[10] However, the most important reason for the proliferation of "sightseeing accounts" beginning in the Northern Song lies in yet another aspect of the development that accompanied the Tang-Song transition: by the late tenth and eleventh centuries, leisure and entertainment had become essential components of Chinese cultural life, especially in larger cities like Kaifeng and Lin'an (or Hangzhou), and it functioned on a level previously unknown.[11] These various entertainments, enjoyed mainly but not exclusively by the wealthy and upper classes, included such performing arts as music, dance, acrobatics, operas, and puppet shows, to name just some examples. Such activities all had antecedents in earlier historical periods. What was different during the Song was the scale on which they were carried out and the prestige they enjoyed.[12] But one aspect of Song dynasty recreational life—undertaken during leisure time away from one's normal duties or responsibilities—that was not widely practiced in earlier Chinese history was sightseeing. Accounts written to commemorate this pursuit, common in Song literary collections, serve as the foundation of *youji* writing during the period.

Literary historians who have written about the development of travel literature during the Song usually compartmentalize *youji* texts into different topical categories based on author type. Mei and Yu, for instance, organize travel-related works—mainly sightseeing accounts—into *youji* written by "philosophers" (*zheren*), by practitioners of "ancient-style prose" (*guwen*) writing, and by proponents of "neo-Confucian" (*lixue*) values. These are then further divided into subcategories that include "reasoned reflections on life" (*ganhuai shuoli*), "scientific investigation" (*kexue kaocha*), "retreat to landscape" (*shanshui huigui*), "myths and legends" (*shenhua chuanshuo*), and "social conditions and customs" (*minqing fengsu*).[13] Wang Liqun, on the other hand, lumps all traditional Chinese travel writing into one massive grouping that he designates as "landscape travel accounts" (*shanshui youji*), which he then subdivides into smaller categories such as "location-oriented" (*yudi*) and "literary" (*wenxue*) travel writing.[14] Still other scholars, such as Zhu Yaoting, essentially present the history of *youji* in anthology format organized into the two general categories of poetry and prose.[15]

Such histories of travel writing focus on the primary source, which is based more on the general literary and historical reputations of a select group of famous authors and less on those texts that are most representative of Song travel literature. Examples of the "famous authors" include major period figures, such as Fan Zhongyan (989–1052), Ouyang Xiu, Wang Anshi (1021–86), and Zhu Xi. Fan Zhongyan's "Account of the Yueyang Tower" (Yue-yang lou ji) and Ouyang Xiu's "Account of the Old Drunkard's Pavilion" (Zuiweng ting ji) are both literary masterpieces still studied today by every middle-school student in China. Moreover, they are anthologized in virtually every collection of *youji* ever published, including Richard Strassberg's influential *Inscribed Landscapes*. But one wonders why these works are classified as *travel* literature—Fan Zhongyan's account contains no travel component whatsoever, and he himself never personally visited the Yueyang Tower in Hunan; and Ouyang Xiu's famous essay, aside from a single line where he mentions "walking up the mountain for six or seven *li*," lacks a travel narrative. As for Wang Anshi and Zhu Xi, both are major figures in Song political and intellectual history, respectively, but neither wrote much *youji*. Nevertheless, Wang's "Account of a Sightseeing Trip to Baochan Mountain" (You Baochan Shan ji) and Zhu Xi's "Account of One Hundred *Zhang* Mountain" (Baizhang Shan ji) are standard selections in *youji* collections,[16] presumably not because of their importance in the history and development of the travel literature genre, but instead because their authors are major writers of the Song period who wrote a few travel pieces. So, to identify representative prototypes of the Song sightseeing essay, we need to look beyond the customary anthology selections found in Bei and Ye's *Selections of Travel Accounts from the Successive Eras* and its numerous analogues.

We begin with a sightseeing account concerning Jade Splendor Mountain (Yuhua Shan), located in modern Tongchuan *xian* in Shaanxi, about 140 miles north of Xi'an. The mountain derives its name from an imperial palace that once stood there and that served as a summer retreat for the second emperor of the Tang dynasty, Taizong.[17] In 651, the palace was converted into a Buddhist monastic complex, and between 659 and 664, it became the base of operations for Xuanzang's famous Buddhist sūtra translation project. In the eleventh century, the architectural remains and cultural relics that still stood on the original site of the Jade Splendor Palace complex began to attract tourists. Among the earliest visitors was a Northern Song official named Zhang Min (eleventh century), who, along with his two brothers and some acquaintances, toured the site in the summer of 1066. His description of the experience is titled "Account of a Sightseeing Trip to Jade Splendor Mountain" (You Yuhua Shan ji):

> If one travels forty *li* southwest of Yijun town, a mountain approaches along both sides of the road. This is Jade Splendor [Yuhua]. South of it is called "Wildfire Valley" [Yehuo Gu]. There are rocks on the mountain that are constantly blazing red. When you gaze at them, they seem to be emitting smoke from a chimney, and yet no one knows where it comes from. West of Wildfire Valley is called "Phoenix Valley" [Fenghuang Gu], which is the ancient site where the Tang built the Jade Splendor Palace. Presumably, when first built, the palace had nine audience halls and five gates, yet those known now by name and location only number six. Its main audience hall is the Jade Splendor Audience Hall. Above it is the Serried Clouds [Paiyun]; also above it is the Felicitous Clouds [Qingyun].[18]
>
> Jade Splendor's main gate is the Southern Wind Gate [Nanfeng Men]. East of the Southern Wind Gate is the residence of the heir apparent. His audience hall is called "Glorious Harmony" [Yaohe]; its main gate is called "Praiseworthy Ceremony" [Jiali]. There is just one instance where the name of a site is known but the location has been lost, and this is called the "Golden Whirlwind Gate" [Jinbiao Men]. Today only a small section of its wall and a few roof tiles remain. I went over to inspect it, but all I saw

was abandoned fields and overgrown weeds, thistles and thorns. West of the palace is called "Coral Valley" [Shanhu Gu]. Presumably, once an auxiliary audience hall stood there. North of Coral Valley Audience Hall is called "Lan Mushroom Valley" [Lanzhi Gu]. Long ago, the emperor Taizong commanded the Buddhist monk Xuanzang to translate Buddhist sūtras here. At first, it was called the "Austere Accomplishment Audience Hall" [Sucheng Dian]. Later it was abandoned and became a Buddhist monastery, or so it is said. Inside the monastery grounds is a rock face standing precipitously, as if it had been wrought by heaven.[19] Below it there is a chamber chiseled into the rock face, which can accommodate several tens of people. A stream tumbles down into the chamber with a force that seems to create flying rain. There are eighteen pine trees circuiting its flanks, all of which have grown through cracks in the rocks. They are probably ten *xun* in height, standing straight up like a firmly held writing brush. To its west and south there is an embankment called "Imperial Tour Stop" [Zhuluan]. When you first enter it, the two walls stand straight up, as if they had been formed by paring the rock. After reaching its interior, it seems as if you are looking at a large-beaked wine jar. On its flanks, a stream flies downward that looks like a suspended piece of cloth that seems to shoot watery gems. It is called the "Water Curtain" [Shuilian]. Slightly to the north there is another rock wall and stream, which resemble the scene here but are somewhat smaller.

On *dingsi* day, in the fifth month of summer, in the third year of the Ordered Tranquility [Zhiping] reign [1066], together with six others I came here for some sightseeing. We sat together on rocks in the shade of a pine tree, listened to the flow of the stream, and tasted its water. In due course, we shilly-shallied about to look over the ancient palace grounds and asked an old farmer about some lost matters of the past. Our spirits were running high and there was no desire to leave, but as for myself and the six others, some of us had office responsibilities and other business to attend to, and so by force of circumstances we could not stay any longer. So, after spending the night, in due course we took our leave. Some of those among us exchanged looks of disappointment, and so I said to them, "However you look at it, the joy of mountains and forests, and streams and rocks, along with sightseeing that is extraordinary and magnificent, is often found in remote and out-of-the-way places, far removed from all human traces. Thus, to find them one must go to places where dwell rustic monks, method masters,[20] and reclusive hermits. And yet, while reclusive hermits are fond of such places, their abilities are insufficient to manage them. Since the doctrines of Buddha and Laozi can indeed move people emotionally, thus their followers often alone have such abilities and can manage such places."[21] As for precipitous pavilions and sprawling manors, and the amusement derived from gazing upon and looking at them, there is no one who preempts the Buddhists and Daoists. Now, if you take up the prosperity of the Tang and its depletion of all wealth in the empire, it built a palace here, which subsequently fell into ruin and vanished. Du Fu, in fact, was a contemporary. When he visited the palace, he had feelings of sadness and grief, so much so that he expressed them in a poem. Information about the monastery today survives only because followers of the monastery monks have passed it down from one generation to the next. Since the Tang commanded power over the entire world, is there anything, then, more humiliating than this? Because of the competence of Taizong and the excellence of his government administration, these accomplishments should be disseminated even more as time goes on. But today if you could ask the elders of yesteryear about Taizong,[22] they would know nothing about him. As for Xuanzang, he is just a monk, yet those who praise him go so far as to use absurd language that is hard to comprehend to extol his accomplishments. Could it be that the way of man is often to find pleasure in wild and distorted speech and behavior and thereby easily forget about what is central and proper? Could it be that in the rise and fall of things each has its fortune, but during the Tang only Buddhism flourished? This is lamentable. But as for the competence of Taizong and his power in the world, still these qualities could not be preserved over the long term. But as for the rest of us, we will indeed be satisfied if we could just get one glimpse at the ancient palaces! Moreover, what need is there on our part to have regrets because they have not lasted very long? As for the desolation of these abandoned embankments and endless valleys, discarded palaces and crumbled ruins, although many years have passed, yet never has there been a single sightseer or two here. But myself and six others all came at the same time, and this indeed is something that can be called a grand occasion![23]

The initial motivation for Zhang Min's trip to Jade Splendor Mountain was to enjoy a day of sightseeing with his two brothers and four of their friends. And even though the trip had to be cut short because members of the group had matters, official and otherwise, that required attention, still Zhang concludes that getting everyone together for an outing is something that can be called a "grand occasion" (*sheng*).[24] Careful readers probably noticed that the structure of "Account of a Sightseeing Trip to Jade Splendor Mountain" does not strictly adhere to the quadripartite structure discussed in chapter 2, which suggests that the structure of the Song sightseeing account had not yet become fixed. Zhang instead begins with a description of the ancient site that reads like an archeological field report. His concern is to first provide a precise and detailed inventory of what physically remains of the Tang palace and later monastery that once stood there (his readers would certainly have been familiar with the general history of the complex, as well as with the famous poem written by Du Fu about its demise). It is not surprising, then, that some modern scholars have drawn on Zhang Min's text in their study of the architectural monuments that once served as Tai-zong's summer retreat.[25] Following his "field report," the author then provides his introduction, which includes the precise date of the sightseeing excursion and the circumstances of its being cut short. Zhang Min's reaction to the "looks of disappointment" on the faces of his fellow travelers then provides a catalyst for him to voice author reaction concerning the antiquities he observed and the historical figures with whom they are associated: Taizong, Xuanzang, and Du Fu. The account closes with a list (not translated) of the names of the six people who accompanied him on the short-lived tour.

Sightseeing journeys with friends to ancient historical sites (*fanggu*) was a common recreational activity during the Northern Song. Two famous examples are Su Shi's prose-poem compositions on the Red Cliff battle site.[26] But Zhang Min tells readers that while many years have passed since the Tang dynasty, "never has there been a single sightseer or two here." Thus, the author and his traveling companions most likely had no idea what they would find on the grounds of the ancient palace/monastery. Typically, when Chinese authors write about antiquities that once represented great accomplishments, deeds, or historical figures but have now turned into "abandoned fields and overgrown weeds, thistles and thorns," they lament the inevitable passage of time with language and imagery that contrasts former greatness with current state of ruin. As an example, consider the opening couplet of Du Fu's poem on the Jade Splendor Palace: "The stream turns, wind is steady through the pines; / Grey rats hide among the ancient roof tiles."[27] This verse is an example of the "reflection on the past" (*huaigu*) topos in Chinese poetry, in which an author visits an ancient cultural site, muses on the passage of historical time embedded in the site, laments its demise, and sometimes even sighs about the passage of personal time (Du Fu does all these things in his poem).[28] Zhang Min, however, reacts to what he observed in a way that few readers would have anticipated: instead of voicing concerns about the brevity of human life and the loss of past architectural monuments, he is more concerned about historical memory; more specifically, the commendable accomplishments of Taizong, reliable knowledge of which, Zhang contends, has not been passed down to subsequent generations.

Zhang Min's main argument, presented in almost lecture form to his traveling companions and readers, runs as follows: some of the most scenic and historically significant areas, like Jade Splendor Mountain, are in remote, out-of-the-way places. Followers of Buddhist and Daoist religious traditions can properly "look after" (ying) such places because they traditionally have taken up residence in remote locations to avoid the congestion and "contamination" inherently found in populated areas. We know this, Zhang Min argues, because they successfully pass down their religious traditions from one generation to the next. In the secular world, however, he says this is not the case. As an example, take the emperor Taizong. Zhang laments that no one really knows about the emperor's accomplishments, not even the "elders of yesteryear." And why is this? Zhang Min says it is precisely because no one cares about what is central and proper (zhongzheng) anymore. In other words, in Zhang's view Xuanzang was just a Buddhist monk, yet he is praised to the limit. The great deeds of Taizong, however, are unknown to posterity. At the close of his address, the author does briefly lament the dilapidated state of Tang antiquities on Jade Splendor Mountain. At the same time, however, he makes clear that what is most important is that "the competence of Taizong and the excellence of his government administration" be identified and disseminated to current and future generations.[29]

Although not frequently anthologized, another good example of the Song sightseeing account is Chao Buzhi's (1053–1110) "Account of a Sightseeing Trip to North Mountain in Xincheng" (Xincheng you Beishan ji). This work was written sometime during the Serene Peace (Xining) reign (1068–78), when his father, Chao Duanyou (jinshi 1053), served as magistrate (xianling) of Xincheng, a town under the jurisdiction of Hangzhou:

> Thirty li to the north of Xincheng, the hills gradually deepen, while the grasses, trees, springs, and rocks gradually become more secluded. At first, we were still able to travel on horseback through the rocky crags.

Everywhere on our flanks were huge pines: those that were bent over resembled carriage canopies; those that went straight up resembled pennants atop a flag pole; those that stood erect resembled people; and those that lay recumbent resembled coiled dragons. Among the grasses below the pines is a spring moving along a marshy bed, now hidden, now in view. It drops into a stony pit, making a tinkling sound. Among the pines were vines several tens of *chi* in length, slithering and writhing like huge serpents. Upon them was a bird as black as a mynah, with a fiery red crown and long beak, which lowered his head and pecked away, cawing with a piercing cry.

A little to the west, by a single peak lofty and sheer, is a footpath so narrow one can barely walk along it. We tethered our horses to the tip of a rock and ascended the footpath, helping one another along the way. The bamboo thicket was so dense that, looking up, we could not see the sun. Proceeding another four or five *li*, we then heard some cackling fowl. A monk dressed in a linen robe and wearing sandals came forward to greet us, but when we addressed him, he gave a start and turned away. He seemed like a roe deer in that he could not be approached.

On the summit of the peak is a building with several tens of rooms. They curve and twist along the cliff wall, forming a railing. Like snails and mice, we trailed and tracked through them until we found a way out. The doors and windows of the building directly face one another. After we sat down, a gust of mountain wind arrived, and all the large and small folly bells in the reception and ceremonial halls began to chime. My companions and I looked around and became alarmed. We had no idea of where we were.

Since dusk was about to fall, we spent the night. The time was the ninth month, when skies are lofty and dew is clear, when hills are deserted and moonlight is bright. Looking up, I scanned the starry dipper. All its stars were brilliant and huge, as if they were right above our heads. Outside the window were several tens of bamboo shafts, knocking against one another with a ceaseless din. Amid the bamboos were plum and palm trees thick-set, seemingly in the shapes of specters and sprites standing in pairs with their brows bristled. My companions and I again looked around at one another, frightened to the soul and unable to sleep. All of us got out of there at the crack of dawn.

Several days later, after returning home, I was still dazed and confused, as if under some spell. Thus, I have recalled and made a record of our trip to North Mountain. Afterward, I never returned to that place again, but I often think about the events that once took place there.[30]

In their commentary on this work, Bei and Ye remark that in both language and style, "Account of a Sightseeing Trip to North Mountain in Xincheng" was "deeply influenced by the landscape *youji* of Liu Zongyuan."[31] Although they fail to mention precisely how this influence is manifested, it is easily spotted on several levels. First, like his Tang predecessor, Chao provides narration of *movement* through a landscape toward a specific destination: the summit of North Mountain. The emphasis of Chao Buzhi's *youji*, however, is not so much on the journey itself but upon describing the physical setting observed along the way to, and at, the travel destination (it will be recalled that this was also the case in some of Liu Zongyuan's "Eight Accounts"). The author executes an evocative description of those features through a register of *guwen* prose that is succinct and yet loaded with action verbs that evoke a word picture of the physical features spied by Chao and his companions. Note also how Chao Buzhi, like Liu Zongyuan, generously employs simile to assist in his delineation of landscape ("Everywhere on our flanks were huge pines: those that were bent over *resembled* carriage canopies; those that went straight up *resembled* pennants atop a flag pole; those that stood erect *resembled* people; and those that lay recumbent *resembled* coiled dragons"). And finally, also observe that Chao closes his account with an author reaction that is markedly unlike anything we saw in the works of his Tang predecessors ("All of us got out of there at the crack of dawn."). This unexpected reaction serves as an excellent example of how "sightseeing" *youji* developed in a new direction during the Northern Song.

Unlike Yuan Jie and Liu Zongyuan, Chao Buzhi does not draw upon landscape to voice personal inner conflicts or express highly emotional concerns. This new direction, which will be followed by Su Shi (in the next selection) and virtually all Song *youji* authors, marks a major turning point in the history of the genre and functions as a key factor in the maturation process that began in the eleventh century. In the case of Chao Buzhi's account, his focus is upon the details of the landscape he and his friends observed and enjoyed during the journey and how they reacted to unexpected events after reaching their destination. In many, if not most, sightseeing *youji* dating from the Song, the reaction is usually praise of the beautiful scenery observed during the trip and the enjoyment derived from

3.1. Fan Kuan 范寬 (*ca.* 960–1030). *Travelers Among Mountains and Streams* (Xishan xinglü tu 溪山行旅圖). Ink and slight color on silk, 6¾ ft. × 2½ ft. The Collection of the National Palace Museum, Taipei.

the social experience of sightseeing with friends.[32] In Chao Buzhi's text, there is certainly a hefty amount of admiration of the scenery around North Mountain, but the author's tone of appreciation disappears abruptly when he and his friends experience the sudden, windy nighttime conditions on the summit. Their fear then transforms trees swaying in the wind outside their window into imagined "specters and sprites standing in pairs with their brows bristled." Not surprisingly, Chao then reports, "My companions and I again looked around at one another, frightened to the soul and unable to sleep."

Chao Buzhi's text also introduces a rhetorical device that is new in *youji*: travel accounts written directly in the form of a recollection. The overwhelming majority of *youji* written in ancient China was of course composed after the journey ended (otherwise, how could one write about a real travel experience that has not yet taken place?). But Chao Buzhi and some of his contemporaries, including Su Shi, are among the first *youji* authors to state outright that they are "retracing" (*zhui*) or "recalling" (*yi*) past events[33] and that they do so to bring emphasis to an *experience* that resulted from that event. Chao's recollection accentuates the deep fear he experienced on the mountain. The coda to "Account of a Sightseeing Trip to North Mountain in Xincheng" no doubt surprised many readers—no earlier account of an excursion taken for pleasure had concluded with the author relating how frightful the experience turned out to be. In Chao's case, he was still reeling from the outing and thinking about it several days after it happened. The author reaction voiced in the closing section of "Account of a Sightseeing Trip to North Mountain in Xincheng" emphasizes the psychological and emotional impact of the trip and the results of the experience on the traveler. Again, this approach to *youji* composition is different from that followed by Yuan Jie and Liu Zongyuan, who preferred to impose their personal feelings and emotions onto the landscape.

Finally, we should also acknowledge Chao Buzhi's skillful use of sound-related imagery, specifically in the closing section of his account. I refer to the sudden racket of wind-blown "folly bells" and the "ceaseless din" of rattling bamboo stalks. Sound imagery like this functions on at least two levels. First, it demonstrates how unexpected sounds in an unfamiliar environment can trigger fear ("My companions and I looked around and became alarmed. We had no idea of where we were."). Second, it helps readers better imagine how a leisurely sightseeing excursion can suddenly be transformed by sound (and by hallucinations of "specters and sprites" outside the monastery window) into a nightmare, which in effect functions as an "attack" on the auditory and visual senses, executed through careful use of specific imagery.

Our third and final example of the Song sightseeing account comes from Su Shi, who, as it turns out, is not only a major Song literary figure but also an important travel writer in his own right. In fact, as I have argued elsewhere, Su was one of—if not *the*—first Chinese author to produce *youji* in a sustained manner over a number of years, and many of his sightseeing essays (discussed below) served as prototypes that helped effect the maturity of travel literature in the Song.[34] Judging from the comments and observations of various anthologists and commentators, however, his reputation as a major *youji* author is based on one text: "Account of Stone Bells Mountain" (Shizhong Shan ji).[35]

Su wrote this work in 1084 while accompanying his son Mai (1059–1119) to the young man's first official post. Therein he notes a claim about which he harbored doubts: that the clanking sound made by water striking rocks at the foot of the Stone Bells Mountain had previously been described by Li Daoyuan and the Tang essayist Li Bo (fl. early ninth century) as sounding like "ringing bells."[36] Since Su's travel itinerary took him and son Mai near Stone Bells Mountain (in modern Jiangxi, on the eastern shore of Lake Poyang), he decided to investigate the situation first hand. His account has rightly been regarded as a masterful literary production and superb example of how some *youji* works dating from the Song reveal an investigative quality that seeks to clear up literary and historical misunderstandings about the names of places by gathering empirical evidence; in this regard, Su's text certainly deserves special recognition. Its "masterpiece" reputation in Chinese literary history notwithstanding, it is *not* representative of Song *youji* in any general sense, nor does it seem to reflect Su's preferred style of writing about his sightseeing activities. Aside from the Stone Bells Mountain essay, Su Shi did not write any other "investigative" *youji*. He did, however, pen many sightseeing accounts, and it is among these texts that we will find those exemplars that serve as a starting point in our search for the prototypical Song dynasty sightseeing account.

Su Shi's surviving prose oeuvre includes seventeen or eighteen *youji* works, most of which are sightseeing accounts.[37] Su seems to have preferred composing more light-hearted, informal accounts to commemorate such outings. A good example is his "Sightseeing Trip to Sand Lake" (You Shahu).[38] Sand Lake was a sightseeing spot outside of Huang county (Huangzhou; modern Huanggang, Hubei):

> Thirty *li* southeast of Huang county is Sand Lake, also called Black Snail Inn [Luosi Dian]. I was thinking about buying some land thereabouts, but upon going there to look over the land I became ill. I heard that Pang Anchang, a native of Maqiao, was skillful in medicine, but was deaf. I therefore went to see him in search of a cure. Although Anchang is deaf, he surpasses all others in intelligence. I drew some characters on paper, writing just a few of them, and he knew my meaning exactly. I said to him jokingly, "I use my writing hand as a mouth; you use your eyes as ears. We are both uncommon men of our times!" When I recovered from my illness, we went together on an outing to Clear Spring Monastery [Qingquan Si]. The monastery is situated about two *li* outside the outer gate of

Qishui town. There one finds Wang Yishao's Washing Brush Spring [Xibi Quan],[39] the water of which is extremely sweet. It overlooks Lan Creek [Lanxi], which flows westward. I composed a song [to mark the occasion] that goes:

> Below the hill, short *lan* buds invade the creek;
> Amid the pines, the clean sandy path is free of mud.
> A sunset storm rages and roars; a cuckoo cries out.
> Who says that in human life youth never comes twice?
> Look! The flowing stream is still able to move westward.
> Stop worrying about white hair and crowing yellow cocks!

We drank heavily that day and then returned home.[40]

Note that in the verse included in "Sightseeing Trip to Sand Lake," which functions as Su's author reaction, he unabashedly rejects any discussion of issues such as the inevitable passage of time or the brevity of human mortality ("Stop worrying about white hair and crowing yellow cocks!"). This exhortation is most certainly an indirect reference to Wang Xizhi's "Preface to the Lanting Poems," in which the famous calligrapher laments the transience, and hence sadness, of human life.[41] Su Shi will have none of this, and instead he closes his account with a simple report that becomes especially poignant when one considers that he wrote his account about Sand Lake while living in political exile in Huang county in the early 1080s: "We drank heavily that day and then returned home."[42] It is precisely this sort of expression about the pleasure derived from sightseeing with friends that functions as the hallmark quality of the Song dynasty sightseeing account.

The three texts by Zhang Min, Chao Buzhi, and Su Shi are not only representative of the Northern Song sightseeing essay, they also exemplify the new directions in which *youji* is now developing. In the tenth and eleventh centuries, most travel accounts were produced to celebrate trips undertaken essentially for *social* purposes—those specifically to gatherings and outings taken together with family, friends, or acquaintances. A few of examples of this practice—that is, pleasure outings to scenic sites taken with friends—survive in Tang prose (Li Bai's "Preface to the Poem 'Boating on Court Gentleman Lake in Mian County'" and some of Liu Zongyuan's excursions in Yongzhou are isolated examples), but such socially oriented *youji* were certainly not common in the Tang. Moreover, the kind of *youji* written by Yuan Jie and Liu Zongyuan, in which personal emotion and career disappointment is fused with landscape, was not imitated by any post-Tang prose travel literature author. What was now new and most important about the sightseeing account is this: Northern Song writers responded to landscape and antiquities in diverse ways. Zhang Min's author reaction to what he observed on Jade Splendor Mountain was sparked and fueled by a passion for the preservation of memory and knowledge of an important historical figure. Chao Buzhi's account, on the other hand, relates a story about a sightseeing excursion with friends that initially was quite enjoyable but ended up turning into a terrifying experience he could not forget. And finally, Su Shi's trip to Sand Lake, undertaken during his exile years in Huang county, closes with a celebratory poem about "eternal youth" and an exclamation on how wonderful it is to spend time touring a temple with a new friend.

RIVER DIARIES

> Everything that is discussed and described in the works [that is, Fan Chengda's travel diaries]—mountains and streams, customs and mores, natural resources and local products, traces of antiquity, or traveling companions—is both delightful and affecting. Fan's notes capture and record the facts; his language is elegant and truthful. When reading the diary, it embodies the historian's method.
>
> LU XIANG (*JINSHI* 1523), "SHIHU JIXING SANLU BA"[43]

Of the two types of diary-format documents—one written essentially for public circulation, the other (the personal diary) describing a non-circulating and private document[44]—our main interest here is with the former: diaries intended for a public readership. First produced on a regular basis during the Northern Song dynasty, many such works survive, with contents that vary considerably. Many government officials kept diaries concerning contemporary political matters and the discussions about them that were conducted at the imperial court.[45] Others, like the famous scholar-official, calligrapher, and poet Huang Tingjian, maintained detailed logs of their routine everyday activities.[46] Still other authors wrote in diary format about the journeys they undertook while traveling to and from office postings in the provinces. One early example is Ouyang Xiu's *Chronicle of Going into Service* (Yuyi zhi), which provides a barebones account—reminiscent of Li Ao's *Register of Coming South*—of his trip in 1036 to an exile post in Hubei.[47] Many other diaries related to travel and dating from the Northern and Southern Song also survive.[48] An especially important text among these works is Zhang Shunmin's (*jinshi* 1065) *Register of a Trip to Chen County* (Chenxing lu).[49]

Zhang was a friend of both Su Shi and Huang Tingjian and an opponent of the reform program of Wang Anshi. When Wang's political faction regained power in the 1090s, Zhang Shunmin and the other members of the "Yuanyou faction" were exiled to various corners of the empire. Zhang was dispatched to Chen county in southern Hunan. *Register of a Trip to Chen County* describes the journey from Kaifeng to his exile site. This work deserves close attention because while Zhang employs the travel diary format used by Li Ao and Ouyang Xiu, at the same time he expands the content to include extended descriptions of attractive landscapes and reports on important paintings and calligraphy specimens (Zhang was an art connoisseur) that he examined in different monasteries along the way and on other observations he made during his journey south. *Register of a Trip to Chen County*, with its expanded format and varied content, is an immediate predecessor of the two prototypical river diaries of the Song: Lu You's *Account of Entering Shu* (Ru Shu ji) and Fan Chengda's *Register of a Boat Trip to Wu* (Wuchuan lu).[50] These works are referred to here as "river diaries" because both describe lengthy trips—roughly eighteen hundred miles each but taken in opposite directions—on the Great River in the 1170s. Lu You's 1170 journey took him from his home in Shanyin (modern Shaoxing, Zhejiang) to a new post in Kuizhou, eastern Sichuan, while Fan's 1177 diary chronicles a journey from Chengdu (in Sichuan), where he had just completed a two-year assignment as military governor, to his home at Stone Lake (Shihu), just outside of Suzhou (modern Jiangsu).

The Southern Song river diaries are an entirely new form of *youji*. Following the lead of Li Ao and Ouyang Xiu, Lu You and Fan Chengda convincingly demonstrate that the travel diary format was an appropriate literary form by which to chronicle an extended journey. They also show—as we will see in examples to follow—that the language and contents of individual entries can be formulaic, simple, and even colloquial at certain times and highly literary and even lyrical at others. The river diaries are notable in several other respects as well. For instance, they are the longest *youji* texts dating from the Song dynasty that describe a single, continuous journey.[51] Lu You's excursion upstream on the Great River took 157 days to complete, while Fan Chengda's journey downstream from Sichuan lasted for 122 days. The great length of time needed to complete these trips explains why Lu and Fan employed a diary format: dated entries provide an efficient and convenient way of organizing a written account of a lengthy trip and keeping track of the key places passed along the way. Fan's *Register of a Boat Trip to Wu* has 110 entries that cover all 122 days of the trip (some entries cover multiple days), while *Account of Entering Shu* covers all but four of the 157 days of Lu You's trip.[52] Individual entries in both works always begin with a date and geographical location reference. For instance, when Fan Chengda decided to moor his boat in Jiazhou (modern Leshan in Sichuan) and to undertake a sightseeing trip to nearby Mount Emei (Emei Shan), his diary entry for that day begins:

> *Guisi* day [22 July 1177]: Set out from Emei town. Leaving by the West Gate, I began my ascent of the mountain.[53]

The similarity between Fan and Lu's diaries and Li Ao's *Register of Coming to the South* and Ouyang Xiu's *Chronicle of Going into Service*, however, ends there. What immediately distinguishes the river diaries from their Tang and Northern Song predecessors is the length of the entries and corresponding detail of information found therein. Consider this: the *Register of a Boat Trip to Wu* entry describing the initial leg of Fan Chengda's ascent of Mount Emei—covering one day, 22 July 1177—runs much longer than most extant sightseeing accounts dating from the Northern Song.

Although the river diary entries reflect the quadripartite structure of *youji* outlined earlier, they differ in significant ways from all earlier travel literature. First, because of its segmented and extended diary format, the river diary is designed to provide the author with a literary vehicle that he can use to write about *multiple places* as his itinerary courses along the Great River (Strassberg calls this format "extended strings of individual travel accounts"[54]). In other words, each time Lu or Fan passed a notable place—and there were many of them along the Great River, including famous mountains, historical landmarks, notable caves and grottoes, and ancient temples—they inevitably would stop to moor their boat and then set off on a sightseeing tour. These side trips usually lasted only a day or two because most of the places visited were close to the Great River. Fan Chengda's trip to the summit of Mount Emei is an exception; it took him ten days to complete his ascent and tour of the mountain.

Second, although the general focus of Northern Song sightseeing essays is upon brief description of, and author reaction to, attractive landscape venues, the river diaries of the Song are essentially designed not only to provide descriptive reports on striking or unusual riparian scenery along the Great River, but also to serve more utilitarian purposes: to provide readers with descriptive accounts of notable historical and literary landmarks along the river, to give reports on their physical condition, and at times to voice critical remarks about, or evaluation of, those sites. Consider the following two passages from the *Account of Entering Shu*, the first of which illustrates the way Lu You describes the mountain peaks in Xialao Pass (Xialao Guan; near modern Yichang, Hubei):

> At the end of the fifth watch, our boat was untied. We went through Xialao Pass. The Great River was hemmed in by a thousand peaks and myriad cliffs. Some rose up in groups competing with one another. Some rose up alone. Some were crumbling away as if about to crash down. Some were perilously near to toppling over. Some were ridden with horizontal crevices. Others had vertical cracks. Some were concave, some were convex. Some had large fissures. All were so strange that they could never be described in full.[55]

Now compare Lu's descriptive passage on Xialao Pass with the following entry, which recounts a visit to a famous landmark, Yellow Crane Tower (Huanghe Lou), situated near modern city of Wuhan:

> As for the Yellow Crane Tower, a long-standing tradition has it that Fei Yi made his flight and ascension to immortality here. Later, he came back riding a yellow crane. Hence, the tower is so named. It is known for having the finest scenic view in the empire. Cui Hao's [d. 754] poem about the tower is the best known, and the marvelous lines Taibai [or Li Bai] got here are especially numerous.[56] Now the tower is already in ruins; its ancient foundation is also gone. I asked an old clerk about its location, and he said it was between Stone Mirror Pavilion [Shijing Ting] and South Tower [Nanlou], directly facing Parrot Isle [Yingwu Zhou]. I can still imagine what it

must have looked like. Only the tower's name placard, written in seal script by Li Jian and engraved in stone, remains. Taibai climbed this tower and sent off Meng Haoran [689–740] with a poem that read:

> "The distant glare of his solitary sail vanishes in deep-blue mountains;
> I see only the Great River as it flows to sky's horizon."

Presumably, the sail and mast shining against the distant mountains was especially worth viewing. Without traveling the river for a long time, however, one cannot know this.[57]

Passages like this are common in the *Account of Entering Shu* and *Register of a Boat Trip to Wu* and illustrate well how Fan Chengda and Lu You engage the past in their diaries. Whereas Zhang Min's sightseeing account deals only with the historical past as it relates to the legacies of Tang Taizong and Xuanzang, Lu's diary entry on the Yellow Crane Tower illustrates well how he and Fan often engage both the historical past (a famous tower now in ruins) and literary legacy (the poems by Cui Hao and Li Bai written there). There were numerous such locations along the Great River, and unlike their Six Dynasties and Tang predecessors, many of whom sought to infuse landscape with personal feelings and concerns, Song river diarists focused much more attention on what I prefer to call "historical-literary heritage sites."[58] Fan Chengda and Lu You were especially fond of citing earlier texts—especially famous poems—and then commenting on how they actually relate to the historical place in question and its current physical state. Zhang Min engages in this practice in his *youji* on the Jade Splendor Palace, but such active engagement with the historical past is not common in the Northern Song sightseeing essay. In the river diaries, however, one can find numerous examples. On the opening pages of the *Register of a Boat Trip to Wu*, for instance, Fan Chengda quotes a quatrain by Du Fu that suggests that there are "plum rains" (*meiyu*) in Sichuan. Fan then disputes this claim.[59] In the example just cited concerning the Yellow Crane Tower, Lu You does not point out or correct a mistake in a text from the literary past but simply observes, "Without traveling the Great River for a long time, however, one cannot know this."

The skill of using language to create cinematic-like word descriptions of places could be applied to help readers to "see" these places, to "be there," and to "share the travel experience," either together with the author or in his place. Another quality that distinguishes the river diary from all previous *youji* was the ability of Lu You and Fan Chengda, perhaps more than any other travel literature authors before or after them, to use words to execute "pictures" of the sights and experiences associated with river travel, as represented in two passages from their diaries. The first comes from the *Register of a Boat Trip to Wu* and describes Fan's passage through Qutang Gorge on the Great River, the first of the famous Three Gorges:

> *Dingsi* day [15 August]: The river had not yet stopped rising. During the *chen* and *si* double hours [7 a.m.–9:00 a.m. and 9 a.m.–11:00 a.m.] we decided to untie our mooring lines. Traveled fifteen *li* and reached the mouth of Qutang Gorge. The water was flat as a mat. Only the crest of Yanyu Heap[60] still appeared and disappeared in the whirlpool. Our boat brushed against it as we passed by; the oarsmen had sweaty palms and the fear of death in their hearts. Their faces were pale. This is probably the most dangerous place in the empire! As we proceeded on this extremely perilous leg of our journey, the onlookers next to me all became alarmed. I was already in the boat, so I entrusted everything to the forces of nature and did not take the time to ask about anything. Leaning against a folding chair, I just sat at the helm and let the boat heave and totter.[61]

A powerful sense of motion is present in this passage, as is the inherent peril of traveling by boat through the gorges. How this danger affected passengers and crew is then highlighted ("The oarsmen had sweaty palms and the fear of death in their hearts."). And as in many of his reports and sightings, Fan closes with a brief author reaction. In this case, he has no choice but to leave everything to "the forces of nature" (*ziran*).

Now compare Fan's account of passing through Qutang Gorge with his description of a meteorological phenomenon that sometimes appears on the summit of Mount Emei. To pious and devout followers of Buddhism, however, this rare spectacle is regarded as a physical manifestation (*xian*) of Samantabhadra (Puxian), the resident bodhisattva on the mountain:

> We paid a second visit to the hall on the cliff and offered prayers. Suddenly, a dense fog arose in the four directions, turning everything completely white. A monk said, "This is the Silvery World" [Yinse Shijie]. A short time later, there was a heavy downpour and the dense fog retreated. The monk said, "This is the rain that cleanses the cliff. The bodhisattva

is about to make a 'Great Manifestation'" [Daxian]. Silvery tūla clouds[62] again spread out below the cliff, gathered thickly, and mounted upward to within a few yards of the edge, where they abruptly halted. The cloud tops were as smooth as a jade floor. From time to time, raindrops flew by. I looked down into the cliff's belly, and there was a great globe of light lying outstretched on a flat cloud. The outer corona was in three rings, each of which had indigo, yellow, red, and green hues. In the very center of the globe was a hollow of concentrated brightness. Each of us onlookers saw our forms in the hollow and bright spot, without the slightest detail hidden, just as if we were looking in a mirror. If you raise a hand or move a foot, the reflection does likewise. And yet you will not see the reflection of the person standing right next to you. The monk said, "This is the Body-Absorbing Light" [Sheshen Guang]. When the light disappeared, winds arose from the mountains in front and the clouds scurried about. In the wind and clouds there again appeared a huge, globular form of light. It spanned across several mountains, exhausting every possible color and blending them into a beautiful array. The plants and trees on the peaks and ridges were so fresh and alluring, so gorgeous and striking, that you could not look at them directly.[63]

Fan Chengda executes his word picture skillfully, alternating between precise descriptive language concerning the scene on the summit, the "manifestation announcements" of the monk who accompanied him, and the author's observations of the weather changes that led to Samantabhadra's "appearance." Descriptive passages like this not only help readers visualize what Fan observed on the summit of Mount Emei, they also endow the river diaries with literary merit that illustrates how adeptly Fan Chengda and Lu You could manipulate language to convey to readers the visual qualities of their travel experiences on the Great River.

Other than literary language and spectacular word pictures, the river diaries are also concerned with the mundane matters related to river travel. For instance, Lu You's report on what happened to one of his boats while negotiating dangerous rapids near Gui county in eastern Sichuan reads:

Our boat started up the New Rapids. Following the southern bank, the boat had gone seven- or eight-tenths of the way when its bottom struck the rocks. I hurriedly sent someone to go and rescue the boat, and it was barely saved from sinking. A sharp rock had pierced the bottom of the boat, which was stuck fast and could not be moved. This happened because some boatmen brought along so much chinaware to sell in Shu.[64]

The river diaries contain numerous similar reports concerning the experiences—some of them quite dangerous and difficult—faced by the river traveler. At times, however, we can also encounter a startling and unexpected commentary or report. For instance, Fan Chengda provides a detailed, gruesome description of a massive sheep slaughter that occurred every year near Chengdu in honor of Grand Protector Li (Li Taishou), who, in ancient times, is said to have expelled an evil dragon and parted the Min River in an effort to control local flooding.[65] And while visiting a monastery on Mount Emei, Fan discovers a written account of the Buddhist monk Jiye's imperially sanctioned trip to the Western Regions (that is, Central Asia and India) in the early years of the Song dynasty. Remarking that "such information is rarely seen in the world," Fan Chengda copied the entire account of Jiye's trip into the *Register of a Boat Trip to Wu* so it could "make up for omissions in the histories of the dynasty."[66]

These various sightings, descriptions, and commentaries, all based on eyewitness observation, are of course of immense value to historians. But in the overall history and development of *youji*, what most distinguishes the river diary is the great diversity of its contents. Therein we find matters concerning historical monuments like the Yellow Crane Tower; detailed lyrical description of riverscape, such as that observed by Lu You in Xialao Pass; and quotations and commentary on literary gems of the past that relate to sites along the river, such as Li Bai's farewell poem to Meng Haoran. At the same time, we also encounter passages that are less literary or more matter-of-fact, such as Lu You's account of his boatman loading too much chinaware to sell in Sichuan, which almost sank one of his boats. We also find reports of local customs that might seem quite strange to readers in Jiangnan, such as the annual sheep slaughter near Chengdu.

Given the diverse content of the river diaries and the different register of language one finds in entries therein, ranging from straightforward, almost colloquial diction (Lu You's chinaware report) to highly literate and lyrical language (Fan Chengda's description of Samantabhadra's "appearance"), it is difficult to classify the river diaries beyond the general designation of *youji*. As far as content is concerned, there is no single focus. And we certainly cannot regard the river diaries as autobiography. They reveal author statements, opinions, and even personal concerns, but they do not disclose inner emotions or feelings on any consistent basis. Ultimately, then, the river diaries must be viewed as a composite form of *youji* that provide a wealth of information to contemporary and later readers, especially regarding historical-literary heritage sites along the Great River. And of course, the *Account of Entering Shu* and *Register of a Boat Trip to Wu* also contain valuable geographical-topographical information, along with numerous observations about local customs and practices. In this respect, the river diaries function as a new form of *youji* whose content represents a union of focus concerning place (*di*), history (*shi*), and literature (*wen*). Few other forms of prose writing in imperial China, if any, could match the thematic breadth of the river diary. Of course, Lu You and Fan Chengda were master prose stylists, and, as we have seen, on occasion they showed off their literary prowess. But the ultimate purpose of the river diary is reportorial, that is, to provide readers with a detailed account of what it is like to travel on the river, one that would give the armchair traveler (and one endowed with a hearty imagination) a chance to travel with the author vicariously and to "see" what he saw and "experience" what he experienced.

EMBASSY ACCOUNTS

> On the contrary, it seems to me that these [embassy] accounts were the product of intellectual and emotional subjectivities rather than written as transparent windows. Their authors were superimposing anachronistic mental maps upon the altered cityscapes they traversed, describing spaces that both they and their readers could only recognize and reconstitute from textual accounts of the Northern Song city. Their accounts of the ruined and blank spaces of Jīn Kaifeng were suffused with nostalgia for what had been lost, and confused by disorientation about what had been erased from physical reality and collective memory in the intervening years.
>
> ARI DANIEL LEVINE, "WELCOME TO THE OCCUPATION: COLLECTIVE MEMORY, DISPLACED NOSTALGIA, AND DISLOCATED KNOWLEDGE IN SOUTHERN SONG AMBASSADORS' TRAVEL RECORDS OF JIN-DYNASTY KAIFENG"[67]

In 1170, seven years before he ascended to the summit of Mount Emei, the river diarist Fan Chengda was selected to serve as a Southern Song emissary to the state of Jīn, which had invaded China in the very same year he was born (1126), besieged and subsequently destroyed the Song capital at Kai-feng, and eventually took control of the general area north of the Huai River. One result of this catastrophic event, known in Chinese sources as the "Calamity of the Settled Salubrity Reign" (Jingkang zhi huo),[68] was a treaty, signed in 1142, that established formalized diplomatic channels that shut-tled government envoys back and forth between the Song exile capital at Lin'an in the south (modern Hangzhou) and the Jīn capital at Zhongdu in the north (modern Beijing).[69] Most of these embassies were perfunctory and ceremonial, charged with such duties as conveying congratulations on an emperor's birthday or sending greetings upon the arrival of the New Year. On some occasions, however, ad hoc ambassadorial missions concerning matters of substance and importance to the exile Song government in the south were also dispatched to Zhongdu.

Song ambassadors to the Jīn routinely wrote reports describing their observations and experiences. These documents provided valuable infor-mation on road conditions, waterways and bridges, major cities, Jīn military fortifications, and even conversations with Chinese refugees in the north, all of which could of course be used by the Song for intelligence purposes. Four texts, written by Song ambassadors in travel diary format, have survived. Listed in chronological order, they are Lou Yue's (1137–1213) *Diary of a Journey North* (Beixing rilu) of 1169–70, Fan Chengda's *Register of Grasping the Carriage Reins* (Lanpei lu) of 1170, Zhou Hui's (b. 1126) *Register of Northbound Cart Shafts* (Beiyuan lu) of 1177, and Cheng Zhuo's (1153–1223) *Register of an Embassy to the Jin* (Shi Jīn lu) of 1211–12.[70] All four of these works have been studied and translated by Western scholars.[71] They are important for many reasons, but one is paramount: they contain the only eyewitness accounts by exile-generation Chinese of the post-Jīn conquest that describe the urban centers of the north, especially the former Northern Song capital at Kaifeng; the general social and political conditions north of the Huai River, specifically as they relate to Chinese refugees still living there under the harsh conditions of Jīn rule; and the architectural layout of the Jīn capital in Zhongdu.[72] For these reasons, they are invaluable historical sources.

And yet, even though the form and content of the four extant embassy accounts certainly accord with how most scholars define *youji*, Mei and Yu and other literary historians, along with Bei and Ye and their fellow anthol-ogists, all fail to regard the Southern Song embassy account as a form or subgenre of "travel writing." I suspect that there are three related reasons for this neglect. First, landscape appreciation and sightseeing for pleasure play no roles whatsoever in these works; second, these texts are not designed to highlight or display the literary talents of the author; and third, those scholars who have written about Song embassy accounts regard them as "political and administrative documents" rather than *youji*, despite their travel-diary format.[73] While there is no denying that some embassy accounts—and here I refer specifically to those written by Song envoys to the Liao—place emphasis on demographic, military, and geopolitical matters and hence read like intelligence reports,[74] the Southern Song embassy diaries served an additional function: they provided a textual format by which Chinese diasporic literati like Fan Chengda and Lou Yue could express nostalgia for a lost historical past and voice disgust over the current "barbarian" occupation of the Chinese homeland.[75] And they did so through the diary format initiated by Li Ao and later adopted by Ouyang Xiu and others during the Northern Song. I regard the embassy account as an important form of Chinese travel literature, one that is unique in the history of *youji* in China. Among the four surviving embassy accounts, two are considerably more detailed and complete than the others: Lou Yue's *Diary of a Journey North* and Fan Chengda's *Register of Grasping the Carriage Reins*. The discussion that follows will thus focus on these texts as exemplars of the Southern Song embassy account.

Unlike the other three surviving ambassadorial accounts, which concerned birthday and New Year missions, Fan Chengda's ad hoc embassy to Zhongdu in 1170 addressed matters of significant importance to the Southern Song emperor Xiaozong (r. 1162–89). Officially, Fan was charged with negotiating a change in the protocol that required the Song emperor to stand while receiving official correspondence from the Jīn envoys. Contrary to the usual embassy procedure, however, Fan was ordered to pursue a second matter that would not be announced to the Jīn in advance: he was to request the return of Chinese territory lost during the Jīn invasions of 1126–27, specifically the area in Henan (near Luoyang) that housed the Song imperial tombs. The possibility of Jīn approval of either request probably seemed remote at best. Still, the fact that Fan Chengda was charged with such an important mission speaks to the emperor's confidence and trust in his envoy.

Following the Jīn-prescribed itinerary for all Song envoys, Fan passed through the former Song capital at Kaifeng, also known during the Northern Song as the Dongjing, or "Eastern Capital," which by 1170 had already been under Jīn control for over four decades. The reportorial style of Fan's prose is unmistakable. The two themes that run throughout his main diary entry on Kaifeng are the former glory days of the Song capital and its present current state of devastation and depopulation. These themes are then juxtaposed with Fan's intense personal loathing for the alien conquerors. His contempt for the northern invaders is expressed by repeated use of a single contemptuous term in reference to them—*lu,* "caitiffs" (literally, "wretched," "despicable," "contemptable"). Fan Chengda and the other Song envoys also paid close attention to the multiple names for places in Kaifeng—the former Song name, the new Jīn name, and so on—"in an attempt to reorient both themselves and their readership with the altered, lost, desacralized spaces he is traversing."[76] The Buddhist monastery mentioned in the following passage from the *Register of Grasping the Carriage Reins* was once the foremost Buddhist monastic complex in the old Song capital:

> Proceeded two more *li* and reached the Eastern Capital [Dongjing]. The caitiffs have changed its name to "Southern Capital" [Nanjing]. Entered New Song Gate [Xinsong Men], which in fact is the Sunrise Aurora Gate [Zhaoyang Men]. The caitiffs have changed its name to read "Universal Humanity Gate" [Hongren Men]. The outer city of Kaifeng[77] is an overgrown wasteland as far as the eye can see. . . . Passed the Great Monastery of the State of Xiang. Its eaves are canted, and its edges are broken off. Never again will it regain its former look.[78]

Especially affecting in embassy diaries are reports of face-to-face encounters and actual conversations with Chinese refugees. The following account, taken from Lou Yue's *Diary of a Journey North,* describes how residents in Kaifeng lined the streets to watch his ambassadorial retinue pass by:

> We passed the Residence of Grand Preceptor [the Duke of] Zheng [Zheng Taizai Zhai],[79] at the southwest corner of which was a small tower. The people of the capital lined up to observe us. Among them was an old woman whose dress and adornment were extremely strange. Many white-haired elderly people were sighing and holding back sobs. Some of them pointed to the deputy envoy saying, "This must be an official from the Promulgated Accord [Xuanhe] reign."[80]

In addition to their embassy diaries, some Song ambassadors also wrote poetry during their journeys to the north. Fan Chengda is most notable in this respect because he composed a parallel narrative of his journey in verse; specifically, seventy-two heptasyllabic quatrains, which together make up chapter 12 of his collected works.[81] To be sure, Fan's prose diary *Register of Grasping the Carriage Reins* and the quatrains are two distinct literary forms that serve different functions. The prose descriptions in his embassy account, as we have seen, are essentially designed to report on the mundane detail of what was observed in the north, the dilapidated physical state of the Kaifeng and other notable landmarks, and the plight of Chinese refugees living under the repressive conditions of Jīn rule.[82] The poems are more reflective, evocative, and lyrical. All of them, in varying degrees, reflect Fan Chengda's disgust with the illegitimate "caitiff" occupation of sacred Song territory. When one reads the diary entries and poems side-by-side, a strikingly vivid and emotionally charged picture emerges that otherwise might be absent if one only read Fan's prose diary entry. Here is an example, which takes us back to the Monastery of the State of Xiang. In his diary entry, Fan only mentions some physical damage to the eaves and projections on the monastery's roof and how it will never again "regain its former look." Compare those comments with his quatrain about that same monastery, which during the Northern Song was famous for its fairs, held several times a month, at which a vast variety of wares and luxury items were sold. Fan's verse is prefaced by the following observation, written in the form of a "prose note":

> The monastery's placard retains Youling's [that is, Emperor Huizong, r. 1100–26] imperial calligraphy. Inside the monastery, various wares are sold, all of which are simply for the barbarians' customary needs.

Fan's quatrain reads:

> Canted eaves and broken-off edges shelter the imperial tablet;
> The gold and blue stūpa is grimed by ancient dust.
> I hear tell that the current dynasty has just reopened the monastery:
> Lambskin coats and wolf-fur caps are now the latest style.[83]

The ultimate line in this poem is especially powerful because it draws a stark contrast between the former glory days of the Northern Song, when the temple market flourished, and its current occupation by the Jīn, which now only caters to "barbarian fashions" such as "lambskin coats and wolf-fur caps."

After leaving Kaifeng, Song envoys proceeded north, following the prescribed itinerary for all Song envoys to Zhongdu. As was the case with their observations about Kaifeng, the revealing glimpses that readers get of conditions in the north are fascinating. For instance, shortly after leaving Song territory, Lou Yue makes the following observation:

> We heard that a new law of the northerners ordered people living along the road to move to a neighboring district, fearing that they might harbor traitors and thieves. Those who disobeyed had their houses burned.[84]

Another issue that receives attention is Jīn conscription practice. In the following passage, Lou Yue quotes from a conversation with a soldier:

> Our generation is three or four people. We plant a little hemp and beans and it is enough for us to survive. It is said that in earlier times, everybody liked a good fight. But now they only fear being conscripted. All things considered, it is good they have quit fighting.

And he further said:

> I have heard fathers and mothers say that the population rate has been harmed by that, and that my generation only exchanges [fighting] for thievery. Because of the high price of things in Henan and Hebei, all have gone further in[land], but they still cannot survive.[85]

Some of the harshest comments about the "caitiffs" were voiced by Song envoys after they reached Zhongdu. Here is Fan Chengda's description of the Jīn effort to construct an opulent capital in the north and how in the process it conscripted and killed a myriad of workers and desecrated Chinese graves:

> Conscription laborers numbering eight hundred thousand and military laborers numbering four hundred thousand worked and labored on the project for several years. The number of those who died is beyond calculation. The lands excavated by the Jīn all housed ancient cairns and barrows [that is, graves], which were dug up and abandoned without exception.[86]

Lou Yue's tone is even harsher:

> The Jīn absorb the fat and blood of the people in order to supply their nests and dens. [Their] treasuries and storehouses are mostly located at places around the Superior Capital [Shangjing; that is, Acheng, a southeastern suburb of modern Harbin]. Thus, the people of Henan are greatly impoverished, and specie is becoming increasingly scarce.[87]

As noted by Stephen H. West in "Discarded Treasures," the Southern Song embassy accounts are the literary product of some "unusual and painful circumstances."[88] No texts were ever written again during the imperial period that describe the experiences of Chinese ambassadors visiting a foreign state that was forcefully occupying a large area—or the entirety—of former Chinese territory. Still, the embassy accounts are important in the history of *youji* because, like the *Account of Entering Shu* and *Register of a Boat Trip to Wu*, they confirm that the diary format was an efficient literary vehicle by which to organize and present a lengthy travel narrative, even one describing travel to a foreign land. One important post-Song text that reflects this practice is Xu Mingshan's (dates uncertain) late-thirteenth-century diary *Account of a Trip to Annam* (Annan xing ji), which describes the events and experiences of a diplomatic mission to the state of Annam (later known as Vietnam).[89] Many similar works describing trips to border regions and foreign states were produced, for various purposes, during the subsequent Ming and Qing periods, and these texts can certainly be viewed as analogues of the Southern Song embassy account.[90] But we should not forgot that that the Southern Song embassy account ultimately served a primary need of traditional Chinese historiography: to discredit the illegitimate and immoral nature of an alien occupation of Chinese territory and to lament what was lost or altered as a result. In this respect, the Southern Song embassy accounts are unique.

ADDENDUM

Why does author reaction vary so much in Song *youji*, especially in the sightseeing accounts? We saw several examples of such variation in this chapter, but many others could have been presented as well. Scholars who have written about this question usually explain it by referencing new intellectual concerns and scholarly trends during the Song.[91] While many of these matters are certainly relevant, it is difficult to assess just how much they may have contributed directly to the development of travel literature. If one looks closely at any large body of similar textual material, some differences and variety will inevitably emerge. This is certainly the case with Song travel writing. At the same time, however, currents and variations also surface. Except for the embassy account, sightseeing for pleasure and/or some investigative purpose is a priority in both the sightseeing accounts and the river diaries, and individual tastes and concerns about, and approaches to, such matters produced different author reactions. We should keep in mind, however, that with just a few exceptions, almost all travel during the Song was initiated by the state. Some modern scholars, like Wang Fuxin, have referred to a "tourist/tourism industry" (*lüyou ye*) in the Song,[92] but this is misleading because it was not a "tourist/tourism industry" in the modern sense. Rather, the infrastructure of travel—that is, the hostel (*lüguan*) and transport systems, the availability of boats for river travel, and so on—were designed and operated almost exclusively for traveling government officials and their families and servants. This situation, however, will change in the late Ming, when a true "tourist industry" will appear in China for the first time.

CHAPTER 4

TRANSITION AND INNOVATION IN THE JĪN, YUAN, AND EARLY TO MID-MING

I once heard a famous literatus from Wu remark, "If you make it to
a certain place or certain mountain, you cannot get away without
taking a sightseeing trip there; if you go sightseeing at a certain
mountain, you cannot get away without writing an account about
your visit."

QIAN QIANYI, *THE BEGINNING LEARNER'S COLLECTED WORKS*
FROM THE SHEPHERD'S STUDIO

THE SONG AND JĪN FORMED A MILITARY ALLIANCE IN THE EARLY
1120s that succeeded in driving the Khitan-led Liao state out of north China
and into Central Asia. Shortly thereafter, however, the Jīn severed its alliance with the Song and mounted a full-scale invasion into the Chinese
heartland. By January 1126, Jurchen troops had reached and besieged the
Song capital at Kaifeng. A second siege followed later that year, and by
early 1127, the city was looted and destroyed. Emperor Qinzong (r. 1126–
27), along with his father, the former Emperor Huizong (r. 1100–26), were
both captured and hauled off to prison in Manchuria, where they died in
captivity many years later. Another son of Huizong, Gaozong (r. 1127–62),
managed to flee to the south, where in 1138, he established an exile capital
(*xingzai*) in Hangzhou. Hostilities between the Jīn and Song eventually
came to a halt when a treaty was ratified in 1142 that forced the Song to
make huge annual indemnity payments to the Jīn in silver and silk.

When Lou Yue, Fan Chengda, and other Southern Song ambassadors
traveled to the north in the twelfth and early thirteenth centuries, then, the

Jurchen state was a superior military force vis-à-vis its former foe, now ensconced in the south. But the Jīn dynasty and its empire, which now included all Chinese territory north of the Huai River, was short-lived. A formidable new military force arrived in East Asia in the early thirteenth century, and this led to yet another great dynastic transition. But this shift was one that China had never experienced: total military defeat and occupation by a foreign military power—the Mongols. After taking control of all Chinese territory, Kublai (or Qubilai) Khan (1215–94), grandson of Genghis (or Chinggis) Khan (*ca.* 1162–1227), was chosen to serve as the first emperor of the new Mongol regime, which the foreign conquerors dubbed "Yuan" (literally, "primary" or "premier"). Despite the auspicious name for the new dynasty, however, the government established by Kublai and his successors was also short-lived by Chinese dynastic standards. It lasted less than a century.

SOME OLD AND NEW VOICES

[Song Lian's "Account of a Sightseeing Trip to Bell Mountain"] is among the more learned of travel accounts; it reflects the increasing tendency of Ming and Qing travel writers to perceive a place as defined by the enduring presence of its past.

RICHARD E. STRASSBERG, *INSCRIBED LANDSCAPES: TRAVEL WRITING FROM IMPERIAL CHINA*[1]

The Song-Yuan dynastic transition was chaotic and violent. Numerous Chinese cities were decimated and their populations essentially exterminated.[2] There were major societal changes as well. Upon taking power, the Mongols immediately suspended the Chinese civil-service-examination system that recruited educated men to serve in government. The system was revived in 1315, but with severe restrictions that favored candidates of Mongol descent. Thus, even for those Chinese scholar-officials willing to serve an alien political regime—and many were not—career entry and advancement in government service posed challenges. Yet despite these and several other upheavals that relate to the Song-Yuan transition, travel literature continued to be produced, by both Chinese and, for the first time, ethnically non-Chinese (or "Sinicized") authors writing in Chinese. One good example of a *youji* text penned by a Jīn author, which dates from before the transition, is Yuan Haowen's (1190–1257) *Account of a Trip to Ji'nan* (Ji'nan xing ji), composed in 1235. Yuan was a descendent of the Tuoba clan that founded the Northern Wei dynasty, and for a time he served as an official in the Jīn government. He was also an accomplished poet and frequent traveler-sightseer. The surviving account of his tour of Ji'nan (Shandong), in which he skillfully describes notable scenic and historical sites around the city and its suburbs, is strongly reminiscent of the reportorial-style prose Lu You and Fan Chengda used in their twelfth-century river diaries.[3]

Another text worth mentioning is Yelü Chucai's (1189–1243) *Register of a Journey to the West* (Xiyou lu).[4] Yelü was an ethnic Khitan (or Qidan; that is, the founders of the Liao dynasty, 907–1125) who served as an official in both the Jīn and Yuan governments. From 1219 until 1224, he accompanied Genghis Khan on a military campaign into the regions west of China. The first section of his account, which describes the cities Yelü visited in Central Asia, is modeled after the prose style that Xuanzang used in his *Accounts of the Western Regions during the Great Tang*, but it is less detailed and does not provide distances in *li* between various stages of the journey.

Finally, among *youji* accounts written during the Yuan dynasty by Chinese authors, Yang Weizhen's (1296–1370), "Account of a Sightseeing Trip to Gan's Hill" (You Ganshan ji) deserves special mention.[5] Unlike Yuan Haowen, Yelü Chucai, and other Jīn and Yuan travel writers who lived and wrote about journeys in north China (or, in Yelü's case, places beyond China's western border), Yang Weizhen was a native of the Jiangnan region in south-central China. Probably composed in the turbulent final years of Mongol rule, when the author sought refuge in Songjiang (near modern Shanghai) from the hostilities, Yang's text relates the experiences of a sightseeing excursion to Gan's Hill, which takes its name from a famous swordsmith of the Warring States period. What is noteworthy about this account is that although the scenery around Gan's Hill is attractive, it is not especially remarkable in any way. Nevertheless, Yang Weizhen takes thorough delight in the sights he observed at Gan's Hill and the various people he encountered there. Here is a representative passage, taken from the closing section of his account:

> At daybreak the next morning, we made offerings at the grave of the Resident Adept West of the Clouds [Yunxi Chushi]. Then set out by boat to pay a visit to Gold Mountain Garrison [Jinshan Wei] and the Daoist adepts Efu and Zheng, but did not find them. Next, following the river's current, we unexpectedly passed the Shi Family's [Shishi] Drunken Madness Gate

[Zuichi Men]. As we playfully grasped at the moon,[6] Li Fen invited me[7] to drink with him in the Stupid Rock Study [Chunshi Xuan]. Yu Jin, known by the sobriquet Ge Yinsheng,[8] joined us. We wrote poems about "Stupid Rock," and wrote calligraphy by the eastern window. We returned that night riding the moon.[9]

Without mentioning a word about the chaos accompanying the fall of the Yuan, Yang Weizhen clearly regards Songjiang as a haven from the disorder that surrounds him. When reading his account, one gets the distinct impression that Gan's Hill functions as a metaphor for Yang himself, standing isolated, alone, and perhaps even vulnerable in the relatively flat, accessible landscape in Songjiang yet nevertheless safe and enjoying himself—at least for the time being.

Some notable differences from the *youji* of earlier periods are present in the three texts just described. First, sightseeing accounts dating from the Jīn and Yuan are generally much longer and more detailed than earlier travel writing. Yuan Haowen's *youji* describing his trip to Ji'nan, for instance, discusses sightseeing activities that took place over twenty days. This practice of composing longer, extended *youji*—some with dated sections or entries, some without—concerning single or multiple destinations, is especially evident in works dating from the mid- and late Ming.[10] Second, Yuan dynasty and transition-period travel literature sometimes also includes extended discussions—or, more precisely, digressions—that are not related in any direct way to travel or sightseeing. For instance, less than one-third of Yelü Chucai's *Register of a Journey to the West* deals with the expedition that took him to Central Asia. The remainder of his text constitutes a blistering attack on a contemporary religious rival, the Daoist patriarch Qiu Chuji (1148–1227).[11] A similar example comes from the Moslem traveler and well-known poet Sadula, also known as Sa Tianxi (*ca.* 1272–1355), whose account—a popular *youji* anthology piece—of a sightseeing excursion to the famous Longmen caves outside Luoyang, essentially functions as a written condemnation of the "false views" of Buddhism.[12] The practice of including religious-based polemical material not related to the journey itself need not concern us further, because it plays no role in subsequent Ming dynasty travel literature.[13] A new type of sightseeing *youji* appeared in the Ming period, however, that included authorial digressions—or more accurately, reactions—that are highly personal. And while they are usually inspired by an attractive landmark, these responses often say more about the author than they do about his travel destination or sightseeing experience.

In their assessment of travel literature composed during the Jīn-Yuan–early-Ming periods, Mei Xinlin and Yu Zhanghua make the following observation: "From the Jīn and Yuan to the early period of the Ming, all *youji* authors essentially fumbled forward under the shadow of the lofty accomplishments of the Song."[14] Without a doubt, in the works of some late Yuan and early Ming *youji* writers, the influence of Tang and especially Song travel writers is noticeably present, and Mei and Yu cite several examples to support their argument.[15] However, some Yuan and early Ming writers produced *youji* of considerable literary merit. Moreover, even though their compositions do not represent any major or groundbreaking developments in travel writing, these works are still worthy of attention, not only because of their intrinsic literary worth but also because they fore-shadow some of the new paths the genre will take later in the Ming. Among these new directions, the most important is the regular appearance of sightseeing *youji* that are significantly longer than the Song dynasty sight-seeing essays and that display increased attention to matters related to historical-literary heritage and empirical verification of geographical details as they relate to individual sites. A good example of a Yuan author who preferred to compose longer accounts of sightseeing excursions is Li Xiaoguang (1285–1348), a native of Wenzhou in southern Zhejiang.

Although for a time he served as an official in the Mongol government, Li Xiaoguang also spent many years living in the scenic Yandang Mountains (Yandang Shan) outside of Wenzhou. He has left a set of travel compositions titled "Ten Accounts of the Yan[dang] Mountains" (Yanshan shiji), which is modeled, in both title and general descriptive style, after Liu Zongyuan's "Eight Accounts of Yongzhou." "Great Dragon Plunge Pool" (Da Longqiu) is situated in a valley on the western side of Yandang Shan. From Linked Clouds Peak (Lianyun Feng) high above that valley, a waterfall cascades down almost 650 feet (about 196 meters), making it still today one of Yangdang's premier tourist attractions. Here is Li Xiaoguang's account of two visits he made there, titled "Account of the Great Dragon Plunge Pool" (Da Longqiu ji):

> In autumn, the eighth month of the seventh year of the Great Virtue
> [Dade] reign [1303], I accompanied the venerable gentleman on his visit to
> the Great Dragon Plunge Pool. For several days and nights, it had rained

continuously. On the day he arrived, a great wind arose in the northwest, and only then were we able to see the sun. Just now the force of the water falling into the plunge pool is enormous. Upon entering the valley leading to the plunge pool, before we even went five *li* or so, we heard a thunderous roar. Those accompanying us were terror stricken. Gazing toward the northwest, we saw a towering crag in the shape of a person looking down at us, which also resembled a huge pillar. After proceeding another two hundred *bu*, we then saw two more sections of the same crag standing upright and facing one another. Upon further advancing another one hundred *bu*, the crag then resembled a folding screen as big as a tree, but the top of it was jagged and pointy, like the two pincers of a crab, which from time to time would seem to stir and pinch. Travelers like us, tense and uneasy, never approach the crag. So we turned and followed along the crag to the foot of South Mountain. Slightly north of there, we looked back, and the mountain peak now resembled a jade tablet that had been planted in the ground.[16] Next, after we turned back and approached Eastern Precipice, we looked up and saw a mass of water plummeting down from the sky, which quickly dispersed. Some water spiraled and coiled for a long time, but did not come down. Then it abruptly burst downward like a sudden peel of thunder. At the foot of Eastern Precipice is the Nakula Nunnery [Nuojuna An]. At a point five or six *bu* from the mountain, we rushed into the nunnery to avoid getting soaked. Residual froth got into the nunnery as if there were a cloudburst. Water beat down on the great plunge pool "bang and boom," like ten thousand people hitting drums. We talked while closely facing each other but only saw our moving mouths and heard nothing because of the din. We then looked at one another and let out a big laugh. The gentleman exclaimed, "How wonderful! In my travels throughout the empire I have never seen a waterfall like this!"

Afterward, I probably visited the plunge pool once every year. Usually, this would be during the ninth month. In the tenth month, the water level always drops, and so the situation here now is not like it was before. This past winter, when there was a great drought, the sightseer[17] reached the stone bridge beyond the nunnery and gradually heard rushing water. I then followed along below the stone bridge and came out amid a jumble of rocks. Only then did I see the waterfall cascading down. The spray spurted and gushed in the form of a blue-green mist, suddenly small, then suddenly huge, and its roar became louder and louder. Rushing water fell into the pool and on low-lying rocks. The surface of the rocks was lashed and pounded by the violent force of the waterfall, which reflected a red luster as deep as cinnabar. In the pool were twenty-some snakehead fish [*banyu*]. When they heard water hitting the rocks, they slowly disappeared into the distance, then leisurely swam back, like recluses free from the world. The houseboys placed a large jug by a rock. As they looked up, intending to fill the jug, the water suddenly danced toward them, doubling in its intensity. Since they were unable now to go back and fetch the jug, they took off their clothes, doffed their caps, and put them on a rock. Then, steadying each other, they made an earnest effort to go back under the waterfall and fetch the jug. Because of this, we all roared and had a big laugh.

On the rocky wall to the southeast were several tens of yellow gibbons [*huangyuan*].[18] When they heard all the commotion, they became alarmed and unsettled. They then withdrew to the top of the cliff and then came down one by one and rested on a tree. They peeped down at us and let out a cry, staring for a long time. When we exited the Auspicious Deer Cloister [Ruilu Yuan],[19] the sun had already gone down. The dark green forest before us was so thick with leaves that we could not find the path and lost our way. All we could see was the bright moonlight, which we greeted like an old friend. The venerable gentleman is known as the "Master of South Mountain."[20]

Unlike the description found in most earlier sightseeing *youji*, which are designed to appeal to the visual aspects of scene, Li Xiaoguang's account draws heavily on the auditory sense, specifically the sound of water moving rapidly and with great force: "A thunderous roar came out of the valley. Those accompanying me were terror stricken. . . . Its roar became louder and louder. Rushing water fell into the pool. . . . The surface of the rocks was lashed and pounded." Li also employs onomatopoeia: "Water beat down on the great plunge pool 'bang and boom,' like ten thousand people hitting drums. We talked while closely facing each other but only saw our moving mouths and heard nothing because of the din."

Li Xiaoguang adeptly draws on visual imagery as well. One way to identify and evaluate the skill of a writer working in any literary genre, but especially in *youji*, is to examine whether he or she uses simile in some new or unusual way. Several such examples are present in "Account of the Great Dragon Plunge Pool." For instance, in his description of the "towering crag" to the northwest, Li uses different similes to describe how its shape and appearance changes as he walks through the landscape. At first, he says, the crag resembles a giant "person looking down on us," but then again it also looks like a "giant pillar." But after moving forward, the two sections of the crag now seem to be "standing upright," after which the appearance changes again: now the rock formation resembles a standing screen "as big as a tree." But the top of it seems "jagged and pointy, like the two pincers of a crab, which from time to time would seem to stir and pinch." Li Xiaoguang also alternates between images related to action ("a towering crag in the shape of a person *looking down*") and immobility (a "huge pillar"); "the two pincers of a crab, which from time to time would [seem to] *stir and pinch*" and a "standing screen." Such alternation of activity and repose not only adds binary variety to the imagery but also helps to evoke a "pulse" to the landscape description that ultimately creates a more lively and evocative scene. Finally, we should also note Li's use of laughter and humor in this piece (the houseboys taking off their clothes to go and fetch the water jug, and so on). Although rare in earlier *youji*, as the joy of affective association finds expanded expression in late Ming *youji*, the more often we will encounter humor.

Another good example of "extended *youji*" is Song Lian's (1310–81) *Account of a Sightseeing Trip to Bell Mountain* (You Zhongshan ji), which runs about eighteen hundred Chinese characters in length. Song Lian was a major political and literary figure of the late Yuan and early years of the Ming and served as an advisor to the first Ming emperor. Bell Mountain, better known today as Purple-Gold Mountain (Zijin Shan), was just a few *li* outside the gates of Nanjing. In the company of two friends, Song Lian spent three days sightseeing on the mountain in late 1361. While it is undeniable that Song's account follows the general structural format of the Song dynasty sightseeing essay, its enhanced length is designed to accommodate what essentially constitutes a scholarly accounting of the mountain's history. Even before mentioning the date of his journey and identifying his traveling companions, Song Lian's first order of business is to explicate the provenance of the mountain's name. "Jinling" and "Moling" are both ancient names for Nanjing. "Great Emperor" (Dadi) refers to Sun Quan (182–252), who founded the state of Wu (222–80) during the Three Kingdoms period (220–80):

> Bell Mountain is known by the alternate name "Jinling Mountain." In
> the late Han, Jiang Ziwen, Commander of Moling, died at the foot of this

mountain while chasing some bandits. The Great Emperor later enfeoffed him as "Marquis Jiang" [Jiang Hou]. Since the Great Emperor's paternal grandfather was named Zhong [or "bell"], Zhong became a taboo word, and so the name was changed again, this time to "Jiang Mountain" [Jiang-shan]. In fact, it served as the bulwark of Yangdu [or Yangzhou].[21] This is the place Zhuge Liang [181–234] referred to as "Bell Mountain, where a Dragon Coils."[22]

The ostensible purpose of Song Lian's visit to Bell Mountain was to undertake an enjoyable sightseeing excursion with friends. But even a cursory reading of his *youji* reveals Song's true intent: to provide a detailed report concerning the mountain's most prominent sites and structures and the many figures and events of the past associated with it in some way. On this point, his description is like many of the entries in Fan Chengda's and Lu You's river diaries. The exegetical tone and detail of Song Lian's prose style is quite evident, even in a brief passage like the following:

> We departed by the East Gate and then passed the Loyalty-to-the-State-Being-at-Peace Monastery [Baoning Si], which is halfway from the city gate to the mountain. The temple was the former residence of the Prince of Shu [Shuwang; that is, Wang Anshi]. The Knoll of Master Xie [Xiegong Dun][23] now hides, now rises behind it. To the west, the monastery faces an earthen mound. This is probably the place where the Prince of Shu fell ill from the dampness and so had a canal dug to drain the accumulated water into the city's river.[24]

And for the first time in the history of Chinese travel literature, we find mention of a contemporary military event; in this case, the Yuan-Ming transition, though it is not clear which "soldiers" destroyed the temple:

> We reached the Gateway to Perfect Enlightenment [Huanwu Guan]. As for the Gateway [or monastery], it was constructed by Abbot Qin during the Song.[25] The Grand Tranquility and Ascendant Nation Monastery [Taiping Xingguo Si] was located there. Before the Liang dynasty [502–57], the mountain hosted seventy Buddhist temples. All of them are gone now. Only this monastery [that is, the Gateway] flourished in recent times. Recently, it was destroyed by soldiers, and all that remains is the outer three gates.

Contrary to the statement at the close of Song Lian's account, where he declares, "Fortunately, with my two companions I have been able to release my feelings among the crannies of these mountains and streams," nowhere does he voice genuine appreciation of the landscape on Bell Mountain. At the close of his long and detailed account, however, the author does express a desire to undertake further excursions to other "famous mountains" in scenic Jiangnan.

> I would not trade this experience for a thousand pieces of gold. If the mountain spirits happen to know about this, they should then allow me to go sightseeing at all the famous mountains south of the Great River.[26]

Ultimately, then, it is neither scenery nor even camaraderie with friends that ultimately attracts Song Lian, but the scholarly exercise of defining historical heritage. This practice, which began in the river diaries of the Southern Song, is distinctly different from the social-recreational sightseeing accounts of the Northern Song. It is essentially designed to showcase the author's command of historical and geographical knowledge, gained from textual sources like gazetteers, which is then corroborated, corrected, or disproven by personal, on-site investigation. Song Lian follows this style closely in his *Account of a Sightseeing Trip to Bell Mountain,* and this preference reflects the Ming dynasty intellectual concern for verification of matters geographical and historical as they relate to place. Travel writing is just one literary outlet of this concern. There are several others.[27]

I have purposely selected *Account of a Sightseeing Trip to Bell Mountain* to introduce early Ming dynasty *youji* because of its de-emphasis on author reaction to pleasing landscape and its focus on the history of place, in this case, Bell Mountain. Song Lian's use of this writing style—which, again, is traceable to the Southern Song river diaries—foreshadows one of the most important new developments in travel literature during the Ming. Many author-travelers, especially in the sixteenth century and thereafter, define places—even scenic mountain environments—not so much by how aesthetically pleasing they are to the eye but by the richness of their historical traditions and legacy. The journey narrative is of course present in these texts, as is some description of scene, but these matters are secondary when compared to the attention given to the history of the place, its institutions, its landmarks, who visited or once lived there, and so on. Also, that Song Lian preferred to visit the famous mountains of Jiangnan rather than notable peaks in other parts of China tells us something important about Ming dynasty *youji*; namely, that much if not most of the travel literature surviving from the Ming describes places in the Jiangnan region—mainly Jiangsu and Zhejiang,[28] though more traditional destinations, like Mount Tai and Beijing (especially after the capital of the Ming was moved from Nanjing to Beijing in 1421), also attracted Ming traveler-writers. In addition to hosting some of China's most beautiful scenery, Jiangnan still served as China's richest and most urbanized region during the middle and late years of the Ming dynasty. In fact, by the mid-sixteenth century, Suzhou was a major national hub for China's burgeoning long-distance commerce industry.[29]

Ming historians have correctly pointed out that travel for nongovernment persons during the early Ming was extremely difficult because of government-imposed restrictions.[30] The history of such regulations extends back to the Warring States era and continued—in various forms—throughout subsequent dynastic periods.[31] During the early Ming, nongovernmental persons, including merchants, were required to apply for a route certificate (*luyin*) when traveling more than one hundred *li* from home, and they faced harsh penalties for violating that law. Travelers were routinely checked when passing through mountain guard posts (*shanguan*) or traversing ferry crossings (*jindu*). Those without route certificates were caned eighty strokes; civil and military personnel who assisted travelers in fraudulently passing through government checkpoints got one hundred strokes, as did the traveler.[32] Movement during the hours of darkness was also strictly forbidden, as was travel abroad, which was a capital offence. In 1370, the emperor ordered the Ministry of Revenue to require that all households register with the government and thereby receive a household certificate (*hutie*) listing all adult male names and ages and the dimensions of the property owned by the family.[33] These laws were designed to curtail the physical mobility of the general populace, which, it was thought, would in turn bring social and economic stability to an agrarian society.

In the end, these government prohibitions had little or no effect. Literate people who were essentially grounded by travel restrictions in the early Ming—literati without examination degrees, merchants, artisans, painters, monks, and so on—in fact never produced any appreciable quantity of travel literature in imperial China prior to the sixteenth century. In the early Ming, then, when private travel was severely restricted, government officials were still—as they had been in previous eras—essentially the only people in society who had opportunities to travel or sightsee and to write about it.

One of the most important developments in the history of *youji* is that private individuals, beginning in the middle years of the Ming, will begin to play a much greater role in the composition of travel literature.

ALBUM *YOUJI*

> You would think me preposterous if I wrote about Mt. Hua without having traveled there. Would it be any less absurd if I climbed Mt. Hua without writing about it?
>
> WANG LÜ, HUASHAN TUCE[34]

As in the first century of Ming rule, the middle years of the dynasty also produced some talented *youji* writers, including Xue Xuan (1389–1464), Zhou Xu (*jinshi* 1418), Yang Shouchen (1425–89), Shi Jian (1434–96), and Cheng Minzheng (1446–99), to name several. Typical of the kind of sightseeing accounts written in the first half of the fifteenth century is "Account of a Sightseeing Trip to Dragon Gate" (You Longmen ji), written by the neo-Confucian scholar and prominent government official Xue Xuan. "Dragon Gate" in the following excerpt refers to a mountain of that name on the western side of the Yellow River in southwestern Shanxi, northeast of modern Hancheng *shi*. Xue was a native of nearby Hejin (modern Hejin *shi*), so the starting point of his sightseeing excursion is his hometown:

> We departed Hejin town by the outer western gate. Proceeded northeast for thirty *li* and reached the base of Dragon Gate Mountain [Longmen Shan]. To the east and west there was nothing but layered chains of mountains and precipitous peaks, spanning across the Milky Way. The Great Yellow River approaches from the northwest through a mountain gorge. Upon reaching here, the mountain is cut off, but the river comes through. The two walls on each side of the river stand majestically aloft, facing one another. The drilling labors by Divine Yu are especially remarkable here.

After reaching the summit of the mountain, Xue continues his report:

> On the summit is the Contemplating-while-Gazing Gallery [Linsi Ge]. Because of the wind and lofty altitude, no wooden structure can be built

there, so the pavilion is made of brick and stone. Leaning on the pavilion gate, we looked down on the Great Yellow River as it swiftly rushed by. Three sides of the mountain's base were struck by its surge. I thought the rocky peaks seemed to be shaking and trembling. To the north we looked back at the giant gorge, with cinnabar-red cliffs and emerald ramparts, where clouds are born, and mists scurry off, where night and day come and go, and where swiftly come myriad changes. To the west, linked mountains twist and turn as they depart; to the east we see a majestic mountain, towering as it floats away to the heavens.

The remainder of "Account of a Sightseeing Trip to Dragon Gate" continues with similar description of landscape. Xue Xuan closes his account with the following report:

> *Bingwu*, or prime year of the Promulgated Virtue reign [1426]; summer, fifth month, twenty-fifth day; while sightseeing, I was accompanied by Yang Jingrui.[35]

Strictly speaking, this work predates the middle Ming by twenty-some years. Still, Xue Xuan's account of Dragon Gate Mountain is presented here because it represents well the general style of *youji* prevalent in the middle years of the Ming. Xue and many of his contemporaries, especially Shi Jian, are quite adept at delineating landscape.[36] Although it may not be immediately apparent in my English translation, Xue Xuan, like Liu Zongyuan, is fond of using "quartets" in his scenic description (here they begin with the line about the Yellow River "swiftly rushing by"), many of which approximate the kind of prose-poetry described in chapter 2. What is fascinating about this piece is that aside from a general undertone of a proud native son describing the outstanding scenery near his hometown, the author-reaction component is minimal, and on this account, Xue Xuan's *youji* is quite like Song Lian's *Account of a Sightseeing Trip to Bell Mountain*. But unlike his predecessor, who was mainly concerned with historical heritage, Xue's entire attention is devoted to landscape description. One might even argue that there is no author-reaction component in this work at all, except perhaps for the admiring tone the author uses when describing Dragon Gate Mountain's stunning scenery. And yet, although there is nothing personal or lyrical in such accounts, Xue Xuan should not be faulted for this "omission." This is because he preferred to compose *youji* in a scenic-descriptive style like some of his distinguished predecessors, most notably by Li Dao-yuan.[37] At the same time, however, we must also recognize that no major new directions in *youji* emerge in this mode of writing, which essentially follows earlier styles and conventions.

But that is not to say that there were no innovations in travel writing during the middle years of the Ming dynasty. In fact, an extremely important development took place precisely at this time, during which an entirely new variety of *youji* appeared in which an individual author, after composing travel writings at one or multiple sightseeing destination(s) (Ming authors call these places *jing* or *jingdian*, terms that are still used today in China's travel industry), would then collect these texts and publish them together under a single title.[38] Compared to Liu Zongyuan's "Eight Accounts of Yong County," these Ming dynasty "sightseeing albums" (*zhuanji*; literally, "specialized collections") devoted to travel writing are much more diversified: some pieces therein might be brief, some much longer; the sites described may be near to or distant from one another; or the assembled texts may have been written over an indefinite period of time.

Several of these albums survive from the middle and late Ming.[39] A good example is Du Mu's (1459–1525), *Accounts of Sightseeing Trips to Famous Mountains* (You mingshan ji), preface dated 1515.[40] Du hailed from Wu (modern Suzhou) in Jiangnan, served in several high-ranking posts in the Ming government, and traveled extensively in that capacity. Du's "famous mountains" album, which consists of numerous compositions on mountains he visited on trips to Ningxia and other places, is notable for its broad geographical scope, which begins with Mount Hua (Huashan) in Shaanxi, the tallest of the Five Marchmounts (Wuyue),[41] and then moves on to describe additional famous mountains in and around Henan, Jiangsu, Beijing, Nanjing, Hangzhou, Hunan, and Suzhou. In his extended travels throughout the Ming empire, Du Mu always tried to visit any notable mountains he passed along the way. His travel-narrative style is straightforward and unembellished; his language is like the prose style we saw earlier in the Southern Song river diaries. The following entry, written in the travel diary format, concerns Mount Song (Songshan) in Henan, the middle or central peak among the "Five Marchmounts":

> *Guiyou*, Eleventh month, first day: I reached Luoyang and desired to devise a plan to go sightseeing on Mount Song [Songshan].
> *Bingyin*, Second day: Reached Yanshi town.

Dingmao, Third day: Departed from Yanshi. Followed the Luo River southeast for five *li*, crossed the river and went on another ten *li*. Ascended to the gravesite of Crown Prince Luling of the Tang.[42] Stone figures of people were arranged around the gravesite. Horses and stones on the exterior were still intact. The single stele was lofty and huge, but the characters on it were worn away and could not be read. Another thirty *li* and I reached Eling Passageway, where two mountains face each other.[43] The stone pathway is rugged and rough. In fact, the opening between the two mountains was cut when Emperor Gaozong of the Tang graced the Shaolin Temple with a visit.[44] After another eight *li* up the mountain, reached the Shaolin Temple.[45]

At the close of his entry on Mount Hua, Du Mu confesses to suffering from an affliction he calls *youpi*, which means something like "sightseeing mania." Since this term is important in the history and development of travel writing during the Ming, a brief digression seems justified. The concept of *pi*, or "mania," is a Chinese cultural idea with a long history. Originally a medical term that referred to a blockage in the digestive track, by the middle and late Ming, *pi* was used mainly in one of two senses: as a term to describe collectors or connoisseurs of special or precious inanimate objects, such as books or rocks; or as a term to describe persons with an extreme fondness for certain human avocations, such as garden construction or sightseeing. In the sixteenth century, *pi*, even in its most extreme forms, became extolled as a mode of behavior to be admired and emulated; perhaps more importantly, it became closely associated with the idea of individualism and self-expression.[46] So when Du Mu confesses to having a "sightseeing mania," he is not complaining. Quite the contrary—he is, in fact, telling readers that "composing *youji* accounts is the way I overwhelmingly prefer to express myself."

But Du Mu, quite unlike Song Lian, is not so much concerned with showcasing his knowledge of historical facts and details. Instead, he desires to share his sightseeing "mania" with readers who, he says, are too preoccupied with "writing and argumentation" (*wenzhang yanlun*).[47] As he openly acknowledges, "I am by nature fond of landscape. Wherever I have been, if there was outstanding landscape nearby, I have never failed to go sightseeing there. And when I go sightseeing, I must write about it. That is the way I learn."[48] For Du Mu, then, the one and only purpose of sightseeing is pleasure (*le*).

What explains the appearance of album *youji* during the middle years of the Ming dynasty, especially in the sixteenth century? Not coincidentally, several diverse types of collections—all related to *youji*—appeared at the same time and with increasing frequency. Yongtao Du has observed that "in the last century of the Ming, private compilation of comprehensive gazetteers (*zongzhi*) flourished. As if in a sudden burst of enthusiasm, almost ten times more such works were published in this relatively short period than in the dynasty's first 150 years, making the late Ming by far the most productive period for this genre since its inception during the Tang-Song transition."[49] The dramatic increase in *zongzhi* production is just one expression of two related trends: increased travel—especially travel related to tourism—in the middle and later years of the Ming; and enhanced literati interest in acquiring and verifying geographical knowledge.

These developments led to increased production and distribution of numerous kinds of texts concerning place, including gazetteers, mountain monographs (*shanzhi*), individual *youji* works and albums, anthologies of travel accounts about visits to famous mountains, route books, and many more. These works all served a common utilitarian purpose: they provided information about what sightseers could expect to find at a given destination. Or, as in the case of the route books, they informed travelers how to get there. Thus, when Du Mu compiled his *Accounts of Sightseeing Trips to Famous Mountains*, he and his publisher knew it would appeal to a sizeable readership. Moreover, the preferred sightseeing destinations of government officials like Du Mu and Song Lian, who in their travels to and from office postings traversed many various parts of the Ming empire, were famous mountains. And as noted earlier, even painters sometimes trekked to remote mountain locations, such as the Yellow Mountains (Huangshan) in Anhui, to get closer to their subjects.[50] But private travelers, especially in the later years of the Ming, overwhelmingly preferred more local and accessible destinations in Jiangnan, such as West Lake (Xihu) in Hangzhou, the beautiful gardens of Suzhou, and the ethereal-like vistas in Yangzhou. The reasons for this preference are discussed in chapter 5.

Related to album *youji* are the pictorial collections of scenic sites produced by Ming artists. The most famous of these collections is one executed by Wang Lü, a late fourteenth-century doctor and painter. His account of a sightseeing trip to Mount Hua in 1381 collectively includes forty separate album leaves, each depicting a notable scene (*jing*) on the mountain, a prose *youji* description of the actual journey itself, and related writings on

4.1. *Painting of the White Marchmount* (Baiyue tu 白岳圖; 1343). 84.4 × 41.4 cm.
Attributed to Leng Qian (fl. fourteenth century). The Collection of National Palace
Museum, Taipei.

painting theory attributed to Wang Lü. One key question of special interest here is, What is the relationship between the author's forty album-leaf paintings on Mount Hua and the prose *youji* account that accompanies them? The title of art historian Kathlyn Maurean Liscomb's monograph on Wang Lü and his Mount Hua album provides her answer to this question: *Learning from Mount Hua: A Chinese Physician's Illustrated Travel Record and Painting Theory*. In Liscomb's view, then, the paintings are intended to function as illustrations of Wang Lü's prose travel account. If Liscomb is correct about this—and my own reading of the text strongly suggests that she is—then what we have here is one of the first illustrated travel accounts in the history of the *youji* genre. Since Wang Lü was a painter, it seems reasonable to expect him to produce paintings illustrating the scenes and sites he observed during his ascent of Mount Hua. But why would he also pen a prose travel account and then use the album leaves to illustrate the sites that are referenced in his *youji*? Liscomb does not provide a definitive answer to this question, although she speculates that Wang's interest in the details of his climb, such as visiting specific buildings, shrines, and so on during his ascent, and what she calls "the limitations of verbal imagery," may explain the need for illustrations.[51] Whatever Wang Lü's motivation, a "travel consciousness" is detectable in many Ming paintings, including works that predate Wang Lü. One famous early—though isolated—example, is a small hanging scroll by Leng Qian (fl. fourteenth century) titled *Painting of the White Marchmount* (Baiyue tu), dated 1343 (see fig. 4.1). This is the earliest-known painting to combine a landscape depiction with a prose *youji* description (prominently featured in the upper right-hand corner).[52] Others followed this practice later in the Ming, including major artists such as Shen Zhou[53] and his disciple Wen Zhengming (1470–1559).[54]

ADDENDUM

Up until the Ming dynasty, travel literature relied completely on authorial verbal skill to create word pictures of visually based phenomena like mountains, water, rocks, and trees. That some Ming painters, especially those, like Wang Lü, who were interested in depicting the realities and dangers of mountain climbing and providing more verbal *and* visual details about the physical challenges of the journey, especially the dangers of ascending an extremely perilous height like Mount Hua, would use paintings to illustrate such details in their *youji* is certainly not surprising.[55] And while topo-graphical paintings that were related to sightseeing destinations continued to be produced in the Qing dynasty, most of which concerned famous mountains and carried inscriptions in verse (rather than prose), albums like that of Wang Lü, which included a prose *youji* describing a real journey to the place depicted in the painting, are in fact rare in the history of Chinese painting. One reason for this, as noted by Cahill, is that "the Chinese tradition of painting contains no single 'realistic' or 'true-to-life' mode of representation," but only some occasional examples.[56] The most critical point of all, however, is this: even though scholars like Kathlyn Maurean Liscomb have been able to find isolated examples in which a pictorial representation of a real landscape includes a prose *youji*, these works had no discernible impact on the development of travel writing. Virtually all Chinese *youji* authors in the Ming and the remainder of the traditional period followed the generic conventions established by their predecessors, and rather than break tradition and begin to append paintings, illustrations, maps, and so on to their prose accounts, they instead continued to utilize and to rely on their verbal skills to describe and "paint word pictures" of their travel experiences.

CHAPTER 5

THE GOLDEN AGE OF TRAVEL WRITING
IN THE LATE MING

The late Ming boom in private travel, spearheaded by merchants but also involving people from other walks of life, suggests that the [travel restriction] policies set up in the early Ming had been reduced to formalities. . . . Meanwhile, the state-sponsored courier system had become barely sustainable thanks to financial difficulties.

YONGTAO DU, *THE ORDER OF PLACES: TRANSLOCAL PRACTICES OF THE HUIZHOU MERCHANTS IN LATE IMPERIAL CHINA*

LITERARY HISTORIANS AND CRITICS ARE UNANIMOUS IN THEIR praise of the late Ming dynasty as "the golden age" of travel writing in imperial China, the era that produced the very best *youji* authors, whose masterpieces represent the exemplars of the genre. There is some justification for such commendation, but the precise reasons for the acclaim beg for adjustment. Two authors are consistently singled out as the "masters" of late Ming travel writing: Yuan Hongdao (1568–1610), a leading literary figure of his generation, and Xu Xiake. Yuan and fellow members of the so-called Gong'an School (Gong'an Pai) are consistently portrayed as the "geniuses" (*cairen*) behind the sudden appearance of a "new" prose form called "vignette," which, we are told, they skillfully adapted to *youji* composition. Xu Xiake, on the other hand, is universally hailed as China's "greatest travel diarist" and the unrivaled master of *kexue kaocha youji*, or "scientific-investigative travel writing."[1] This characterization likewise requires some critical tweaking.

The first problem with subsuming late Ming *youji* into the dual categories of vignette (Yuan Hongdao) and scientific-investigative (Xu Xiake)
travel writing is that it oversimplifies the disparate nature of a large body of
textual material. Diversity in style and content is evident on multiple levels.
For instance, some compositions are quite lengthy, while others are as brief
as a paragraph. Some works stress scholarly exegesis of historical and literary
traditions associated with place, while others prioritize individual expression. This corpus of material, as that addressed in previous chapters,
includes late Ming textual prototypes that demonstrate new directions in
the style and content of travel writing. Ming travel literature comprises three
topical perspectives: recreational-sightseeing, scholarly-commentarial, and
geographical-investigative. These three broad rubrics serve only as guide-
posts to help isolate textual exemplars, however, and not all late sixteenth
and early seventeenth century travel writing is subsumed under them. Also,
it is essential to be aware that the developments in late Ming travel writing
did not take place in a vacuum; they are intimately connected to a series of
remarkable social, economic, and intellectual developments in the last
seventy years of Ming rule. Awareness of these influences is essential to
understanding how and why *youji* changed so dramatically in the late sixteenth and early seventeenth centuries.

PROLIFERATION OF TRAVEL WRITING

> The late Ming was a time of widespread enthusiasm among the
> gentry for travel—not on official assignment but for their own
> pleasure.
>
> TIMOTHY BROOK, *THE CONFUCIANS OF PLEASURE:*
> *COMMERCE AND CULTURE IN MING CHINA*[2]

Two major societal changes in the late Ming directly affected the development of travel writing. First, largely thanks to an improved land and water
transportation system—inspired by an expanding commerce-driven
economy already well in place in the sixteenth century—all levels of society
became more mobile than in any previous period of Chinese history. The
static and stable agrarian society promoted by Hongwu (or Zhu Yuanzhang,
1328–98; r. 1368–98), the founding emperor of the dynasty, was no more.
What eradicated early Ming travel restrictions was economic pressure.
Many people, including scholars with and without imperial examination

degrees, merchants, common tourists, religious pilgrims, and even migrant
workers now had professional and personal reasons to travel extensively.
Even if the central government desired to restrict their mobility, in the wan-
ing decades of the Ming it was powerless to do so.

Directly related to enhanced opportunity to travel was the rise of tourism, which expanded tremendously and to levels unheard of in the past.[3] To
most Western readers, the idea of a thriving tourist industry existing any-
where in the world around the same time that the *Mayflower* landed on
Cape Cod (1620) probably seems preposterous. But it was precisely around
this time that the notion of sightseeing for pleasure first flourished in China.
To get some perspective on just how massive the scale of tourist activity
became in the late Ming, consider several observations by Zhang Dai, himself an important literary figure and accomplished *youji* author.[4] When
Zhang visited Mount Tai, the "Eastern Marchmount," in 1631, he reported
that eight to nine thousand tourists flocked to the mountain daily, and during the spring months, this number could swell to twenty thousand.[5] He
also mentions that local officials imposed a "mountain fee" (*shanshui*) on
sightseers of one mace (*qian*) and two candareen's (*fen*) of silver,[6] accumulation of which over a year's time could swell the local government's coffers
by twenty or thirty thousand mace. "Package tours" with sedan chairs were
available for wealthy sightseers like Zhang Dai, as were three levels of "con-
gratulatory banquets," each more extravagant and expensive than the next,
for those wanting to celebrate their successful ascent to the summit. Several
huge inns catered to tourists in Tai'an, the nearby town, each with twenty
kitchens or more, hundreds of servants, opera performers, and scores of
courtesans (entertainer-prostitutes).

Zhang Dai was not at all happy with his Mount Tai tourist experience;
he openly grumbles about the numerous beggars present at every stage of
the ascent, as well as tourists desecrating the sacred landscape of Mount Tai
with their "hackneyed graffiti."[7] One additional indication of the surge in
tourist activity during the late Ming is that for the first time in Chinese
history, women were actively engaged in various capacities in sightseeing
and tourism.[8] Travel for pleasure was serious business in the late Ming, and
it was not cheap, especially at frequent destinations like Mount Tai or at
popular tourist spots in Jiangnan. So even though one may justifiably refer
to the Ming as "the great age of travel" in imperial China, only tourists who
had the financial means could actively engage in sightseeing at famous
places like Mount Tai. Still, however, Zhang Tai's observations confirm that

5.1. General Sketch Map of Mount Emei. From Huang Shoufu 黃綬芙 (d. 1886) and Tan Zhongyue 譚鐘嶽 (late Qing), *Xinban Eshan zhi chong huitu* 新版峨山志重繪圖 (Chengdu: Rixing Yinshua Gongyeshe, 1936). Courtesy of the C. V. Starr East Asian Library, University of California, Berkeley.

there were multitudes of tourists who could afford to visit such destinations in the late sixteenth and early seventeenth centuries.

Accompanying the surge in tourism was a corresponding increase in the number of *youji* being produced by literate sightseers, the details of which have been studied by several scholars.[9] Of course, given the considerable number of surviving individual collections, albums, anthologies, geographical works, gazetteers, paintings, and other sources of travel literature, it is impossible to determine even an approximate number of the travel works composed in the late Ming. We can be sure, however, that the number easily runs into the thousands. The distinguished historian-geographer Zhou Zhenhe has gathered some fascinating data concerning *youji* production during the Ming. In a survey conducted by Zhou and his colleagues at Fudan University in Shanghai of approximately one thousand individual-author literary collections (*wenji*) from the Ming, 450 *youji* works by 115 authors were identified, of which 310 titles date from 1582 or thereafter.[10] These figures, which by no means are complete, along with comments from contemporary Ming observers such as Jiang Yingke (1556–1605),[11] strongly support the claim that travel writing expanded considerably during approximately the last sixty or seventy years of Ming rule. Attractive sketch albums of famous scenic sites, such as Yang Erzeng's (fl. early seventeen century) *Extraordinary Sights within the Seas* (Hainei qiguan; 1609) and Wang Qi (*jinshi* 1565) and son Wang Siyi's illustrated encyclopedia *Collection of Schematic Images from the Three Realms* (Sancai tuhui; 1609), appeared in the late Ming as well, which not only helped to satisfy the desires of armchair travelers but also probably inspired many readers to engage in real sightseeing activity themselves. One important consequence of this expansion of travel writing was the compilation and publication of numerous *youji* anthologies,[12] along with increased awareness—in the form of commentary and criticism—of travel writing as a distinct prose genre.[13]

RECREATIONAL-SIGHTSEEING *YOUJI*

> Among the ancients who wrote about landscape, the most superior
> is Li Daoyuan, and following him is Liu Zihou [or Liu Zongyuan].
> In recent times, it is Yuan Zhonglang [or Yuan Hongdao].
>
> ZHANG DAI, *WRITINGS FROM THE MAGIC BOOK REPOSITORY*[14]

> In some ways, he [Zhang Dai] represented the culmination of the
> trends of what may be called the late Ming dissident style: a disdain
> for conventions sometimes bordering on iconoclasm, an emphasis
> on individuality and originality, and a readiness to reveal the self
> to a greater extent than ever before.
>
> PEI-YI WU, "AN AMBIVALENT PILGRIM TO T'AI SHAN IN THE
> SEVENTEENTH CENTURY"[15]

As we have already seen, sightseeing undertaken for recreational purposes has a long history in China, extending at least back to the Six Dynasties period and probably much earlier. These trips are typically of short duration—usually a day or two—and are almost always taken in the company of family members, friends, or local officials. The late Ming travel boom accelerated sightseeing activity, and with it came a flurry of *youji* production. When compared with earlier sightseeing accounts, however, one significant difference stands out: most late Ming authors of recreational-sightseeing *youji* overwhelmingly favored travel to well-established, easily accessible, and comfortable urban or suburban destinations in Jiangnan rather than remote, difficult-to-access locations, especially sites with primitive or limited tourist facilities. Here is a good example of a late Ming recreational-sightseeing account of travel to a popular urban tourist attraction called the Lake Heart Pavilion (Huxin ting), located on a small island in Hangzhou's scenic West Lake:

> In the twelfth month of the fifth year of the Exalted Providence [Chong-zhen] reign [1632], I was staying at West Lake. There was heavy snow for three days, completely cutting off all sounds of man and birds from the lake. After the first watch had passed,[16] clad in a large fur overcoat and holding a small brazier, I took a small boat and alone headed off to the Lake Heart Pavilion to marvel at the snow scene. A boundless expanse of hoarfrost covered the trees. The sky, merging with the clouds, hills, and water, above and below was a blanket of white. The only shadows on the lake were cast by a trace of the long embankment and my single-mustard-seed boat. In the boat, it was only me and two or three specks.[17] When I reached the pavilion, there were two people there sitting across from one another on a felt rug. A servant boy was preparing some wine, which had just warmed. When they saw me, they were greatly surprised and said, "How could this fellow be out on the lake as well?" They pressed me to join them in a drink. I drained three large cups and then took my leave. I asked their names and learned they were from Jinling [Nanjing] and had come to do some sightseeing. When I got back to my boat, the boatman mumbled, "Say not that my lord is crazy, for there are those who are just as crazy!"[18]

This brief composition is representative of the kind of *xiaopin*, or "vignette," *youji* that was much in style during the late Ming. What most distinguishes the *xiaopin* as a format for writing is its brevity. In this example, Zhang describes—in less than two hundred Chinese characters—an evening excursion to a local tourist destination. But Zhang Dai's composition differs in several ways from the Song dynasty sightseeing accounts discussed in chapter 3. Rather than present an elaborate, extended description of the snow scene on West Lake, Zhang, following the usual vignette practice, provides only a sketch comprised of selected details. And again, unlike sightseeing accounts of the Song in which authorial reaction is most often presented in the form of a response to the scene just described, the focus here is commentary about the author himself. This is a key point and essential to understanding the nature and purpose of vignette *youji*: the sightseeing experience functions essentially as a catalyst designed to inspire authorial reaction of a personal nature.

The catalyst in Zhang Dai's vignette is the act of his arrival at the pavilion. If a typical Song dynasty *youji* author were writing about the same kind of experience, at this point he would react with commentary about the difficulty and danger of boat travel on a lake in whiteout conditions or by executing a much more detailed description of the snow scene and how it inspired his feelings or emotions in some way. Zhang Dai, however, turns his attention to the two unnamed tourists discovered on the island, and he even quotes their brief conversation. This then sets the stage for the light-hearted, humorous "punch line" from the boatman. This casual, informal *youji* style is not unlike some of Su Shi's shorter travel pieces discussed in chapter 3, but the emphasis in Zhang Dai's account is entirely on the author's own personal engagement with the sightseeing experience. That Zhang Dai in this vignette contrasts the vastness of the sky and scene before him with his own little "speck" and tiny "single-mustard-seed boat" in a "boundless expanse of white" makes a salient point: his very presence on West Lake is not only quite insignificant, but, as muttered by the boatman, Zhang is also quite "crazy" for even being there (in a blizzard) in the first place (as were the two sojourners from Jinling).

Comedic, self-deprecating humor like this, which often finds expression in late Ming *youji*, represents an entirely new form of authorial reaction in travel writing. This response mode is in fact a form of self-representation that became a part of literati life in the late Ming and, by extension, functioned as an essential element of sightseeing *youji*.[19] Historian Timothy Brook is correct when he argues that "from the mid-sixteenth century onward, more and more well-educated men preferred the rigors and rewards of travel to those of office." He further contends that "travel was an integral element in scholarly cultivation."[20] The implication of Brook's keen observation is important: by the late Ming, the essential nature of sightseeing had changed. What was once a primarily recreational activity to be shared with friends had become a part of self-cultivation and self-representation that, in turn, functioned as a key element in literati identity. Moreover, the very act of composing prose and verse *youji* was now part of *shidafu* culture and functioned as a method of self-refinement that brought prestige to the writer-traveler. This "self-representational" aspect in sightseeing *youji* is also present in scholarly-commentarial and geographical-investigative travel writing, which will be discussed later in this chapter.

Now as for the vignette, there is no question that it was a popular form of composition in the sixteenth and early seventeenth centuries, and this trend continued well into the Qing dynasty. But there is a problem with what literary historians and critics often identify as "vignette travel writing." Much of it fails to meet the definition of travel literature proposed in this study. Simply put, most of what has been identified as late Ming "*xiaopin youji*" lacks a travel narrative.[21] Here I will cite just one prominent example, culled from the so-called travel vignettes of Yuan Hongdao. This selection concerns Tiger Hill (Huqiu), a famous tourist attraction in Suzhou mentioned earlier. In the following passage, Yuan Hongdao describes the sights he observed at Tiger Hill during the Mid-Autumn Harvest Moon Festival in 1597:

> Whenever this day arrives, so does every family in the city, shoulder to shoulder. From fine ladies and elegant gentlemen down to shanty dwellers, all put on their finery, and the women don makeup. They spread out layers of mats and drink wine by the roadside. From Thousand Men Rock to the Temple Gate, they crowd together like teeth on a comb, like scales on a fish. A hill could be formed from all the sandalwood clappers; the wine drains from goblets like rain from clouds. Observed from a distance, it looks like geese flocking along sandy banks, like mist blanketing the Long (or Great) River, like thunder rumbling or lightning crackling— I could not fully describe it.[22]

Zhang Dai makes similar "tourist observations" (that is, all description and no physical movement on the part of the author) of West Lake in one of his most often-cited *xiaopin* compositions, titled "West Lake during the Mid-Summer Festival" (Xihu qiyue ban). This work is highlighted in practically every *youji* anthology ever compiled,[23] but again, these are the remarks of an onlooker rather than someone who was physically engaged in sightseeing activities. The reasons that most *xiaopin youji* lack a travel narrative are easy to identify: first, to include journey-related information would extend the length of the composition and thereby violate the hallmark quality of the vignette, which is conciseness; and second, vignette authors writing about tourist destinations were not generally interested in providing travel details. The whole point of the composition was to provide the author with an opportunity for personal expression, which may or may not have been related to sightseeing.

Vignette writing from the late Ming did not attract critical attention and acclaim until the first half of the twentieth century, and the background to this development involves complicated issues that have been discussed at length elsewhere.[24] For my part, I will offer just one observation: the main reason that vignettes like Yuan Hongdao's "Tiger Hill" and "West Lake" pieces are classified by literary historians and *youji* anthologists as travel writing is the same as it was for Ouyang Xiu's "Account of the Old Drunkard's Pavilion" and Fan Zhongyan's "Account of the Yueyang Tower." Like their two Song counterparts, Yuan Hongdao and Zhang Dai are major literary figures of the Ming. Thus, the presence of their compositions in travel anthologies brings familiar, major literary names to those collections, which of course attracts reader attention. That is not to say that Yong Hongdao, Zhang Dai, and other writers of the late Ming did not pen some outstanding *youji* in the vignette style. They did. But to find these works, we need to look beyond the standard anthology pieces.

As for Yuan Hongdao, his writings reveal a man who loved to travel and sightsee, but he had no taste for wild and remote mountain scenery. Instead, he overwhelmingly preferred "refined" sites such as West Lake, Tiger Hill, or the famous Brimming Well (Manjing) northeast of Beijing. Yuan visited this last-mentioned tourist spot in the winter of 1599, when he was serving as an official in the capital. "Yan" (or "Yanshan") is an ancient name for the area around modern Beijing. This is one of Yuan Hongdao's best vignette *youji* compositions:

> The land of Yan is cold. Following the Festival of Flowers,[25] the intense cold lingers. Sometimes a freezing wind blows, and when it blows, sand flies around and gravel darts about. Cramped inside a single room, I wanted to go outside but could not. Every time I went out and braved the wind, before going a hundred *bu*, I would always turn back. On the twenty-second day, it got a bit warmer, so in the company of several friends I went out Dongzhi Gate and visited the Brimming Well. Lofty willow trees lined both sides of the embankment, and the fertile soil had a tiny bit of moisture. I glanced once at the vast openness, and it seemed as if a swan had escaped from its cage. The frozen river had just begun to melt, and

the shine on the water had just started to shimmer. Through layer upon layer of fish-scale-like waves, I could see all the way to the bottom, which was bright and brilliant like a newly opened mirror whose refreshing radiance had just been released from the inside of a dressing case. The mountain chain, bathed by sun-drenched snow, seemed as if its beauty had been revealed. Its fresh, vivid, and brilliant charm seemed like a beautiful woman who had washed her face and just combed her hair into a bun. The willow branches were about to extend but had not yet extended. The soft tips of their branches fluttered in the wind. Wheat fields looked like horse manes, about an inch in length. Although there still were not many sightseers, from time to time there were some drawing spring water for tea, some pouring wine and singing, and some wearing gaudy outfits while riding donkeys. Although the force of the wind was still strong, yet even walking with hands free one still sweated profusely. Birds sunning themselves on sandy shoals and fish frolicking on the waves were carefree and content. There was an air of joy among all the birds and beasts. Only then did I realize that spring had arrived everywhere in the suburbs, but those living in the city still did not yet know about it. Well now, among those who did not shirk their official duties due to sightseeing yet felt totally unrestrained among the hills and rocks, plants and trees, there is only this one government official! Moreover, it is fortunate that Brimming Well is close to where I am staying. My plans for sightseeing in the suburbs have begun right here, and so how could I not chronicle the experience? *Yihai* day of the second month.[26]

As with most of Yuan Hongdao's *youji*, the actual journey component in this piece is minimal ("in the company of several friends I went out Dongzhi Gate and visited the Brimming Well"). Virtually all the author's attention is focused on describing the wintry scene at Brimming Well. But aside from the "went out" (*chu*) and "visited" (*zhi*; literally, "reached") in the line just cited, there are no motion or action verbs in this composition. In other words, Yuan is not narrating movement through the snowy scene but describing it from a fixed position. What really distinguishes this composition, however, is the author's skillful use of language. For instance, on several occasions, Yuan employs simile in an unusual way, such as likening the snowy "vast openness" outside Beijing to a "swan that had escaped from his cage" and describing the shimmer on the overflowing water of the well to a "mirror whose refreshing radiance had just been released from the inside of a dressing case." Not unusual in Chinese poetry but rare in *youji* prose is the use of nominal or noun phrases to describe actions. Yuan Hongdao employs this rhetorical device in the line "birds sunning themselves on sandy shoals and fish frolicking on the waves," which in the original literally reads, "birds that are exposed to the sun; fish that sip on the waves." Even more unusual in pre-late Ming travel literature, but what now has become quite common in vignette *youji*, are comparisons of attractive landscapes—in this case a mountain chain—to a beautiful woman: "Its fresh, vivid, and brilliant charm seemed like a beautiful woman who had washed her face and just combed her hair into a bun." And finally, the introductory portion and the closing author-reaction component of "Account of a Sightseeing Trip to Brimming Well" make it quite clear that aside from the author's verbal skills and evocative word picture, the focus of this composition is about Yuan Hongdao finally being able to escape from the confinement forced by Beijing's harsh winters and thus do some sightseeing in the suburbs. This is an expression of the self-representational aspect of late Ming *youji* mentioned earlier.

SCHOLARLY-COMMENTARIAL *YOUJI*

The subtype *xueren youji* (literally, "scholarly *youji*"), which refers to travel writing composed by exceptionally capable men of letters, is a variety of travel writing concerned mainly with scholarly exegesis about place, presented in the context of a journey narrative. Song Lian's *Account of a Sightseeing Trip to Bell Mountain* is an early Ming example of scholarly-commentarial *youji*. In the late Ming, however, a few exceptionally gifted authors brought this style of travel writing to full maturity. Among them, the most important and influential are Cao Xuequan (1574–1646) and Qian Qianyi.

Although Qian Qianyi was best known among his contemporaries as a poet, scholar, and literary historian—and as a government official who betrayed the Ming by serving the alien Manchu Qing dynasty—his verse and prose accounts of a journey made to the Yellow Mountains in 1641 have received much attention in recent years.[27] Cao Xuequan, on the other hand, is hardly noticed at all in Western scholarship on the Ming, even though he traveled extensively and composed a hefty collection of travel writing. He also compiled an important geographical work titled *Extensive Accounts of Shu* (Shuzhong guangji; 108 *juan*). Since Qian Qianyi's only prose *youji* composition—the account of his journey to the Yellow Mountains just mentioned—has already been studied and translated by Stephen McDowall, we will examine a composition by Cao Xuequan titled "Account of a Sightseeing Trip to Wuyi" (You Wuyi ji) that illustrates scholarly-commentarial *youji*.

The main range of the Wuyi Mountains is in northern Fujian along the border with Jiangxi. There is also a separate spur, separated from the main range by less than twenty miles. A waterway called "Nine Bends Stream" (Jiuqu Xi) connects the range and spur, and tourists traveling by boat on the stream could view scenic sites at each of the "Nine Bends."[28] Cao's text recounts just such an excursion, though from time to time his boat would stop and moor so he could explore and visit scenic sites not visible from the stream. Ever since the Song dynasty, there has been a strong community presence on Wuyi that has perpetuated various cults, beliefs, and legends associated with religious Daoism. In the Daoist pantheon of sacred mountains, Wuyi ranks as the sixteenth *dongtian*, or "cavern heaven."

On the day before the Seventh Night,[29] I set out from Jian Stream [Jianxi], traveled one hundred *li*, and arrived at Myriad Years Palace [Wannian Gong],[30] where I paid a visit to the Jade Emperor [Yuhuang], Supreme Dame [Tailao], and ranks of the Thirteen Immortals [Shisan Xian].[31] Walked around the Han dynasty sacrificial altar, which in fact refers to "making sacrificial offerings of dried fish to Wuyi at the time of the Martial Emperor of the Han" [Han Wudi; r. 141–87 BCE].[32] As our boat floated along the stream, I gazed at the many mountain peaks towering in the distance. The first to emerge was Great King [Dawang].[33] The next one, slightly more expansive, was Canopy Pavilion [Manting]. According to the *Annals*,[34] Wei [Wang] Ziqian assembled the Thirteen Immortals and, as master of the land, had the Ascendant Truth Abbey [Shengzhen Guan] built on the summit of Canopy Pavilion Peak. The scenic sights there include Celestial Mirror Pool [Tianjian Chi] and Tracing Crane Rock [Mohe Yan]. In the second year of the First Emperor's reign [220 BCE; the second year after he declared himself First Emperor], the Lord of Wuyi fashioned a rainbow bridge and held a feast, at which all his "great-grandsons" sang "Sorrowful is the Human World" [Renjian Ke Ai].[35] Today, one cannot climb up to Canopy Pavilion by means of the Great King's Ladder [Dawang Ti], and nothing is left except for autumn cicadas droning and buzzing in the grasses. Several *li* below Jade Maiden [Yunü] and Helmet [Doumou] Peaks there is Single Thread Sky. As for [Chen]

Youding's [1330–68] ancient city,[36] because there is a tiger in the area, sight-seers dare not go too far inside. The distance between the two cliffs is about one *li*, in which there is barely a thread of sunlight. The Wind Cavern [Fengdong] is here, where Bai Yuchan decapitated the snake.[37] He is worshipped today, and the solemn atmosphere of the snake's execution still exists, or so it is said.

Our drifting boat passed Great Repository Peak [Dacang Feng], where we visited the Imperial Tea Garden [Yucha Yuan], then ascended its myriad stone steps. The mountain peak looks like a bird's nest. Presumably, this is where the Wei Wang [Ziqian] removed all his clothing to climb Celestial Pillar [Tianzhu], which became the Changing Clothes Terrace [Gengyi Tai]. Crossed the bank and paid a visit to Master Zhu's Study [Zhuzi Dushu Suo].[38] Bowed to his portrait and lingered and loitered there for quite a while. Went directly into the Cloud Nest [Yunwo], where Chen Danshu refined and purified his elixirs.[39] His stone elixir brazier survives.

Came out of Great Hidden Screen [Dayin Ping] to head west. Climbed Welcome-the-Bamboo-Shoots [Jiesun], proceeding along the path with wooden ladders and iron cables. Looking up, we were terrified of losing our footing; looking down, we were terrified of vertigo. After a thousand turns crossed Dragon Spine [Longji] and thereupon reached the Immortal Chess Pavilion [Xianyi Ting], where we could rest. Beyond the various bamboo and droning cicadas, yellow caps[40] were just opening and closing their cinnabar chambers [*danfang*]. Even though Heavenly Journey [Tianyou] is towering and imposing, we passed it, but far off and away from the peak, one can take a sedan chair up to One Glance Terrace [Yilan Tai] and thereby count off on one's fingers the sights of the thirty-six peaks. When that was accomplished, our boat proceeded about one *li* and passed a narrow mountain pass, which forms Sinking Rock Hall [Xianshi Tang], where there is a small bridge amidst a flowing stream. Passed a stone gate and came to a farm in the wilderness, where we heard chickens and dogs. Could this be something like the land of Wuling?[41] We thereupon gazed at Drum Peak [Guzi Feng], which was nearby, and then passed through a bamboo grove for five *li*, where catwalks made of timbers and stone connected with one another. We knocked on the cliff-face rock, which went "boom" like a drum. Below the cliff is the Cavern of Master Wu [Wugong Dong],[42] and beside it is a Daoist abbey. As it turned out, during this sightseeing trip we reached all Nine Bends in the proper order.

We then returned to the Myriad Years Palace, and from the foot of
the mountain proceeded twenty *li*. Visited Water Curtain [Shuilian]
Cavern and descended from the waterfall at Jumbled Precipice [Luanya].
Our clothes seemed bluish-green in color and were completely soaked.
We then took our leave from a mountain ravine that led us out onto
the Chong'an Stream [Chong'an Xi] road to Xi [or Jiangxi] and Chu [or
Hunan].

Cao Xuequan remarks: I have investigated the *Annals of Religious Rites
for Wuyi*. What detail there is in its accounts! And from these details I
have deduced that the rulers of men have always been obsessed with
immortals. The First Emperor dispatched the alchemist Xu Shi to search
for immortality on the high seas, and yet there is nothing in the *Annals*
about the Lord of Wuyi. What is the reason for this omission? Moreover,
the reports about Wei [Wang] Ziqian meeting up with Zhang Zhan and
the Thirteen Immortals, and holding a feast with his "great-grandsons"
on Canopy Pavilion Peak—all these events supposedly took place in the
second year of the First Emperor's reign. How grandiose they were! And
yet the mountains descended into obscurity later. Now, that this is not
a case where a mountain's spirit has been altered because of these shortcomings is indeed clear! There is a saying that goes, "Previous glory and
honor can be restored and realized." Perhaps this is the point here?

Structurally, Cao Xuequan's account conforms to the quadripartite
structure of *youji* that first appeared in the works of Yuan Jie and Liu
Zongyuan: there is a dated introduction, description of landscape, authorial
reaction, and a closing section. His travel itinerary, taken mainly by boat,
followed a prescribed course designed to take him past the Nine Bends
along the waterway, each with its own assembly of scenic peaks and hidden
caverns. And not surprisingly, virtually every site, person, and event mentioned by Cao Xuequan has a connection to Wuyi's Daoist tradition. Cao
was not a follower of Daoism, but he was thoroughly familiar with its connections to Wuyi, and this is because authors writing *youji* in the scholarly-
commentarial style always read sources about their travel destination before
they journeyed there. These materials would typically include local gazetteers and other travel accounts. Although he probably consulted such
sources if they were available to him, Cao does not mention them by title.
On two occasions, however, he references the text *Annals of the Religious
Rites for Wuyi* (Wuyi sidian zhi).[43]

On the surface, the itinerary and landscape description in Cao Xuequan's account is like most Song and Ming sightseeing *youji*. In other words, he follows the usual tourist itinerary past each of the Nine Bends, and he describes—in straightforward language—what he observes. But note that there is practically no aesthetic appreciation of landscape. The focus of Cao's travel narrative is upon places (mainly peaks and caverns), people (mainly deities and adepts), and events related to the mountain's Daoist tradition. What most distinguishes scholarly-commentarial *youji* from the more common sightseeing accounts is a process whereby the author compares his on-site observations with a (presumably reliable) textual source (or sources) and then comments on the differences or discrepancies between them. The "commentary" I refer to here, in fact, functions in scholarly-commentarial *youji* as the fourth and closing section of the text, which in this case is introduced by the phrase "Cao Xuequan remarks." Readers familiar with historical writing in ancient China will likely associate this practice with Sima Qian, who, in many chapters of the *Shiji*, appended commentaries that essentially passed moral judgment on the behavior and actions of historical figures. Cao Xuequan is essentially following the same commentarial style, but his only concern is how places, persons, and events associated with Daoism on Wuyi are described (or not) in the *Annals of the Religious Rites for Wuyi*.

As with almost all description—especially commentary—the author's views concerning the subject matter at hand are easily discernible. This is certainly the case with Cao Xuequan. Comments such as "nothing is left [of the Great King's Ladder] except for autumn cicadas droning and buzzing in the grasses" and Great Repository Peak is now "looking like a bird's nest" reveal Cao's not-so-subtle criticism: the heyday of the Daoist presence on the mountain ended long ago. It is precisely this observation that stirs Cao Xuequan's commentary in the closing section of his *youji*. His main concern is omissions concerning major figures, such as the Lord of Wuyi—who tradition claims "found the Way" on the mountain—and the complete absence in later sources of reference to the dated events that allegedly took place there, such as the "feast" convened in 245 BCE by Wang Ziqian on the summit of Canopy Pavilion Peak. Of course, the implication here is that these events probably never took place at all. Cao, however, does not pursue the myth-vs.-history issue. Instead, he comes to the defense of the mountain's reputation, declaring, "This is not a case where a mountain's spirit has been altered because of these shortcomings." The operative word here

5.2. A section of Nine Bends Stream today. https://commons.wikimedia.org/wiki/File:
Punting_9bends.JPG.

is *ling*, which refers to the essential spirit or soul of the mountain. Further-more, Cao argues that "glory and honor" does not need to come from myths and fabrications" but are traits that can be "cultivated and realized" over time.

The late Ming scholarly-commentarial travel writing style of Qian Qianyi and Cao Xuequan is an expression of the late Ming ideal of schol-arly research based on ancient texts *and* personal visitation to the promi-nent places, such as the Wuyi Mountains, mentioned in those works. And the manner in which Cao Xuequan and Qian Qianyi's travel writings display the scholarly acumen and historical knowledge of their authors is yet another manifestation of the late Ming concern for self-identity and self-expression. "Scholarly-commentarial" travel writings continued to thrive in the Qing period, especially in *youji* written by prominent literary figures and promoters of *kaozheng* (textual investigation) like Wang Fuzhi (1610–92), Huang Zongxi (1610–95), and Gu Yanwu, all of whom promoted careful textual study and critical thinking as the hallmarks of sound scholarship.[44]

GEOGRAPHICAL-INVESTIGATIVE *YOUJI*

> [Xu Xiake's] spirit of inquiry is so startlingly modern that it alone
> would have ranked him as the earliest leader of modern geography
> in China.
>
> V. K. TING, "ON HSÜ HSIA-K'O, EXPLORER AND GEOGRAPHER"[45]

Geographical-investigative travel writing, like the scholarly-commentarial style discussed in the previous section, is a variety of *youji* that has its genesis in the late Ming concern for verification of textual sources concerning place. The two most accomplished contemporary practitioners of this category of writing are Wang Shixing (1547–98) and Xu Xiake. In some ways, however, this is an odd pairing of authors. This is because while the latter has been canonized as China's greatest travel writer (except among specialists working in the field of traditional Chinese geography), Wang Shixing is practically unknown.[46] On the other hand, Xu Xiake never held public office and indeed might even be described as the quintessential Ming dynasty "private traveler" in that he came from a wealthy family (his mother managed a successful weaving business that supported his travels) and chose to spend a lifetime following his primary intellectual interests, geography and history. Wang Shixing, on the other hand, served in a long succession of government administrative posts in almost every corner of the Ming empire, including Sichuan and Yunnan.

Yet despite these marked contrasts, the two writers had much in common. One of Wang Shixing's distinctions as a writer-traveler is that he personally visited each of the Five Marchmounts, as well as numerous other scenic and historical sites throughout China. The scope of Xu Xiake's travels is equally remarkable: his journeys, most often undertaken on foot, took him to sixteen of China's modern provinces. Wang Shixing and Xu Xiake also each produced a large body of travel writing. Wang's most important works are his *youji* album *Drafts of Sightseeing Trips to the Five Marchmounts* (Wuyue you cao) and a separate but related work, written in his later years, titled *Sorting Out My Extensive Jottings* (Guangzhi yi).

Xu Xiake's surviving *youji*, all written in diary format, are massive. Estimates vary, but according to one modern scholar, they collectively include about 404,000 Chinese characters.[47] Another source gives the number "over 600,000 characters."[48] In either case, modern editions of his surviving travel writings fill two hefty volumes. Without a doubt, Xu's extensive

5.3. Title page of the 1808 edition of Xu Xiake's travel diaries, preserved in the Watery Heart Study (Shuixin Zhai 水心齋) of the Qing dynasty bibliophile Ye Tingjia 葉廷甲 (1754–1832). Courtesy of the C. V. Starr East Asian Library, University of California, Berkeley.

travels and huge surviving corpus of *youji* help explain why he has been venerated by so many, including some of his contemporaries. To cite just one example, in his biography for Xu Xiake, the distinguished late Ming literary figure Qian Qianyi praises his good friend's *youji* in the highest terms possible: "[They are] the very best among travel accounts, both ancient and modern."[49]

Before we turn to Wang Shixing and Xu Xiake's respective contributions to geographical-investigative travel writing in the late Ming, a key point needs emphasis: it is misguided to categorize Wang and Xu's extensive collections of travel writings solely in terms of the geographical-investigative or any other distinct style. This is because their *youji* embody several different language formats, which clearly reveal the influence of earlier exemplars of the genre. For instance, on more than a few occasions, both authors employ the sort of reportorial-style description we saw in the Southern Song river diaries, which, it will be recalled, is designed to provide readers with historical and literary background on place. A good example of this style is Wang Shixing's introductory remarks in his account of a visit to Mount Lu:

> The *Commentary on the Waterways Treatise* says, "The source of the Lu River is the [Mount of the] Three Sons of Heaven Metropolis.[50] It flows into the Great River west of Pengze town."[51] Presumably, this refers to Mount Lu. Someone also said that during the Yin and Zhou dynasties, there was one Master Kuangxu who lived as a recluse on this mountain. After he left the mountain to become an immortal, only his cottage remained behind. For this reason, the mountain was so named.[52] When I was young I read Master Yuan's account and Venerable Ouyang's "Mount Lu on High" [Lushan Gao]. This is how I came to know about the mountain. . . . Proceeded onward for ten *li* and reached the Kaixian Monastery [Kaixian Si]. The monastery is nestled against and below Crane-Calling Peak [Heming Feng]. As a child, Li, the Middle Ruler of the Southern Tang, was fond of transcendent matters, and afterward conferred upon the monastery the name Kaixian.[53]

Wang Shixing begins his account by citing relevant historical information from an ancient source (as did Fan Chengda and especially Lu Yu in their individual entries on scenic or historical sites), in this case a quotation from the *Commentary on the Waterways Treatise*. By the middle and late Ming, the practice of citing earlier texts regarding place names became a customary practice in almost all *youji*, especially in sightseeing accounts, and this can be regarded as another sixteenth- and seventeenth-century expression of Ming concern with geographical precision and exegesis. Another late Ming practice that also has its genesis in Lu You's and Fan Chengda's river diaries is citation of earlier *youji* accounts and/or poems concerning the place one is visiting. In this case, two authors are mentioned: "Master Yuan" refers to Huiyuan, the Six Dynasties monk and reputed author of "Preface to the Poems about a Sightseeing Trip to Stone Gate by the Lay Buddhists from Mount Lu"; and "Master Ouyang," which refers to Ouyang Xiu.[54] While it is undeniable that Song *youji* authors were mindful about the historical-literary heritage sites they were visiting,[55] late Ming travelers—and here I refer specifically to authors such as Wang Shixing, Wang Jiusi (1468–1551), Qian Qianyi, and Xu Xiake—were especially attentive about earlier geographical, historical, and literary works as they related to places on their travel itinerary. Xu Xiake is known to have carried a copy of the *Great Ming Gazetteer of the Unified Realm* (Da Ming Yitong zhi; completed in 1461) with him, and during his travels, he purchased gazetteers to serve as reference sources.[56]

The *youji* of Wang Shixing and Xu Xiake also reveal indebtedness to the type of landscape delineation introduced by Yuan Jie, refined by Liu Zongyuan, and later imitated by numerous authors—that type of description in which the author charges his language with action and motion verbs while narrating movement through a landscape. The following example comes from Xu Xiake's account of his second trip to the Yellow Mountains, undertaken in 1618. At this point in his itinerary, Xu had reached one of the mountain's premier scenic sites: Heavenly Capital Peak (Tiandu Feng). A local monk named Chengyuan, who also served as a tour guide, tries to dissuade Xu from making the climb because there was "no path" (*wulu*) to the summit. Here is the late Ming traveler's response to the monk's exhortation:

> I did not follow his advice, for I was determined to sightsee[57] on Heavenly Capital, and so I coerced Chengyuan and the servants to accompany me down the same trail into the gorge as before[58] until we reached the side of Heavenly Capital. Like snakes we slithered over streams and boulders. Clambering through weeds, we pulled our way through brambles, and where boulders arose in clusters we would climb over them on our knees, and where the rock cliffs were slanted and sharp we would brace ourselves on the cliff walls as we proceeded. Each time we reached a spot with no place for our hands or feet, Chengyuan would necessarily first ascend and lower an outstretched hand to help me. Whenever I thought about the ascent being as difficult as this, I wondered if the descent would be bearable! But there was no time to think about it. After several dangerous encounters, we finally reached the summit of the peak.

And here is Xu's description of the scene he spied after reaching the summit. Lotus Flower Peak (Lianhua Feng) is another notable sightseeing landmark that stands next to Heavenly Capital Peak:

From time to time, a dense fog would move in and move off. When the first bank of fog moved in, nothing could be seen. Looking out toward the various crags of Lotus Flower, most of them were enveloped in fog. As I alone[59] ascended to Heavenly Capital, when I moved to the front of it, the fog would retreat to the back of it, and as I crossed over to the right, the fog would then exit from the left. As for the pines, they were still twisted and upright, sweeping this way and that. The cypresses, although as big as a man's arm, all clung flatly to the surfaces of rocks in the manner of lichen. On such lofty heights the wind is formidable, and the foggy mists come and go as they please. Looking at the various peaks below, at times they appeared as emerald isles, while at other times they were completely enveloped in a silvery sea. But looking further down the mountain, I beheld a completely different view: there the sunlight glittered brightly and brilliantly. As the sun gradually set, we put our feet forward while our hands braced us from behind, and slid down on our backsides. When we reached a dangerous spot, Chengyuan used his hands and shoulders to help me. By the time the danger had passed, we had reached the col of the mountain. Dusk had fallen, and once again we followed the canyon and traversed a plank walkway to ascend to the Mañjuśrī Close [Wenshu Yuan], where we stopped to spend the night.[60]

This passage is representative of Xu Xiake's best descriptive landscape prose. Above all else, emphasis falls on narration of the journey. When executed well, as it is here, this writing style produces a veritable word picture of the human experience of moving across a landscape. As was the case with examples of this technique described in earlier chapters, what makes it work is skillful deployment of action and movement verbs (fog *moving* in and out, pine trees *sweeping* this way and that, cypress trees *clinging* to rocks, peaks *enveloped* by a silvery sea of fog and mists, and so on), which gives the imagery in his prose—and Xu Xiake himself as an actor or participant in the action—a sense of constant motion. Again, the idea here is to re-create, via narration of physical movement and description of scene, the physical experience of the journey.

Although Xu's word picture makes appeal to various human senses, the emphasis in the Huangshan diary entries is on the visual wonder and charm of the landscape. No scenic detail is omitted. No physical difficulty of the ascent goes unmentioned. In his best scenic-description prose, Xu Xiake has little interest in utilizing prose *youji* to engage philosophical, moral, or introspective life issues. Neither is he a simple observer, recalling some leisurely outing to a scenic spot with some friends. Instead, Xu—by choice—plays the dual roles of narrator and actor, telling readers in a narrative, literary way exactly what is going on, and actively and physically engaged in all the action. With a little imagination and a willingness to participate, the attentive reader can undertake the same journey.

The works by Wang Shixing and Xu Xiake that are most important in the history of travel writing in traditional China are their geographical-investigative *youji*. Wang Shixing, in the Preface to the *Drafts of Sightseeing Trips to the Five Marchmounts*, declares, "What I have witnessed of all the Fashioner-Creator's changes in the heavens and on the earth, human feelings and the principles of things, and the result of encounters with tragedy and joy, both favorable and contrary—none of these has been ignored in the accounts of my travels."[61] This declaration sums up the two primary foci of Wang's attention as a writer-traveler: the natural environment and the changes that take place therein ("the Fashioner-Creator's changes in the skies and on the earth"); and how people and society relate to natural environments. The key word here is "change" (*bian*); that is, how change in environments affects people and society. Wang Shixing's main interest, then, was human geography.

Now, although Wang Shixing's *youji* certainly falls into the broad category of the geographical-investigative style of travel writing described earlier, the bulk of his commentarial work and contributions to human geography are found in his *Sorting Out My Extensive Jottings*. This work was written later in life as a response to his earlier observations made during trips to the Five Marchmounts and other famous sites. What distinguishes his travel writing—especially the *Jottings*—is that Wang Shixing critically interprets the data gathered from his observations of place. His desire to compose investigative-scientific *youji* was inspired in no small part by the limited nature of (and many mistakes in) Ming geographical texts like the *Great Ming Gazetteer of the Unified Realm*. Government-sponsored works like this were not based on firsthand observation but rather on earlier, essentially out-of-date geographical and historical works.

The new geographical-investigative work of Xu Xiake and Wang Shixing represents a major break away from such traditional geography, which mostly concerned the evolution of administrative institutions and matters relating to economy, customs, and culture. It was also heavily influenced by geopolitical constructs and Confucian moralistic ideals that stressed order and balance in the state above all else. Examples of this approach are found in the monographs on geography (*dili zhi*) in the dynastic histories, which present geographical information in a way that supports and reinforces the hierarchal political-administrative organization of the state. Essentially, then, the dynastic monographs and works such as the *Great Ming Gazetteer of the Unified Realm* were designed to collect and present information to facilitate political control, not (strictly speaking) to enhance geographical knowledge. In other words, the state controlled and manipulated geography for its own administrative-political purposes.

However, as Yongtao Du and others have correctly observed, state control of geography waned in the late Ming because it was challenged by the local (or private) production of gazetteers, especially comprehensive gazetteers.[62] The authors of these works made significant effort to provide complete and accurate information that would, among other purposes, facilitate the sightseeing boom in the late Ming.[63] Wang Shixing was certainly a proponent of this sort of comprehensive geography, and his *youji* provides information that was undoubtedly useful to sightseers. But his priority, especially in his *Jottings*, was interpretative—specifically, how changes in environment affect people, society, and the various by-products of social organization, such as customs, culture, religion, dialects, folklore, local products, and communication. Wang Shixing's concern with human geography, then, immediately distinguishes him from the traditional "Confucian" statecraft approach. The platforms for this new direction in writing about place are Wang's *youji* and his *Jottings*.

As an example of Wang Shixing's concern with human geography, consider the following excerpt from his *Jottings*. This passage illustrates well how the author stressed the differences in society and customs that result from variations in the natural environment:

> The southeast benefits from having a plentiful supply of marine resources and non-glutinous rice. The Central Counties[64] and the land of Chu have a plentiful supply of fish. The southwest has a plentiful supply of silver ore, precious stones, beautiful shells, amber, cinnabar, and mercury. The south has a plentiful supply of rhinoceros, elephant, pepper, perilla,[65] and various forms of foreign currency. The north has a plentiful supply of oxen, sheep, *lei*,[66] and felt.[67] The southwest, Sichuan, Gui, Qian (or Guizhou), and the Guangs have a plentiful supply of great torreya and

camphor trees. Jiangnan has a plentiful supply of firewood, so the people there get their fuel from trees. North of the [Great] River there is a plentiful supply of coal, so the people there get their fuel from the ground. In the northwest, where the mountains are high, people travel overland and there are no boats; in the southeast the waterways are extensive, and people travel by boat and rarely by cart or horse. On Hainan, people eat fish and shrimp, but northerners hate the pungent smell. People north of the frontier eat cheese, but southerners despise its smell. Northerners eat onions, garlic, and leeks, but in Jiangnan people fear hot and spicy food. But no one is consciously aware of these differences, which are practices gained over time from natural environment and climate, and so we cannot force everyone to be the same.[68]

In a way, Wang Shixing was redefining the places he wrote about in his *youji*. He was unique because no contemporary or earlier travel writer ever wrote commentary separate from their travel accounts. The central message in Wang Shixing's writings—one that was never voiced in earlier travel writing—is that there is much more to know and consider about place besides physical environment. More specifically, Wang argues that human phenomena vary from region to region because of differences in the physical environment, and these individual differences on the regional or provincial level can also be viewed as part of a global human-environment system. As Zhou Zhenhe has observed, Wang Shixing was an "out-and-out environmental determinist."[69] His views concerning human geography would go on to influence major Qing dynasty thinkers such as Gu Yanwu.[70]

In the case of Xu Xiake, it is certainly the geographical-investigative aspect of his travel writing that has attracted the most attention from scholars and geographers, beginning with V. K. Ting's (Ding Wenjiang; 1887–1936) seminal essay "On Hsü Hsia-k'o, Geographer and Explorer," first published in 1921.[71] Subsequent scholars have argued that the hallmark quality of Xu's travel diaries—especially his reports on places in the southwest written later in life—is their great literary merit, but perhaps his greatest contribution to the evolution of travel writing is found in his geographical-investigative accounts. These works take *youji* in an entirely new direction.

Xu Xiake's geographical-investigative writings fall into one of two broad categories, which may be described as scrutiny of specific, unresolved questions related to geography; and compilation of empirical data and evidence, also related to geography. Xu's most famous "discovery," which is mentioned in almost everything ever written about scientific investigation in traditional China, occurred while he was traveling in Guizhou in 1638. His travels and investigations there led Xu to conclude that the true source of the Great River was not the Min or the Yalong Rivers (Yalong Jiang) in Sichuan, as had been claimed in old geographies, such as the "Tribute to Yu" (Yugong) chapter of the classical Confucian text *Shujing*, or *Documents Classic*. Instead, he identified the source as the Jinsha (literally, "Golden Sands") river system in Qinghai.[72] As it turns out, though he did not pinpoint the precise geographical location, Xu Xiake was correct in identifying the source to be in the upper reaches of the Jinsha river system. What is now recognized as the scientific, geographical, and officially accepted source of the river—in southern Qinghai province on the Tibetan Plateau (at elevation 5,170 meters; coordinates N32°36′14″; E94°30′44″)—was not finally confirmed until 2005.[73] Xu Xiake's contributions to locating the source of the Changjiang and other rivers in southwest China have been acknowledged and extensively written about ever since the Qing dynasty,[74] but their significance to systematic investigations of karst (*yanrong*) topography in Guilin have received far less attention.

Xu Xiake visited Guilin, an area famous for its karst spires and caverns, in 1637. Over a two-month period, he documented visits to more than one hundred underground karst caverns in the region. Thus, to Xu Xiake goes the distinction of being the first person "to undertake real scientific exploration of karst and karst caves in south China."[75] Joseph Needham, in his *Science and Civilisation in China*, remarks of Xu: "He had a wonderful power of analyzing topographical detail, and made systematic use of special terms which enlarged the ordinary nomenclature, such as staircase (thi [*ti*]), basin (phing [*ping*]), etc. Everything was noted carefully in feet or *li*, without vague stock phrases."[76] In fact, Xu's extended trip to southwest China that began in 1636 was specifically undertaken to study the geomorphologic and underground features of karst landscape.

Xu Xiake's "empirical evidence gathering and description" is illustrated in the account of his first visit to Seven Stars Cavern (Qixing Dong) in Guilin (Jingwen is a Buddhist monk who accompanied Xu on many of his trips):

Second day [fifth month, 1637]: After breakfast, along with Jingwen and
Servant Gu, packed some food provisions and, carrying our bedding,
headed out east through Floating Bridge Gate [Fuqiao Men]. Crossed the

Floating Bridge [Fuqiao] and proceeded further east, crossing Flower Bridge [Huaqiao]. Turned east at Flower Bridge and immediately turned north, following along the base of the spire. The hill[77] stood erect, northeast of Flower Bridge. Along the eastern shore of Flower Bridge there is a small rock formation that juts out at the end of the bridge.[78] The slender stream that adorns the nearby village is especially bedazzling to the mind's eye as it moves off to the east. The contours of the hill's crags and cliffs are surprisingly inferior to the peaks along the narrow passageways in the southeast. Seven Stars Spire, in fact, towers up right here. Altogether, it is only one *li* or so from the Floating Bridge. The spire faces west, and below it is the Eternal Buddha Monastery [Shoufo Si]. In fact, it is to the left of the monastery where one ascends the spire. First, there is a pavilion with extended wings [or eaves] aloft that welcomes visitors. It is called Pluck the Stars [Zhaixing] and was constructed and had its name plaque written by Cao Nengshi.[79] A cliff spans and soars high above it. Along our path there was barely enough room for one foot, but when I looked downward at the battlements and West Precipice [Xiyan], it looked very spacious. To the left of the pavilion, in fact, is a Buddhist hermitage facing the entrance to the spire, but going in you do not realize there is an entrance. I asked a monk from the monastery about the location of the entrance to the spire. He pushed me from behind through a door leaf that led me inside.

Xu now enters the cavernous interior of Seven Stars Spire:

Passed through various levels in my ascent, for about three *zhang*. At the entrance to the cavern is a hermitage hidden in pitch-black darkness. Suddenly, we turned and headed northwest, where unexpectedly there was a passageway. Above it formed a dome; below it was flat. Inside were numerous aligned stalagmites,[80] hanging down like suspended columns, crispy and cool, dripping and leaking. This is the upper cavern, which is Seven Stars Spire. From the right, we proceeded in stages downward, where we thereupon entered the lower cavern. This is the Nesting-in-Roseate Clouds Cavern (Qixia Dong). It is spacious and sonorous; grand and imposing. Its entrance also faces the northwest. Looking out into the distance, the view is grand and sublime. On the ceiling of the cavern there is a single crack that runs across it. The "stone carp" there seemed like it was about to leap down from the crack, covered in scales from head to tail. Even if someone had carved a stone to fashion such a carp, it could not so closely resemble a real one as this does. Next to it are intertwined canopies in the shape of coiling dragons—stunning, scintillating, and penta-colored. To the northwest, a storied terrace rises high aloft in layers. We ascended in stages following along its fringe. This is Venerable Lord Terrace [Laojun Tai]. From the terrace we headed north, where the cavern seemed to divide into two sections. To the west was a high terrace; to the east, it followed along the interior of a deep ravine. Proceeded along the terrace and then entered a single gate, and then went straight north until we reached a pitch-black area. Above was a dome without any cracks. Below was a sunken depression, where a pool had formed. The wall of the huge cavern was split into two halves. What had been flat suddenly turned dangerous.

About to penetrate the dark recesses of the cavern, Xu Xiake now engages the services of a local guide:

It was at this point that I engaged a guide for the first time. So we might enter the cavern, we lit pine torches that shined all the way to the bottom. The guide did not accompany us along the terrace, so there was no time to catch up and follow him. We also did not know if this was a place where we could not light torches.[81] We then descended from the terrace and, as before, reached the bottom of the cavern. The guide, carrying a torch, hurried forward. Following the terrace eastward, we proceeded through a ravine and only then caught sight of the terrace. The veins in its wall were now together, now asunder, like an ornately designed tapestry. To be provided with such miraculous variations makes one feel even more so that they have come down from the heavens above. Continued due north and entered the Single Heaven Gate [Yitian Men], whose stone pillars droop straight down so only one person can pass. After we entered, the cavern became even more vaulted, lofty, and distant. To its left there was a stone balustrade spanning crosswise. Below, it sank down into deep darkness, so obscure you cannot see to the bottom. This is the Marmot Pool [Tazi Tan]. The guide said that its abyss leads to the sea, but this is not necessarily so. It is more probably a case that this is the place where Venerable Lord Terrace plummets down to the northeast, but when it reaches here, its great height and depth change positions, and the terrace intersects where it is thick and hollow, going on to form a separate environment.

Inside it are consecutive entrances to two Celestial Gates [Tianmen]. The path gradually turns to the northeast. Therein you find the rock forms Bamboo-Stuck-in-a-Flowery-Vase [Huaping Chazhu], Withdraw-the-Net [Chewang], Chess [Yiqi], Eight Immortals [Baxian], and Steamed Bun [Mantou]. On both sides are images of Sudhana [Shancai Tongzi]; inside is an image of Guanyin.[82] The guide proceeded on with great haste, insisting that we pause to make close examinations but to be aware that there is too much to take in all at one time. But what I desired to observe is not here. Next, we moved past a precipice wall and ascended. To its right is a pool—a black abyss just like the Marmot Pool, but in magnificence and grandeur even surpasses it. This is called Dragon River [Longjiang]. Its dome connects through to Marmot Pool. Next proceeded toward the north, passing Red Felt [Hongzhan] and White Felt [Baizhan]—hanging "blankets" that looked like abandoned "fur coats." Their "wrinkles" seemed like they had been woven. Next, along the path eastward we passed Phoenixes-Frolicking-in-Water [Fenghuang Xishui], where we began to pass through a single cavern entranceway. A chilly wind swished and soughed, which blew out the torch, while the cold stabbed at our bodies. Presumably, the wind came in from outside the cavern, and when it reached here, its collective force became even greater. When we exited, we suddenly saw a single globe of white light. Inside it was an image of a deep ravine. It was hazy and misty, just like when dawn is about to break. We thereupon exited from the east to the rear cavern. There was a stream from the northern section of the cavern that flowed in a circle. We entered the cavern from the south. My guess is that what follows below constitutes Dragon River. Straddling a small rock bridge, we ascended to it, which is said to have been built by the Song dynasty prime minister Master Zeng Bu. We crossed the bridge and whisked by the cavern to a precipice wall on the right, which is where the inscription of Master Zeng's account is located. It was only then I realized that the cavern was formerly named Cold Water Precipice [Lengshui Yan]. Master Zeng served as commander of Gui. While searching for wonders in the cavern he constructed the bridge.[83] Only then was the precipice's name changed to Master Zeng Precipice. Presumably, Dragon River and Nesting-in-Roseate-Clouds are connected as one subterranean cavern, and it is only that their two respective entrances have distinctive features. I stood for a long while on the bridge.

Xu Xiake often gathered information from local informants. In the next section he quotes a response to a question he asked about the source of a subterranean stream:

When I looked down into the gully, I saw someone washing and drawing water. I inquired, "This stream comes from the northeast. Can one enter the cavern when going against its current?" One of them said, "One can go deep inside cave with water for several *li*. Therein is some notable scenery. If you compare it to other caverns, it has double the number of paths and double the number of scenic wonders. If the cave has water, there is no way to tell its depth. One can only wade through it during the winter months, and this is not that time." I immediately demanded that person serve as our guide. He then returned to fetch some pine torches. I followed him out of the cavern and then to the right, where we found the Felicitous Forest Abbey [Qinglin Guan]. He used the satchel he was carrying to store the torches. We temporarily deposited our satchels and packs there and requested that the monks cook some yellow millet to feed us. I thereupon followed the guide in, again from the East Gate of the mountain pass. Only after passing Phoenixes-Frolicking-in-Water and squeezing by the two Felts, Red and White, did we proceed northward on a side path. Inside were lions sporting with balls, elephants with curled trunks, camels with long necks and burgeoning humps. Since there were sacrificial utensils for use at earthen burial mounds, swine whiskers and goose feet were set out in front; since there were *luohans* [*luohan* is the Chinese word for a Buddhist *arhat*, referring to a perfected being who has attained nirvana] present at the feast, there were golden goblets and a silver stand arranged below it. High above it there is an image of mountain spirit, about one *chi* in length, flying and sitting on the overhanging precipice. Where it is deepest, there is an image of Buddha, but only seven *cun* in height and placed to the side of a bodhisattva with both hands clasped, half way up the wall, sitting cross-legged, and meditating on a Chan couch in a niche. In front of a Guanyin statue, Fazang's single prayer wheel seemed as if it was about to start spinning.[84] In the deep part of the cavern again there was pitch blackness where by a bridge a torrent flowed upwards. When we reached this place, the guide would not dare go in, saying, "I'll carry the torch and lead the way, but even if we spent several days, we could not reach the end of it. However, no one has ever

gone in here, let alone just after the time when the water in the stream has
risen." We thereupon turned around and went back, following along the
Red and White Felts and Phoenixes-Sporting-with-Water and then exiting
the cavern.

And finally, following his customary practice, Xu Xiake closes with a summary of the distance he traveled and brief assessment of what was observed.

I figure that first, from Nesting-in-Roseate Clouds to Master Zeng's Spire
[Zenggong Yan], altogether we covered about two *li*, and later, from where
we entered and then exited Master Zeng's Cavern [Zenggong Dong], we
made a circuit of about three *li*. However, as for the surpassing scenery in
the two caverns, we saw everything there was to see."[85]

The modern geographer Bang Bohu has observed that Xu Xiake's
contribution to research in karst falls into three areas: explanations of
karst processes, classifications and descriptions of individual karst landforms, and analysis of the regional characteristics of karst. I agree with
Bang that among these, the most important is the second.[86] The passage
above is a superb example Xu Xiake's geographical-investigative descriptive
technique.

Nowhere in earlier *youji* do we find description of place that even
approaches this level of precision and detail. At least some of the motivation
that produced it is evident in his travel diaries, which reveal that he was
dissatisfied with much of the content in the old geography books because
they were riddled with mistakes, the sources of which were either myths
and legends or else geographies that were simply copied from one generation to the next without verification. Comments by Xu's friend and biogra-
pher, Qian Qianyi, also make it clear that Xu was aware that he was creating
new knowledge and that he wanted that knowledge to be passed on to future
generations. Xu Xiake, then, was a man on a mission to produce precise
description of place through pragmatic and protoscientific methods of
inquiry. Moreover, he believed that the huge corpus of travel writing he
produced would ensure his legacy as a "great traveler" and thereby entitle
him to a place in the pantheon of China's greatest travelers, which for Xu
included Zhang Qian, Xuanzang, and Yelü Chucai.[87]

One useful way to appreciate Xu's precision as an observer and composer
of geographical-investigative travel writing is to read his description of the

karst formations in Seven Stars Cavern as a "mapping" process. The central idea behind this technique is quite simple: the data one accumulates by mapping multiple landmarks (in this case, karst caverns) is formulated into documentation that can later be analyzed quantitatively or qualitatively and from which conclusions can be drawn. Of course, these are the essentials of empirical investigation. What makes Xu Xiake's surveys even more fascinating is that he made them without the sophisticated measuring instruments available to the modern geographer or geologist undertaking field work. He seems to have never owned or used a compass. Armed only with brush, paper, and words (there are no sketches in his surviving diaries), Xu Xiake turned to various descriptive techniques that he drew from earlier travel writing. Especially important in this regard is his close attention to compass direction and distances between landmarks. In his account of Seven Stars Cavern, Xu reveals an extremely strong impulse to observe and record in the most precise manner possible ("Headed out east through Floating Bridge Gate. Crossed Floating Bridge and proceeded further east, crossing Flower Bridge. Turned east at Flower Bridge and immediately turned north and followed along the base of the hill."). It is unclear how he determined precise direction underground without a compass, but studies by several twentieth-century experts in karst studies have confirmed the general accuracy of his observations.[88]

Distances in *li* and *zhang* between key landforms and places are also noted, but these are always given in approximate numbers ("Passed through different levels in my ascent, for *about* three *zhang*"; "From Nesting-in-Roseate Clouds to Master Zeng's Spire, altogether we covered *about* two *li*."). I suspect that Xu himself or Servant Gu paced off distances whenever possible, but probably they used visual estimation as well. Or he may have gathered distance information from local guides or informants. Contributing to the "mapping" process is notation of prominent landmarks in the cavern as they relate to compass direction and distance ("Continued due north and entered the Single Heaven Gate, whose stone pillars droop straight down so as only one person could pass. After we entered, the cavern became even more vaulted, lofty and distant. To its left there was a stone balustrade spanning crosswise. Below, it sank down into deep darkness, so obscure you cannot see the bottom. This is the Marmot Pool."). Concern for direction and distances is also common in the Southern Song river diaries, especially in Lu You's *Account of Entering Shu*, but not extended in this manner nor even near this level of topographical detail.

Closely related to compass direction and distances is Xu Xiake's technique of narrating movement through space, which, when tallied with his distance and direction indications, also serves to help map the cavern. As we have seen with Li Daoyuan, Yuan Jie, and Liu Zongyuan, spatial movement is narrated by careful use of action and motion verbs ("From the terrace we *headed* north, where the cavern seemed to *divide* into two sections. To the west, it *led* to a high terrace; to the east, it *followed along* the interior of a deep ravine. *Proceeded along* the terrace and then *entered* a single gate, and then *went straight* north until we *reached* a pitch-black area."). When there is a pause in movement, it always serves a special purpose. For instance, if a cavern landmark has distinguishing physical features, Xu will usually stop his motion narration to describe it ("Continued due north and entered the Single Heaven Gate, whose stone pillars droop straight down so as only one person could pass. After we entered, the cavern became even more vaulted, lofty and distant."). Note how closely Xu Xiake's perimorphic description of karst stalagmites ("Inside were lions sporting with balls, elephants with curled trunks, camels with long necks and burgeoning humps.") resembles Liu Zongyuan's delineation of rock forms in "Account of Little Hillock West of Flat-Iron Pool" ("Those that descend, toppling downward in layer upon layer, resemble livestock drinking at a creek; those that ascend, poised to charge upward in pointed ranks, resemble bears clambering up a mountain.").[89] And on other occasions, Xu will pause the travel narrative to make an observation or voice an opinion ("The guide said that its abyss leads to the sea, but this is not necessarily so. It is more probably a case that this is the place where Venerable Lord Terrace plummets down to the northeast, but when it reaches here, its great height and depth change positions, and the terrace intersects where it is thick and hollow, going on to form a separate environment.").

In his investigations of karst caverns, Xu Xiake also provides information on the distribution and relationships of karst in southwest China, and on some occasions, he even collected sample mineral deposits. He was also especially interested in hydrology, specifically, subterranean streams and lakes as water resources ("There was a stream from the northern section of the cavern that flowed in a circle."); and wind movement ("A chilly wind swished and soughed, which blew out the torch lights, while the cold stabbed at our bodies. Presumably, the wind came in from outside the cavern, and when it reached here, its collective force became even greater.").

In a recent essay, the New Zealand-based scholar Yi Zheng argues that "spatial-movement" in Xu Xiake's travel writings "made" a kind of new, systematic, and empiricist-based knowledge. Professor Zheng makes earnest effort to link Xu's "spatial movement" descriptive method with intellectual changes in the late Ming and to distance Xu's *youji* from the "lyrical expression, affective association and intellectual meditation" that characterize the travel writings of his contemporaries.[90] Zheng offers some good insights into understanding the scientific achievements of Xu Xiake, but he misses the key link between Xu's "spatial movement" *youji* and its precursors.

Like many of his predecessors, Xu Xiake mines earlier *youji* and from those works draws various narrative techniques to suit his own purposes. His highly literary descriptions of landscape ("Next to it are intertwined canopies in the shape of coiling dragons, stunning, scintillating, and penta-colored. To the northwest, a storied terrace rises up high up in layers.") could easily be mistaken for an excerpt from Li Daoyuan's extended descriptions in the *Commentary on the Waterways Treatise*. And Xu's employment of motion and action verbs to propel his narrative through the caverns of Guilin, thereby helping to make the reader a participant in the action, can in fact be traced all the way back to Huiyuan's "Preface to the Poems about a Sightseeing Trip to Stone Gate by the Lay Buddhists from Mount Lu." There is little here, then, that was entirely new to travel writing. What Xu Xiake did, however, was to meld these earlier elements into a new form—"geographical-investigative" *youji*—that is ultimately designed to produce new knowledge. If Xu Xiake were alive today, he would likely take immense pride in Joseph Needham's remark that Xu's travel accounts "read more like those of a twentieth-century field surveyor."[91] The detail of his mapping and the precision of his description—not written *post eventum*, but drawn from his daily logs—are a written testimonial to his skill at depicting and analyzing topographical detail. Xu Xiake was fond of portraying himself as a "commoner" who only needed "a walking stick and sandals" to head off on his next expedition.[92] But he was no commoner. Xu was a skilled writer, a careful observer, and a passionate traveler who succeeded in making his mark on the world. He did so in grand fashion, and in many ways, his contributions to new knowledge have surpassed those of Zhang Qian, Xuanzang, and Yelü Chucai, his traveler-heroes of antiquity.

ADDENDUM

Although space limitations and practical considerations have necessitated that I conclude this study with a chapter on Chinese travel writing in the late Ming, this act of closure is in no way meant to suggest that the genre somehow waned or declined in the Qing period that followed. It did not. In fact, travel and travel writing expanded considerably under Manchu rule, during which time an ever-increasing number of government officials and private individuals traveled widely and wrote extensively about their experiences.

The period from the mid-seventeenth to early twentieth centuries is a pivotal era that bridges earlier traditions of *youji*, especially the scholarly-commentarial travel writing practiced by Song Lian and Qian Qianyi, which continued to be written and valued by many early Qing authors such as Gu Yanwu, Huang Zongxi, Wang Fuzhi, Qu Dajun (1630–96), and Zhu Yizun, and a new or "modern" form of travel writing produced by major late Qing intellectuals such as Wang Tao (1828–97), Kang Youwei (1858–1927), and Liang Qichao (1873–1929). What was different about the *youji* written by Wang, Kang, Liang, and others in the second half of the nineteenth and early twentieth centuries was its subject matter and content. Unlike earlier traditions of travel writing, late Qing authors now penned accounts of visits to foreign lands, places essentially unknown to them and their readers. Liang Qichao's itineraries, for instance, took him to Japan, Australia, Hawaii, Canada, and the United States. His five-month tour of America in 1903 even included meetings with President Theodore Roosevelt and the financier J. P. Morgan. The travel writings produced by Liang Qichao and his contemporaries not only described unfamiliar foreign lands and people, they also included commentaries on how their observations abroad related to the disastrous political situation at home—a situation that had been precipitated largely by the decaying Manchu government's inability to resist military incursions into its territory and systematic appropriation of its sovereignty by Britain, the United States, and other imperialist powers.

As we have seen, Ming dynasty and earlier *youji* authors rarely mention contemporary political matters. For them, travel and travel writing served other purposes—recreation, lyrical expression, or scholarly exegesis. In the late Qing, however, the content of travel writing expanded to include descriptions and critical evaluations of foreign countries and serious matters of state, including China's place—even its survival—in the modern world.[93] Many Western scholars have written at length about "China's response to the West" in the period following the first Opium War (1839–42), but few have mined the rich catalog of *youji* dating from that era, which offers unique perspectives on how leading intellectuals like Wang Tao, Kang Youwei, and Liang Qichao voiced different ideas about how that response should be translated into concrete political reform and change.

POSTFACE

The use of traveling is to regulate imagination with reality, and
instead of thinking of how things may be, see them as they are.

SAMUEL JOHNSON (1709–1784), *LETTERS*

"TO BE INSCRIBED ON THE WALL OF THE WEST FOREST MONAS-
tery" (Ti Xilin bi) is a well-known but often misunderstood quatrain by Su
Shi. In just four lines of verse, Su captures what is the most essential and
enduring quality of Chinese travel writing:

橫看成嶺側成峰，	Looking from the side it forms a range, from the end it forms a peak;
遠近高低總不同。	From far away or nearby, up high or down below, it's never the same.
不識廬山真面目，	I cannot discern Mount Lu's true face and features,
只緣身在此山中。	And this is simply because I am amidst the very mountain itself.[1]

Note especially how Su Shi perceives images, shapes, and contours, and
the way he delineates the physical landscape of Mount Lu from different
perspectives—now from the side, now from the end; now from far away,
now from up close; now from up above, now from down below. The poet is
never stationary. Hence, his view is never static. The mountain is never
described from a distance. And even though language itself, poetic or otherwise, does not inherently embody the physical act of motion, Su Shi's
poem is nevertheless charged with energy in the form of ever-shifting *movement*. This explains why his view of the mountain is "never the same." It
also reveals why he cannot get a fix on the "true face and features" (*mianmu*,
literally, "face and eyes") of Mount Lu. When Su says that he is "amidst the
very mountain itself," the idea is that he is observing the physical features

of the mountain *as he moves through it.* It is precisely this quality of an ever-shifting perspective, characterized by the experience of motion through space toward an identifiable destination, that most effectively defines Chinese travel writing from the imperial era.

The idea of preparing a written record of notable events in the order in which they occurred can of course be traced back to Sima Qian's *Historical Records.* But later, as we have seen, the account, or *ji,* form expanded to treat other types of "notable events," including the experiences associated with travel and sightseeing. A key implication that results from the *youji* prototypes and exemplars identified and discussed throughout this book is that Chinese travel literature reveals an overwhelming concern with experience; specifically, human interaction with the things and events (*wu*) observed in the physical world during periods of movement. The purpose of these trips, as we have seen, is usually either aesthetic and social, such as a trip with friends to, and appreciation of, a lovely landscape; or reportorial, such as a tour through, and description of, a prominent landmark or historical-literary heritage site. Direct, real-life experience, then, is the basic stuff of all Chinese travel literature.

Of course, no two writers ever view the external world in precisely the same way, so how Chinese authors experience and describe landscapes, ancient sites, snowy lakes, or even karst caverns can, and did, vary considerably. For this reason, there is great diversity in the way *youji* authors recount their experiences. Some, like Liu Zongyuan and Zhang Dai, followed a practice of what the late Qing dynasty and early Republican-era scholar Wang Guowei described as "observing the physical world (or nature) through the self" (*yiwo guanwu*).[2] Others, like Fan Chengda and Xu Xiake, followed a different approach, one that chords well with what the Northern Song philosopher Shao Yong (1012–77) described as "observing the physical world [nature] by means of the physical world" (*yiwu guanwu*; that is, through its own principles).[3] The main distinction between these preferences is that with the former, the author uses the experience of sightseeing and landscape observation to voice personal inner concerns or even conflicts (Liu) or simply to poke fun at himself through a brief self-portrait (Zhang). The second approach, prominent in the Southern Song river diaries and the scholarly-commentarial and scientific-investigatory travel writing of the Ming, puts much less emphasis on the role of "self" and instead focuses on description, analysis, and verification of what is observed during the journey. The preference for this second approach, especially during the period from the Southern Song to the Ming, and later in the Qing, reflects the idea that empirical inquiry—through a process of observing, recording, and ultimately "classifying the things in the physical world" (*gewu*)—functions as part of an ongoing process of self-cultivation and identity building. This idea of gaining knowledge of the world through the experience of travel, which can help a young scholar prepare for entry into government service, can also be traced back to Sima Qian, who journeyed extensively in his youth and later credited those experiences with helping him secure an official post in the imperial palace.[4] Without a doubt, many young men—especially during the Ming and Qing periods—who hoped to one day gain entry into government service also undertook similar tours for the same purpose.

Chinese travel writing is also distinguished by its informal nature as a literary form. Aside from the basic requirements of the genre (narration of a journey to a real place, description of a specific location, author reaction), *youji* is otherwise a highly malleable form of writing. This quality gives authors great flexibility in how they write about travel experiences and especially the kind of language they use to describe their journeys, to relate what they heard and saw, and to express how it might have affected them. Thus, some writers, like Yuan Jie, compose in a highly literary style, while others, like Lu You, prefer reportorial language. Still others, like Song Lian, infuse their *youji* with historical and geographical references designed to confirm or reject traditional accounts about heritage sites like Bell Mountain. And some traveler-writers, like Wang Shixing and Xu Xiake, even adapt the genre to fit an entirely new form of travel writing: "scientific-investigatory" *youji*. Few prose genres from the imperial period in China, if any, provided more independence to serve an author's personal and literary needs. It is precisely this freedom that endows Chinese travel literature with its dynamic quality.

Another result of this expressive freedom is that *youji* often reveals an individual writer's distinct sensibility. Among the many writers in this study, Liu Zongyuan, Su Shi, and Zhang Dai are three prominent examples. Each commanded a signature style in their travel writing that reveals much about themselves and the perspectives they had on the difficulties and challenges of the times and circumstances under which they were forced to live (political exile, dynastic change, personal misfortune, and so on). Chinese travel literature, then, which presents factual accounts in an organized temporal format told by a first-person narrator, is in fact an important form of *autobiography*. Xuanzang's record of his trip to India is just one example of how a *youji* text can reveal informative and revealing details about the life of a historical figure told from his own perspective. At the same time, however, we must keep in mind that *youji* also served an important utilitarian purpose; namely, to function as a literary medium for the acquisition and dissemination of knowledge about places that many readers could probably never personally visit. As we saw in chapter 5, during the mid- and late Ming, increased opportunities for travel, coupled with heightened literati interest in tourism, led to increased production and distribution of numerous kinds of texts relating to place, including individual *youji* works, albums, and anthologies of travel accounts about visits to famous places (this trend continued later in the Qing). The practical purpose of these works was to satisfy public demand for firsthand, reliable information on what sightseers could expect to find at a given sightseeing destination.

During the Ming dynasty, the phrase "to know everything about the empire [or the world] without ever leaving home" (*bu chumen er zhi Tianxia shi*) was used to describe those who were admired and respected for the vast erudition they accumulated simply by remaining at home and reading great volumes of books. I am sure that none of the travel writers discussed in this book would take issue with the idea that beneficial knowledge can be gained through serious study. At the same time, however, I am also confident that they would unanimously agree with Dr. Johnson's exhortation, quoted in the epigraph, concerning the great benefit of travel: rather than sitting around at home and imagining what the outside is like, get out, travel, and thereby gain experience and knowledge that can expand your thinking and "regulate" your ideas about what the world is really like. Ultimately, then, Chinese travel literature can be viewed as serving two very diverse purposes: to provide descriptive accounts to armchair travelers who do not, or cannot, undertake journeys themselves; and to inspire those who have the means to get out of the house and "instead of thinking of how things may be, see them as they are."

NOTES

Introduction

Epigraph: *Hanshu*, 69.2975.

1 *Li Bai ji jiaozhu*, 14.863.

2 *Cihai*, 2:2239. Earlier editions of the *Cihai* and the *Ciyuan* (Origins of words; this is another comprehensive and authoritative Chinese-Chinese dictionary) did not include a definition of *youji*.

3 Some scholars and critics have gone to great lengths to either identify "the very first" occurrence of the term *youji* in ancient Chinese letters or have sought to identify "the very first" *youji* work and thereby pinpoint the precise textual source of the genre. Some of these identifications are discussed in chapter 2.

4 *Shuowen jiezi*, 140xia.

5 For additional information on these sorts of mind travels, see Mei and Yu, *Zhongguo youji wenxue shi*, especially 3–7.

6 Ward, *Xu Xiake*, 98.

7 Although the preface and table of contents of Chen's anthology are extant, the contents have been lost. Many of the texts listed in its table of contents, however, have been preserved in other collections.

8 Wujiao (literally, "corner of a house") appears to be the name of a mountain, but I have not been able to determine its location.

9 These are two well-known verses in the *Songs of Chu* (Chuci), China's second oldest anthology of poetry.

10 The Yi is a famous waterway in Shandong.

11 "Zhang" refers to Zhang Shi (1133–80), a leading intellectual of the Southern Song. When his father died in 1164, Zhang buried him at the foot of Mount Heng (Hengshan) in Hunan and subsequently lived there in mourning. The famous neo-Confucian scholar Zhu Xi (1130–1200) supposedly visited Zhang Shi at Mount Heng in 1167 and convinced him to return to official life.

12 Chen Renyu's preface is preserved in Tao Zongyi's (fl. 1360–68) *Compendium of Travels: The Continuation Volume*, 7 (reprint pagination). See fig. I.1.

13 Ma Dibo's account is translated in Strassberg, *Inscribed Landscapes*, 59–62. Strassberg (58–59) notes that this work "appears to be the earliest extant narrative of a journey told in the first person." He is correct.

14 Tao Yuanming is one such example. In addition to his biography, Chen Renyu also includes Tao's famous "Account of the Peach Blossom Spring" (Taohua Yuan ji), which tells the story of a fisherman's discovery of a lost paradise. Since this is an imaginary work, it seems that Chen was not averse to including fictional travel literature in his collection (or perhaps he thought that such a place once existed?). As for Sima Guang's "Account of the Garden of Solitary Delight," Chen Renyu probably included it because it is well known and written in the *ji*, or account, form, as was much travel-related literature in China during the Tang and thereafter. I shall have more to say on this and related matters in chapters 2 and 3.

15 Mei and Yu, *Zhongguo youji wenxue shi*, 63. Li Daoyuan (*ca.* 469–527) is the author of the *Commentary on the Waterways Treatise* (Shuijing zhu). His prose style is discussed in chapter 1.

16 Here I refer mainly to the following publications: "Some Preliminary Remarks on the Travel Records of the Song Dynasty (960–1279)"; the entry on "*Yu-chi wen-hsüeh*" in *The Indiana Companion to Traditional Chinese Literature*, 936–39; and the entry on "Travel Literature" in Mair, *The Columbia History of Chinese Literature*, 555–59.

17 Frye, *Anatomy of Criticism*, 247–48.

18 "Traditional approach" here refers to the so-called "structuralist" methodology, in which diverse types writing—the sonnet and the novel, for instance, each with discernible structural characteristics—are classified and studied as components of a larger taxonomic system of literary texts.

19 Derrida's ideas that aim to deconstruct traditional genre theory can be found in his seminal essay "La Loi du genre."

20 Moessner, "Genre, Text Type, Style," 131.

21 De Geest and van Gorp, "Literary Genres," 33–50.

22 Ibid., 4.

23 Ibid., 39–40.

24 The English term "prose," from the Latin *prosa*, meaning "direct" (speech), is difficult to define precisely as a form of writing. This is especially the case in the history of prose travel literature in China, in which the content and style changes over time. I consider "prose" as a form of what Chinese literary historians call *sanwen*, or "relaxed writing," as opposed to *yunwen* ("rhymed writing") and *pianwen* ("parallel-prose writing"). "Relaxed" in this context refers to a language style that is loose and irregular as opposed to one that is restricted and standardized by a set of rules governing grammatical structure, tonal euphony, rhyme, and embellished diction.

25 The definition of travel literature offered here is heavily indebted to the *Cihai* gloss cited and discussed earlier. Essentially, I have fine-tuned the *Cihai* definition to serve my own critical purposes. I have also drawn on views expressed in some of my earlier publications (see the bibliography) and on some recent book-length studies of *youji* published in China, especially Mei and Yu's *Zhongguo youji wenxue shi*.

26 One notable exception to this statement is Qing dynasty ethnographic accounts of various non-Chinese and unfamiliar borderland places and peoples, which have been studied in detail by Laura Hostetler in her book *Qing Colonial Enterprise*.

27 Several useful studies have been published on how Qing dynasty imperialist expansion affected travel writing. See, for instance, Xiaofei Tian, *Visionary Journeys*, and Emma J. Teng, *Taiwan's Imagined Geographies*.

28 Tian, *Visionary Journeys*, 3.

29 Cong Ellen Zhang, in her seminal study about travel and culture in the Song dynasty, discusses in some detail how the cave became a literary pilgrimage site for numerous generations of traveling literati. See her *Transformative Journeys*, 169–75.

30 Illustrations and drawings were not used in Chinese travel literature until the Ming dynasty. I shall have more to say about this development in chapter 4.

31 These various ideas are outlined in Yu Kwang-chung's essay "Zhongguo shanshui youji de zhixing," 23–40.

32 The terms "place" and "space" as they relate to traditional *youji* in China are different from the complicated, theoretical concerns of many modern geographers and cultural anthropologists. My own take on these concepts in their Chinese travel literature context is that "place" refers to an environmental setting with identifiable traits, such as a distinguishing name, special topographical or meteorological features, unique buildings, monuments, and/or specific historical, cultural, and literary associations. A country inn in New Jersey bearing a sign saying "George Washington slept here," then, is a "place." One key assumption of this study is that traditionally, the Chinese attached cultural memory and value to places—more to some than to others. In the context of traditional Chinese travel literature, "space" is at once a larger construct with area and volume, through which movement occurs toward a place. So, works classified in this study as *youji* are literary accounts of movement—brief or extended—through space toward a specific destination.

1. Harbingers in the Six Dynasties

Epigraph: Entry on *Xu Xiake youji* (Travel accounts of Xu Xiake), in *Siku quanshu zongmu tiyao*, 2:1539.

1 "Stone Tablet" refers to Stone Tablet Mountain (Jieshi Shan), located along the coast of modern Hebei.

2 Cao Cao, *Cao Cao ji*, 10–11.

3 China historians refer to the period from the fall of the Han dynasty in 220 to the Sui reunification of China in 581 by a host of different names. The three most common designations are "Six Dynasties," "Period of Disunion," and "Early Medieval Period." Hereafter, I will consistently use "Six Dynasties," except when a more precise reference is necessary.

4 See Holzman, *Landscape Appreciation in Ancient and Early Medieval China*, especially 1–24 and 121–54.

5 The Chinese understanding of why landscape assumed a new role and took on new meanings during the Six Dynasties can be summarized as follows: as a result of a sudden revolution in taste against the "reigning Daoist verse" (*xuanyan*) of the period—sometimes called "the poetry of metaphysical words" or "the poetry of arcane discourse"—which stressed, among other things, discursive reasoning,

philosophical argument, metaphysical language, and allusions to Zhuangzi and the *Canon of the Way and Its Power* (Daode jing), "nature poetry" suddenly emerged in the Six Dynasties and produced China's first great "nature poet," Xie Lingyun (385–433).

There is now consensus in the field that the idea of a "sudden emergence" of "nature poetry" or "landscape verse" in China during the Six Dynasties is inaccurate. Many scholars in recent decades have challenged this traditional reading and have come up with alternate explanations. These new understandings about the origins of "nature poetry" in China also have their limitations in that they depend entirely upon how one defines that term. J. D. Frodsham, for instance, almost sixty years ago argued that "nature poetry" is "verse inspired by a mystic philosophy which sees all natural phenomena as symbols charged with a mysterious and cathartic power." Furthermore, although he does regard Xie Lingyun as a "nature poet," he sees Xie's verse as the culmination of a process that began in "Daoist (*xuanyan*) poetry" centuries earlier (see Frodsham, "The Origins of Chinese Nature Poetry").

In his *Murmuring Stream*, however, published later in 1967, Frodsham broadens his definition of "nature poetry" considerably, saying it is "that genre which uses landscape, whether majestically rugged or charmingly rustic, as a means of conveying ethical principles." See his *The Murmuring Stream*, 1:88.

Kang I-sun Chang, on the other hand, sees the political instability of the Six Dynasties sparking poetic inspiration and creativity. Moreover, she observes "a growing concern (in poetry) with the splendors of the physical world in general, obviously a reflection of the poet's urge to enlarge his 'self' into a broader focus. Poetry may continue to be primarily an expression of internal feelings, but the poetic self is externalized to see nature, often a detailed view of it, as a major part of his lyrical domain. The poet's great compulsion to orient, to reorient, himself in the external world brings about a new breadth of scope in poetic creation: at one end of the spectrum stands an individualized 'expression' of feelings, and at the other end the visual 'description' of natural phenomena." Chang, *Six Dynasties Poetry*, xii.

For our purposes, what is most important is that by the fourth century CE, the natural world became part of the poet's "lyrical domain" in a way that it had never functioned before, and this concern also found expression in other types of writing, including prose. Landscape could be appreciated simply for its physical beauty and not just because it had some religious or "mysterious" quality.

6   Although depiction of landscape in Chinese pictorial art certainly predates the Six Dynasties, there is some textual evidence that suggests that artists actively painted and valued landscape painting during that era. For more information on Chinese landscape painting during the Han and Six Dynasties, see Soper, "Early Chinese Landscape Painting," and Michael Sullivan, *The Birth of Landscape Painting in China*, especially 114–27. The surviving titles of several Six Dynasties paintings and scrolls indicate that they were executed specifically to illustrate lyric poems and especially Han rhapsodies on capitals and hunting parks, royal progresses, as well as legendary figures and stories associated with famous mountains, such as Mount Lu (Lushan) in Jiangxi. Sullivan (124) cites a painting intended to accompany a

poem, titled *Wandering by a Clear Pool* (You Qingchi tu). This would appear to be a pictorial representation that describes a journey (*you*) of some sort.

7   Knechtges, *Selections of Refined Literature*, 1:329.

8   Xie Lingyuan, *Xie Lingyun ji jiaozhu*, 318–19.

9   Possible alternate translation for this line: "Rose stone (*meigui*) and cyan jade (*bilin*)."

10 Knechtges, *Selections of Refined Literature*, 2:91. "Mr. He's jewel" refers to a crude or uncarved block of jade (*puyu*) that was once discovered by one "Mr. He" (Heshi) in the mountains of Chu. Later, when the matrix was cut and polished, a precious gem emerged.

11 Rhapsodies (fifty-five works in all) comprise the first nineteen chapters of the *Literary Selections*. Complete and annotated English translations of these texts are provided in the first three volumes of Knechtges's *Selections of Refined Literature*.

12 I use the word "celebratory" because the main purpose of such works was to praise—in the highest terms possible—the glorious benefits and extravagant nature of imperial rule.

13 Xiao Tong also includes twenty-three *youlan*, or "sightseeing poems," and thirty-six "travel" (*xinglü*) verses, all written in the *shi*, or lyric, form.

14 The one exception, found among the three "sightseeing" rhapsodies, is Sun Chuo's (*ca.* 314– *ca.* 371) "Rhapsody on Roaming in the Tiantai Mountains" (You Tiantai Shan fu). Although his *fu* in places does describe the physical attributes of the Tiantai Mountains in Zhejiang, in the preface to his rhapsody, Sun makes it clear that his journey is imaginary, taking place only in his mind. Thus, in his "ascent," Sun Chuo imagines himself roaming (*you*) in the company of Buddhist deities and Daoist gods. In this regard, his composition is related to a type of *shi* poetry written during the Six Dynasties and later called *youxian*, or "roaming with immortals." For additional information on *youxian* poetry and how Sun Chuo's rhapsody relates to this tradition, see Kirvova, *Roaming into the Beyond*, especially 227–41. For a complete translation of Sun Chuo's *fu*, see Mather, "The Mystical Ascent of the T'ian-tai Mountains"; Watson, *Chinese Rhyme-Prose*, 80–85; and *Selections of Refined Literature*, 2:243–53. It seems, then, that the compiler of the *Wenxuan* did not distinguish between literary works that chronicle real journeys and those based on spiritual inspiration. It should also be mentioned that, with just a few exceptions, most of the so-called travel works found in the second-century poetry anthology, *Chuci*, also describe imaginary ascents of sacred mountains or fantastic flights to mystical realms inhabited by gods or extraterrestrial creatures. As Xiaofei Tian demonstrates in her *Visionary Journeys*, especially in chapter 1, "Seeing with the Mind's Eye," study of imaginary journeys is certainly a worthwhile and fruitful area for research. My view, however, is that the structure, purpose, and language modes used in imaginary literary journeys are quite different from those found in *youji* accounts to real places in real time. As mentioned in the introduction, the focus in this study is the latter variety.

15 The rhapsodies by Liu Xin and Lu Ji mentioned here are not included in the *Literary Selections* but can be found in Zhang Qiao (*jinshi* 1213), *Guwen yuan*, 5.37–40, and *Quan Shanggu*, 2:96.2010, respectively.

16 *Quan Shanggu*, 2:96.2010.

17   Knechtges, *Selections of Refined Literature*, 2:197.

18   That is, verbs that take you from one place to another: walk, run, swim, fly, and so on. Cf. Ward, who calls them "active verbs" (*Xu Xiake*, 111–12).

19   "Action verbs" are like "motion verbs" in that they relate what the subject is doing, but they do not move the physical action from one place to another. In the last excerpt from Pan Yue's "Rhapsody on a Distant Western Journey," "turn my back" (*bei*) and "observe" (*guan*) would be examples of "action verbs"; "float" (*fu*) and "leading on" (*dao*), however, are "motion verbs." Both varieties are common in Chinese travel literature.

20   What I have described here as "motion" or "action" verbs are sometimes called "verse (or line) eyes" (*juyan* or *juzhong yan*) in Chinese. K'ang I-Sun Chang has observed that they are common in the landscape poetry of Xie Lingyun, especially in his parallel verse couplets that are "action oriented," and that "they connect or give vigor to the noun segments of the line" ("Description of Landscape," 125). I agree with this observation, but I would just add that in travel writing, the added "vigor" is designed to suggest a sense of movement to the journey being described.

21   Knechtges, *Selections of Refined Literature*, 2:181, note.

22   In a single nighttime attack at Xin'an in 201 BCE, Xiang Yu supposedly massacred two hundred thousand Qin soldiers. See *Shiji*, 7.310.

23   Knechtges, *Selections of Refined Literature*, 2:191. "Lord Liu" refers to Liu Bang (256–195 BCE), founder of the Han dynasty.

24   Ibid., 2:237.

25   *The Limited Views Collection*, 4.313. "Limited Views" is Ronald Egan's translation of the title of Qian Zhongshu's famous collection of essays. See Egan's *Qian Zhongshu, Limited Views*.

26   Sima Qian was castrated because he became embroiled in court politics and in the process offended a relative of the emperor. For additional details and a fascinating, in-depth study of Sima Qian's letter to Ren An, see Stephan Durrant et al., *The Letter to Ren An & Sima Qian's Legacy*.

27   This collection, abbreviated in my notes as "*Quan Shanggu*," is the most complete and authoritative assembly of prose works that predate the Tang dynasty. Altogether, it comprises 746 chapters and includes the works of almost 3,500 authors.

28   A good example is a pair of letters written by Cao Pi (187–226) to his friend Wu Zhi (178–230), in which Cao nostalgically recalls the good times they once shared together while also lamenting their long separation. See *Cao Pi ji jiaozhu*, 258; also in *Wenxuan*, 42.924–26 and *Quan Shanggu*, 2:7.1089. For a translation, see Burton Watson, "Cao Pi: Two Letters to Wu Zhi."

29   Richter, *Letters and Epistolary Culture*, 8–9.

30   Details of the parallel-prose style are discussed later in this chapter.

31   It should be mentioned here that most Six Dynasties authors of letters preferred relaxed prose rather than parallel prose. But anthology compilers seem to have overwhelmingly favored works in the parallel-prose form, perhaps because they thought it better reflected reader taste.

32 Su, "An Annotated English Translation of Bao Zhao's 'Letter,'" 20 (with changes). For the original text of the letter see Bao Canjun, *Bao Canjun jizhu*, 2.36–41.

33 Su, "An Annotated English Translation of Bao Zhao's 'Letter,'" 20–21.

34 Ibid., 21 (with changes).

35 Ibid., 22.

36 Ibid., 20–24. There is also a translation of Bao Zhao's letter in Strassberg, 74–76. I have chosen to use Su's version because it seems to better reflect Bao's parallel-prose style.

37 The idea here is that if scholar-officials, always busy managing matters of state, glanced just once at this beautiful scenic environment, they would forget all about returning to their government posts.

38 *Quan Shanggu*, 4:59.3305–06. In some collections, this work is titled "Letter to Song Yuansi" (Yu Song Yuansi shu). In making my translation here, I have benefitted from consulting Richard E. Strassberg's translation in *Inscribed Landscapes*, 31–32, and Ye Yang's translation of Wu Jun's letter in Luo Yuming, *A Concise History of Chinese Literature*, 225–26. The tripartite structure of most personal letters—opening salutation, main body, and closing—was followed in ancient China's epistolary culture, but oftentimes, later editors would excise the opening and closing sections (this apparently happened in the case of Wu Jun's letter), while some modern translators regrettably choose to ignore them.

39 I borrow this phrase from Cohen's *Grammar Notes for Introductory Classical Chinese*, 16.

40 For an English rendition of this important work, see Rickett, *Wang Kuo-wei's Jen-chien Tz'u-hua*. On the concept of *jing* (scene) as it relates to *qing* (emotion), see especially Rickett's comments on 23–31.

41 See her "Naturalness in Xie Lingyun's Poetic Works," 361. See also Chang, "Description of Landscape in Early Six Dynasties Poetry," 111, who adds that "mountains and water" imagery in the early Six Dynasties "began to serve as the basis of parallelism that was reflected to be the symmetry perceived in nature."

42 Cao Daoheng, "Guanyu Wei Jin Nanbeichao de pianwen he sanwen," 31.

43 James Robert Hightower distinguishes between three categories of parallelism: metrical, grammatical, and phonic. The example here is grammatical, the most basic type. For additional information, see Hightower's "Some Characteristics of Parallel Prose."

44 Other examples include Tao Hongjing's (456–536) "Letter in Reply to Chamberlain of Central Documents Xie" (Da Xie Zhongshu shu), Wu Jun's "Letter to Gu Zhang" (Yu Gu Zhang shu), and Zu Hongxun's (d. early 550s) "Letter to Yang Xiuzhi" (Yu Yang Xiuzhi shu). The last-mentioned work is translated in my *On the Road in Twelve Century China*, 13.

45 Wang Liqun, *Zhongguo gudai shanshui youji yanjiu*, 49.

46 The "Lanting" preface is translated in Strassberg, *Inscribed Landscapes*, 65–66. Although traditionally attributed to Wang Xizhi, authorship remains a contentious topic among China scholars.

47 The meaning of this line is unclear. Shi Chong might be referring to the various entertainments and activities provided for his guests, which required them to leave their carriage and then reboard it, thus causing them to "frequently change seats."

48 *Quan Shanggu*, 2:1651. The "Lanting" preface is modeled in style and content directly after this text. In making my translation, I have benefitted from consulting the translations of Hellmut Wilhelm, "Shih Ch'ung and His Chin-ku-yüan," and Richard Mather, "Preface to the Golden Valley Poems."

49 The distinction between parallel prose and relaxed or "free" prose is not finite. The main difference is that parallel prose generally favors parallel lines (*duiju*) and relaxed prose does not. This difference was already evident during the Wei-Jin period.

50 There is disagreement among scholars regarding the year mentioned in the first line of Tao Yuanming's preface. Some say it refers to the year 401, others argue it should be 414.

51 Tiered Citadel was in the northern section of Mount Lu; Slanted Creek was probably situated at the foot of that mountain.

52 "South Mountain" (Nanfu) is another name for Mount Lu.

53 "Numinous Mountain" refers to Mount Kunlun (Kunlun Shan), an important peak in Chinese mythology where immortals were said to dwell. Tao Yuanming clearly liked the name "Tiered Citadel," and so he thought of Kunlun because it too supposedly had a peak of the same name.

54 *Tao Yuanming shiwen huiping*, 60. I have benefited from consulting Xiaofei Tian's translation of this preface in her *Tao Yuanming & Manuscript Culture*, 143, though in places our reading of the original text is different.

55 Reading *changran*, "chagrined" or "dissatisfied," in this line to mean that Huiyuan and his traveling companions had previously (for some unstated reason) not been able to go sightseeing at Stone Gate. Now, however, they are in "heightened spirits" (*zengxing*) because they are finally on their way there. This reading is based on a gloss in Ni Qixin et al., *Zhongguo gudai youji xuan*, 10n20. Cf. Strassberg's translation: "our uncertainty only increased our sense of rapture" (*Inscribed Landscapes*, 68).

56 *Quan Shanggu*, 3:2437. This is only a partial translation. For a complete English rendition of Huiyuan's preface, including the poem that follows it, see Strassberg, 68–71.

57 Tian, *Visionary Journeys*, 3.

58 *Shuowen jiezi*, 53xia. The comments on *ji* that follow on the pages below draw heavily on He Li, *Tangdai jiti wen yanjiu*, especially 5–8.

59 That is, pairs of characters that are phonetically and graphically similar, the meanings of which are related in some way. For example, *lao* 老 and *kao* 考 are visually similar and both mean "advanced in years" or "old." Such characters are also called "derived cognates."

60 *Shuowen jiezi zhu*, 3.18shang. For more details on the etymology of the word *ji*, see He Li, *Tangdai jiti wen yanjiu*, 5–8. He distinguishes three meanings of *ji* that

evolved over time: to commit something to memory; to make a written account of something; and to make a written account of something and then explain or interpret it. In this study, our main concern is meaning 2; that is, *ji* that are written and designed to be read.

61 Sima Qian, in his "Suoyin" commentary to the *Historical Records*, explains the genre of history writing known as *benji*, usually translated as "basic annals," as follows: "*Ji* means 'to make an account.' You trace to the basis of an event and then make an account of it. Thus, they are called 'basic annals'" (*Shiji*, 1.1). Note: the graph *ji* 紀 originally referred to the action of separating silk filaments or threads. The idea of "distinguishing selected parts from a whole" is fundamental to the basic meaning of both *ji* 紀 and *ji* 記, and this explains why the two words, by about the end of the Han, became synonyms meaning "to make an account." For additional information on the etymological relationship between these two graphs, see the glosses and examples in Wang, *Guci bian*, 708–09.

62 It should also be mentioned that another notable work dating from the Six Dynasties, Liu Xie's *The Literary Mind and Carving of Dragons* (Wenxin diaolong), also has much to say about literary genres, but nowhere does it identify *ji* as an independent form of prose.

63 The translations provided for the various prose forms in the *Literary Selections* listed here are those of David R. Knechtges. See his *Selections of Refined Literature*, 1:21.

64 The *ji* chapters in the *Choice Blossoms* collection are discussed in chapter 2.

65 This is confirmed by the extensive list of works with *ji* in their title listed in the "Canonical and Other Texts" (Jingji) bibliography included in the dynastic history of the Sui (581–618). See *Suishu*, especially 33.982–87. See also Wang, *Zhongguo gudai shanshui youji yanjiu*, especially 64–67.

66 The famous prose stylist Ren Fang (460–508) once compiled a collection with this very title, which included *diji* works by 84 authors in 252 *juan*. Unfortunately, this text was lost during the Song dynasty.

67 There are two complete translations of this work available in English: Jenner, *Memories of Loyang,* and Wang, *An Account of Buddhist Monasteries in Lo-yang.*

68 Although numerous literary historians and critics have identified Tao Yuanming's text as a *ji* and as an important and influential work in the history of traditional travel Chinese literature, it is neither. Despite the presence of the word *ji* in the usual title, it is a preface to a poem (I suspect that using *ji* rather than *xu* in the preface title is probably the work of some later editor). I prefer to not regard this work as related to *youji* because a sizeable portion of its excursion component appears to be imaginative rather than an account based on a real journey to a real place. Also, no later *youji* text that I know of reveals having been influenced by Tao Yuanming's "Account." For those interested, a good English translation is available in Birch, *Anthology of Chinese Literature*, 167–68.

Scholarship in Chinese on Tao Yuanming's famous account is summarized well in Chen Fei's *Zhongguo gudai sanwen yanjiu*, 189–93. Chen (190) says that the "Account of the Peach Blossom Spring" was "relatively influential" on the development of *youji* during the Wei-Jin period, but he fails to demonstrate how this influence is discernable in the works of other writers.

69 This work is lost, but portions of it are preserved in several texts. See, for instance, Wang, *Shuijing zhu*, 34.1074. The loss of this work is truly lamentable, because we know that Yuan Shansong's descriptive style had a major influence on Li Daoyuan, author of the *Commentary on the Waterways Treatise* (discussed in the next section below).

70 Quoted in *Shuijing zhu jiaozheng*, 34.7b–8a. My understanding and translation of the last line in this passage differs substantially from that of Strassberg in *Inscribed Landscapes*, 90. The lines cited here are either quoted from or paraphrase a passage in Yuan's "Yidu ji" (see below). Yidu is the name of a commandery (*jun*) on the Great River not far from Shaman Mountain (Wushan) and visually is one of the most spectacular sites in the region. Yuan Shansong once served as Governor (Taishou) of Yidu and presumably wrote the "Yidu ji" while serving in office there.

71 He Li, "Tangdai jiti wen yanjiu," 17–20.

72 Strassberg, *Inscribed Landscapes*, 59.

73 The original text for Ma Dibo's account is preserved in the *Hou Hanshu* chapter on sacrifices "Jisi zhi," 7shang.3166–67. Here I quote the translation by Strassberg in *Inscribed Landscapes*, 59.

74 "Nine Rivers" refers to what is now the Gan River (Ganjiang) and its eight major tributaries.

75 *Lushan lueji*, 1a–b. In making my translation I have benefitted from the notes in Zhou and Zhao, *Lushan youji xuan*, 3.

76 The textual sources of the surviving portions of the *You mingshan zhi* are discussed in Zhao Shugong, "Xie Lingyun *You mingshan zhi* bianming yu yiwen," 175–77.

77 In *Xie Lingyun ji jiaozhu*, 390–407. The translations that follow of Xie Lingyun's "Notes" are based on this text.

78 Ibid., 398n1.

79 Ibid., 390. The entire preface is translated in Mather, "The Landscape Buddhism," 64, and in Strassberg, 30.

80 Stone Chamber Mountain is located near modern Yongjia *xian*, Zhejiang. Traditionally, it was considered a "Daoist mountain" because of its identification as one of the "blessed sites" (*fudi*) in Daoism.

81 The Chinese name *huangjing* (literally, "yellow abstract") probably refers to *huangzhi*, or "yellow polypore." This is a plant whose pliable stalk was used to make an herb that some people thought could extend human life.

82 Spring Mountain is also known as Pure Source Mountain (Qingyuan shan), and is in Quanzhou, Fujian.

83 The line "With just one person guarding the island peak, a thousand men could not take it" is quoted from Zhu's biography in the *Hanshu* (referred to here as *Hanshi*), 64shang.2792.

84 New Creek was in what is now Dongqing *xian*, Zhejiang. Purple Creek was in Lin'an *xian*, outside of modern Hangzhou.

85 This tower was situated in Shining *xian*.

86 "Changjiang" at the close of this entry does not refer to the Great River but rather the Puyang Jiang in Zhejiang, also known today as the Cao'e jiang (*Xie Lingyun ji jiaozhu*), 405n38.

87 Chang, *Six Dynasties Poetry*, 49.

88 The inspiration for Kang's identification seems to be the preface to the *Lidai youji xuan*, 3, which also identifies Xie as the "progenitor" (*shizu*) of the "landscape travel account."

89 Although Faxian's account is usually referred as the *Foguo ji*, or *Accounts of the Buddhist Kingdoms*, like many works dating from Six Dynasties, it is also known by several alternate titles. For instance, some editors call it *Biography of the Eminent Monk Faxian* (Gaoseng Faxian zhuan) or simply *Biography of Faxian* (Faxian zhuan). On these and other titles by which the text was alternately known, see *Faxian zhuan jiaozhu*, 5–7. The title *Foguo ji* appears first in the bibliographic chapter of the *Suishu* (completed in 636 CE) but was not used consistently in collectania (*congshu*) until the Ming dynasty. There are numerous translations of Faxian's account available in English, in various European languages, and in Japanese. Probably the most useful and available among the English renditions is James Legge's *A Record of Buddhistic Kingdoms*. The most detailed scholarly version (with copious notes) is Max Deeg, *Das Gaoseng-Faxian-Zhuan als religionsgeschichtliche Quelle*.

90 Boulton, "Early Chinese Buddhist Travel Accounts as a Literary Genre," 69.

91 This phrase comes from Tian, *Visionary Journeys*, 3. Tian's reading of Faxian's text is centered on a discussion (96ff) of what she calls the "hell / paradise paradigm."

92 *Faxian zhuan jiaozhu*, 177; Legge, *A Record of Buddhistic Kingdoms*, 116.

93 Translation adapted from Legge, *A Record of Buddhistic Kingdoms*, 12 (with changes).

94 The term "multilingual interpreters" (*jiuyi*; sometimes rendered as *chong jiuyi*) was used to describe foreign (that is, non-Chinese) visitors whose speech needed to be translated numerous times before it could be understood in Chinese. Faxian's use of the term here seems to mean "numerous." In other words, according to numerous accounts (*ji*), neither Zhang Qian nor Gan Ying got as far as the Indus River in their travels. Gan Ying is a Han dynasty military ambassador who was supposedly dispatched to Rome in 97 CE but never reached his destination. He may have gotten as far as the Black Sea, but details about his journey are sketchy. On Zhang Qian, see text below.

95 Legge, *A Record of Buddhistic Kingdoms*, 26.

96 Ibid., 26–27 (with changes).

97 While describing his journey, Faxian never narrates in the first person; instead, he always remains in the background and only on a few rare occasions expresses emotion. He did so because the purpose of his *ji* is to report on the details of his journey.

98 Boulton, "Early Chinese Buddhist Travel Accounts," 387–88. Boulton (381) speculates that this plain style of prose is the result of years spent studying and translating Buddhist scriptures into Chinese, and this influenced both the content and style of Faxian's *Accounts*.

99 *Shiji*, 123.3808; here I use Burton Watson's translation in *Records of the Grand Historian of China*, 2:266, with some minor changes.

100 Knechtges and Chang, *Ancient and Early Medieval Chinese Literature: A Reference Guide*, 1:481.

101 This gorge is more commonly known as Qutang Gorge (Qutang Xia).

102 *Shujing zhu jiaozheng*, 33.777.

103 "Town" (*xian*) here refers to Yong'an (Yong'an *xian*), also known as White Emperor City (Baidi Cheng). It was located high on a hill at the starting point of the Three Gorges.

104 *Shuijing zhu jiaozheng*, 33.777–78. Chang Qu, mentioned at the end of this passage, is the author of the fourth-century geographical treatise *Chronicle of the Land South of Mount Hua* (Huayang guo zhi). The quotation ascribed to him here is presumably cited from this work, but it does not appear in modern editions (at least those available to me). Zuo Si's "Rhapsody on the Shu Capital," however, is preserved in *Wenxuan*, 4.82–92. It is translated in Knechtges, *Selections of Refined Literature*, 1.341–71. The line referenced by Li Daoyuan reads, "Hidden dragons lie coiled in the marshes; / Responding to the sounding drum, they cause rain to fall." *Wenxuan*, 4.85; Knechtges, *Selections of Refined Literature*, 1:349.

105 *Shuijing zhu jiaozheng*, 33.778. The reason that gibbons and ferret-badgers avoided living on the north bank of the Three Gorges is unclear.

106 Ibid., 34.790.

107 Mei and Yu, *Zhongguo youji wenxue shi*, 59.

108 While it is undeniable that the *Shuijing zhu* is written for the most part in relaxed prose, in his literary descriptions of landscape, Li Daoyuan on occasion turns to the parallel-prose style. For instance, in his commentary on the Su River (Sushui) and Salt Road Mountain (Yandao Shan), he writes, "To its west are rocky cliffs one thousand *xun* high; to its east, then, Pan Stream (Panxi) ten thousand *ren* deep. Around flat-top mountain ranges, cloud forms whirl; above marvelous peaks roseate clouds stir; by solitary treetops a florescence emerges. Shade blankets the assembled mountains: blue-green cypresses shade the peaks, while clear springs consecrate their summits" (*Shuijing zhu jiaozheng*, 6.171).

109 It is impossible to determine whether Li Daoyuan's description of the Three Gorges is based on his firsthand experiences or on information gathered from earlier written sources. I suspect it is a combination of the two.

110 Two useful studies of pre-Song dynasty manuscript culture are Tian, *Tao Yuanming & Manuscript Culture*; and Nugent, *Manifest in Words, Written on Paper*.

111 Frye, *Anatomy of Criticism*, 247–48.

112 De Geest and van Gorp, "Literary Genres," 40.

113 Ibid., 41–42: "It is not at all uncommon for a text to share only a few characteristics with the prototypical generic model while it is still recognized as a genuine though rather atypical member of the genre category, even if it bears more resemblances to another neighboring category."

2. Articulation in the Tang

Epigraph: John Muir, *Our National Parks* (Boston and New York: Houghton Mifflin Company, 1901), 91.

1   The most comprehensive study of *ji* composed before and during the Tang dynasty is He Li's 2010 doctoral dissertation, "Tangdai jiti wen yanjiu." Also useful is Chu Binjie, *Zhongguo gudai wenti gailun*, especially 362–70. One reason for the popularity of *ji* about pavilions was certainly the fact that Tang men of letters, like their predecessors during the Six Dynasties and descendants in the Song and thereafter, were fond of constructing pavilions at scenic sites, especially spots that overlooked attractive landscapes. These pavilions, which cost less to build than other more elaborate structures, such as galleries or towers, provided a convenient place where literate men could socialize and compose poetry near an attractive physical environment.

2   The significance of physically inscribing texts on landscape features such as rocks and cave walls is discussed with great insight by Robert E. Harrist Jr. in his *The Landscape of Words*. See also the introduction in Strassberg's *Inscribed Landscapes*, especially 5–7.

3   On names and naming as they relate to Tang dynasty essays concerning physical structures and scenic spots, see Yang, "Naming and Meaning."

4   Almost without exception, modern literary historians and critics of traditional Chinese travel writing identify the title of Liu Zongyuan's first Yongzhou essay as the textual origin of the expression *youji* and as the single prose work that marks the "birth of travel literature." This attribution is highly questionable because, as made clear by the editors of the *Choice Blossoms* anthology, the last three Chinese characters in the title of Liu's first Yongzhou account should be parsed *yanyou ji* (and not *yan youji*). Note: the earliest occurrence of the term *yanyou* in a Chinese text appears in the *Jinshu*, 13.392, compiled in the seventh century, but there, *yanyou* indicates an *activity*, not a form of prose writing. A closely related term essentially bearing the same meaning, *youyan* (literally, "outing banquets"), also has a long history, extending back to the Han period. For instance, see *Hanshu*, 78.3284.

5   *Wenyuan yinghua*, 822.4343.

6   I do not mean to suggest that description of place in Tang literature only appeared in the account, or *ji* form. This was not the case at all. For instance, in some of the prefaces composed by major writers of the early Tang, one can find sustained description of place, especially scenic landscapes. Just one well-known example is Wang Bo's (fl. mid-seventh century) "Preface to the Gallery of Prince Teng" (Tengwang Ge xu). For a translation, see Strassberg, 106–09. For the most part, such works are written in the parallel-prose style and were not recognized as a distinct literary genre dealing mainly with place. There are some works of the eighth century, such as Li Bai's prose preface to the poem "Boating on Court Esquire Lake in Mian County" (Fan Mianzhou Langguan hu) and Wang Wei's (701–61) "Letter from the Mountains to Pei Di, the Budding Talent" (Shanzhong yu Pei Di xiucai shu), which are written in a "looser" variety of prose; that is to say, with fewer restrictions on how many characters there should be in each line and how many lines should comprise a section or paragraph. This style will find full expression later in the works of Liu Zongyuan. Li Bai's preface is translated and discussed later in this chapter. Wang Wei's *ji* is translated in Strassberg, 113–14. The various texts mentioned here, and their analogues

found in the *Choice Blossoms* collection, indicate that writing about scenic places in the preface and letter form, which first appeared in the Six Dynasties, continued during the Tang.

7   Wu, *The Confucian's Progress*, 7.

8   Xuanzang's journey to India, as recounted in the *Da Tang Xiyu ji*, is also important because it inspired the famous Ming novel *Journey to the West* (Xiyou ji; sometimes also referred to as "*Monkey*"). This association, however, does not relate to the development of travel literature in China.

9   Xuanzang was not consistently traveling during his sixteen-year trip. He spent many years living in various places in northern and southern India.

10 I am aware that Xuanzang's translation assistant and disciple, Bianji (619–49), is sometimes credited as author or coauthor of the *Accounts of the Western Regions*. This is because Xuanzang apparently dictated at least some of his travel experiences to Bianji, who in turn then copied them out. I strongly suspect, however, that Xuanzang himself was actively engaged in the preparation of the text, which, after all, had been commissioned by the emperor himself. I find it hard to believe that Xuanzang simply recited the details of the trip to Bianji, who then edited all this information into a single text. And I highly doubt that the numerous facts and figures cited in the *Accounts of the Western Regions*, the accuracy of which has been confirmed by Sir Aurel Stein (1862–1943) and other Central Asian explorers, were recalled solely from memory. Moreover, it is certain that Xuanzang collected local documents during the journey, which he took back to China. The Tang monk certainly drew on these sources for information when compiling the *Accounts of the Western Regions*. Here I will not pursue the authorship issue any further and, for the sake of convenience, hereafter regard Xuanzang as the sole author.

11 The best-known surviving example of this form is Yijing's *Biographies of Eminent Monks who Sought the Dharma in the Western Regions during the Great Tang* (Da Tang Xiyu qiufa gaoseng zhuan). For a description and assessment of Yijing's account, see Boulton, "Early Chinese Buddhist Travel Accounts," 129–57. Such works do include a narrative of a religious tour through India, but it is presented in the form of a biography, told in the third person, by the monk who made the trip.

12 These and many similar accounts, almost all of which are now lost, are listed in *juan* 57 and 58 of Song, *New Documents on the Tang* (Xin Tangshu). One of these works that may have been inspired or influenced by Xuanzang's account is *Illustrated Chronicle of the Western Regions* (Xiyu tuzhi) in sixty *juan*, prepared by emissaries of the Tang emperor Gaozong (r. 649–84). The court official Xu Jingzong (592–672) supervised the editing of these materials, which were presented to the throne in 658.

13 Some scholars have questioned the authenticity of *Shiji* 123. See, for instance, Hulsewé, "The Problem of the Authenticity of *Shih-chi*," and Lu Zongli, "Problems Concerning the Authenticity of *Shih-chi* 123 Reconsidered."

14 This term was applied to a breed of superior horse from Ferghana whose blood vessels reportedly would burst when it was in a sustained, hard gallop.

15 The orthography for "grape" in the *Shiji* (*putao* 蒲陶) is different from the modern form, which is written 葡萄.

16   Sima Qian makes this very clear in the opening line of *juan* 123: "Traces of knowledge about Ferghana is observed through Zhang Qian" (*Shiji*, 123.3157).

17   There were practical reasons why Taizong wanted Xuanzang to write an account of the Western Regions: the more accurate and detailed the description, the more this would benefit the Tang emperor and his military commanders if they were to engage in military operations in unfamiliar territory west of China. But again, to rehearse a critical point made earlier, the contents of the *Accounts of the Western Regions* do not reveal a military intelligence concern on the part of Xuanzang.

18   Wriggins, *The Silk Road Journey with Xuanzang*, 192. On the types of documents Xuanzang collected in India, see also Barthélemy-Sanit-Hilaire, *Hiouen Thsang in India*, 52.

19   This famous dictum is often used by Chinese historians when describing Xuanzang's rigorous pursuit of reliable and useful information. The expression has its origin in *Hanshu*, 53.2410.

20   *Da Tang Xiyu ji jiaozhu*, 2:12.1035.

21   "Bulujia guo" likely refers to the walled city of Perspire (Bulushashiluo), which was in modern Peshawar just west of the Khyber Pass in Pakistan. See my *Riding the River Home*, 117n292.

22   The term *baolong*, which I have translated literally as "ferocious dragons," here indicates avalanches. Also, I have taken some liberty in translating the line that follows. My "one should never approach them" literally means something like "one cannot (*nan*) intrude and encroach upon (*lingfan*) [the ferocious dragons]."

23   Precisely how or why the "taboos" of wearing reddish-brown clothing or the presence of gourds (filled with water?) might start an avalanche is unclear.

24   *Da Tang Xiyu ji jiaozhu*, 1:1.67.

25   Xuanzang's translation skills—working from Sanskrit to Chinese—have been praised for their accuracy. See the comments on this in Wriggins, *The Silk Road Journey with Xuanzang*, 195. For a convenient list of Xuanzang's translations and original works, see Lusthaus, *Buddhist Phenomenology*, 554–73.

26   In ancient China, the term *hu*, often translated as "barbarian(s)," was used as a generic for non-Chinese people.

27   *Da Tang Xiyu ji jiaozhu* , 1:1.87–88. The Čākar, also known as Tchakas and Chāch, were a race of people from nearby Tashkent known for producing outstanding soldiers. The Chinese term (*zhejie* in Modern Chinese) is a transliteration of "Čākar," which in the language of the Čākar people meant "warrior."

28   Although Xuanzang followed different routes in his trip to, and journey home from, India, the sequence of entries in the *Accounts* still follows his itinerary.

29   The influence of Indian Buddhist literature on the travel accounts composed by Chinese monks who visited India, both in subject matter and style, deserves much further attention. So far, my limited reading on this subject indicates that Yijing is the only Chinese author to include poetry in a prose travel narrative, and this style may have been patterned after a similar practice evident in some Indian texts, such as the *Vimalakīrti-nirdeśa-sūtra* (generic abbreviated title in Chinese: *Weimo jing*), *Lotus Sūtra* (*Saddharma-puṇḍarīka-sūtra*; Chinese: *Fahua jing*), and *Amitabha*

Sūtra (*Smaller Sukhavati-vyuha*; Chinese: *Amituo jing*). This format of mixing prose narrative of a journey, real or imagined, with poetry, was unknown in China before the introduction and influence of Buddhist literature. In China, the earliest example of this style of alternating prose and poetry is the *bianwen*, or "transformation texts," discovered at Dunhuang in the early twentieth century, which date from the Tang. This mixing of prose and poetry later became a distinguishing feature of Yuan dynasty opera-drama (*zaju*) and subsequently in vernacular fiction in China, perhaps most notably in the *Journey to the West*. But this style of mixing prose and poetry never developed in Chinese travel literature. Many authors wrote about journeys in both prose and verse, but such literary activities are almost always kept separate.

30 Numerous poetry prefaces by these and other early Tang writers that relate to travel are cited in Mei and Yu, *Zhongguo youji wenxue shi*, 70. The three authors mentioned here, along with Lu Zhaolin (634–ca. 684), are often collectively referred to as the "Four Eminent Writers of the Early Tang" (Chu Tang sijie).

31 This text is translated in Strassberg, 106–09. For background details on Wang's preface, see Timothy Wai Keung Chan, "Dedication and Identification in Wang Bo's Compositions on the Gallery of Prince Teng."

32 The gathering described here took place in Hanyang (in the title of Li Bai's poem, Hanyang is referred to as Mian county, its name during the Tang dynasty), which is now part of the modern city of Wuhan. "South Lake," renamed "Court Gentleman Lake" by Li Bai, was in the southeastern corner of Hanyang. Beyond the information provided here, "Master Du" (Dugong) and "Master Wang" (Wanggong) are not further identified. Mention about the "restoration of peace in the empire" refers to the An Lushan Rebellion, which began in 755. Li Bai's celebratory comments here are premature, for the rebellion was not finally quelled until 763.

33 In other words, they left no poems or other writings describing their visits.

34 The term "Chariot Archer" (*puye*), like "Court Gentleman," is a government office title. Thus, Li Bai is saying here that there is a precedent for adopting an office title to be used as a place name.

35 Li Bai, *Li Bai ji jiaozhu*, 20.1189–90. I have taken some liberty in translating the last line of Li Bai's preface. Literally, it reads: "Thus, it will wear away together with Big Divide Hill." The hill referenced here was situated just northeast of Hanyang. *Li Bai ji jiaozhu*, 20.1191, note.

36 *Quan Tangwen*, 345.3505.

37 Ibid., 433.4419–20.

38 Quoted in Wang, *Zhongguo gudai shanshui youji yanjiu*, 123.

39 As for works in English, the most detailed and informative study of Yuan Jie's prose essays on landscape is Yang, "Naming and Meaning." English translations of "Account of Rightside Creek" and "Account of the Winter Pavilion" are included in Strassberg, 117–18.

40 For instance, see the comments by Bei and Ye in *Lidai youji xuan*, 2, on "Account of Rightside Creek." Bei and Ye view this text as a "relatively mature example of the

landscape travel account" and a continuation of the style Xie Lingyun used in his *Notes on Sightseeing Trips to Famous Mountains.*

41 Qing Lingwen was in fact the magistrate (*xianling*) of Jianghua. "Grand Master" (*dafu*) seems to be used as an honorific designation for this office.

42 The reference here is to the Xiao River (Xiaoshui).

43 The term *dashu*, or "Severe Heat," is one of the twenty-four solar periods on the lunar calendar, referring to the hottest period of summer, just before autumn.

44 Yuan Jie, *Yuan Cishan ji*, 9.7a–b.

45 Strassberg, *Inscribed Landscapes*, 117, suggests an approximate date: "*ca.* 764."

46 Yuan Jie, *Yuan Cishan ji*, 9.5b. "Account of Rightside Creek" is also classified under the subheading "*yanyou*" in the *Choice Blossoms* anthology, and the editors of that collection placed it directly after Liu Zongyuan's "Eight Accounts." See *Wenyuan yinghua*, 823.4345. Note: it is also worth mentioning that in Chen Renyu's *Youzhi* there are eight *ji* works by Liu Zongyuan, six of which are selected from the Yongzhou essays. However, Chen Renyu includes no selections from Yuan Jie. This omission was corrected later, however, by Tao Zongyi. His anthology includes four prefaces and three *ji* by Yuan Jie, one of which is "Account of Rightside Creek." See *Youzhi xubian*, 18–23.

47 The quadripartite organizational format I describe here was inspired by comments by Nienhauser, in *Liu Tsung-yüan*, 71, though I have added an "authorial commentary" section to Nienhauser's original three-section structure (a prose introduction; a verse or rhymed parallel-prose descriptive section(s); and a short prose epilogue).

48 For an example of moral and valedictory concerns in one of Yuan Jie's landscape essays, see Yang, "Naming and Meaning," 88.

49 Yuan Jie, *Yuan Cishan ji*, 9.5a–b.

50 Yang, "Naming and Meaning," 84.

51 On the other hand, it is also certainly possible—and in my view perfectly acceptable—to translate *li* consistently throughout this text with the same English word. Thus, something like "manage" or "management" would also work here.

52 Note that *li* and *shu* (incomparable) each appear precisely five times in Yuan Jie's text. One conceivable way of looking at this is that each of Ma Xiang's *li* talents matches up perfectly with the five occurrences of *shu*, or "extraordinary," which are also related to Ma Xiang, his talent, deeds, and so on.

53 Liu Zongyuan, *Liu Zongyuan ji*, 30.800.

54 Charles Hartman, "Han Yu," in Nienhauser, 398. The most detailed study in English on Han Yu and Liu Zongyuan, and their roles in promoting *guwen*, is still Madeline Kay Spring, "A Stylistic Study of Tang 'Guwen.'" For an informative summary of the various phases or stages of the so-called Ancient Prose-Style Movement, see Chen, *Images and Ideas*, 1–13.

55 Spring, "A Stylistic Study of Tang 'Guwen,'" 272.

56 Liu Zongyuan, *Liu Zongyuan ji*, 29.762.

57 Edward H. Schafer discusses the dangers and perils of banishment to the south in his *Vermilion Bird*, 37–44.

58 Liu Zongyuan, *Liu Zongyuan ji*, 29.770.

59 Ibid., 29.764.

60 For a detailed discussion of how Liu Zongyuan uses the image of a "prisoner" to describe himself during the Yongzhou exile years, see Sun, *Liu Zongyuan zhuan lun*, 144–53.

61 He, *Yongzhou baji daodu*, 84.

62 See the comments in Strassberg, *Inscribed Landscapes*, 33ff.

63 Cf. my article "Clearing the Apertures and Getting in Tune: The Hainan Exile of Su Shi (1037–1101)." *Journal of Sung-Yuan Studies* 30 (2000): 141-67, where I argue that Su Shi used this same survival strategy during his three years living as an exile on Hainan Island. For additional information on political exile during the Tang as it relates to landscape essays in general, and especially to Liu Zongyuan, see Spring, "T'ang Landscapes of Exile," 312–23.

64 This well-known title notwithstanding, there are in fact nine *ji* from Yongzhou, the traditional eight (*Liu Zongyuan ji*, 29.672–73) and an additional one titled "Account of a Sightseeing Trip to Creek of the Spirit Huang " (You Huangxi ji) (29.759–62). Also, the origin of the title "Eight Accounts of Yong County" is unknown. He Peixiong, *Yongzhou baji daodu*, 3, speculates that it may date from the Qing period. Neither issue has any direct bearing on the discussion below, so there is no need to pursue them any further.

65 That is, the pool and the hillock. In the history of Chinese travel literature, the idea of going out to explore and discover (*de*) previously unknown and thereby unappreciated landscapes and then taking possession (*you*) of them in some way (occupation, purchase, and so on) is largely restricted to Liu Zongyuan's Yongzhou essays. This motif is rare in later travel literature, where writer-travelers overwhelmingly prefer to visit well-known sites, both scenic and historical, rather than purchase them.

66 The four place names mentioned here were all popular sightseeing spots around the Tang capital at Chang'an.

67 Liu Zongyuan, *Liu Zongyuan ji*, 29.765–66. The translation here, with some minor changes, follows the one in my *On the Road in Twelfth Century China*, 20–21. The discussion of Liu Zongyuan's "Eight Accounts" that follow draws generously on comments in my *On the Road in Twelfth Century China*, 22–25.

68 These similarities have been noted and discussed previously in Nienhauser et al., *Liu Tsung-yüan*, 68–69.

69 Spring, "A Stylistic Study of Tang 'Guwen,'" 274–75, presents several different examples of parallel structure used in Tang dynasty *guwen*.

70 Mei and Yu, *Zhongguo youji wenxue shi*, 107ff.

71 Liu Zongyuan, *Liu Zongyuan ji*, 29.762.

72 Ibid., 29.763

73 Ibid., 29.767.

74 Following the order of the "Eight Accounts" in *Liu Zongyuan ji*, 29.762–73, the first four were composed in 809. The next four date from 812 (the reason for the three-year gap between the first four and second four compositions is not clear). The "ninth account" ("You Huangxi ji") dates from 813. For additional details on these and related matters, see He Peixiong, *Yongzhou baji daodu*, 3–5.

75   At the close of his "Account of a Sightseeing Trip to Creek of the Spirit Huang" (You Huangxi ji), Liu remarks, "After returning from my trip, I composed an account to inform those in the future who are fond of sightseeing" (*Liu Zongyuan ji*, 29.770). And in "Account of Rocky Rivulet," he writes about an attractive spot he acquired so that future "landscape connoisseurs" will be able to easily find it (*Liu Zongyuan ji*, 29.770). In still another account Liu reports on finding a beautiful secluded spot, but he says he "would not dare to keep it to himself" but would instead prefer to "share it with the world" (*Liu Zongyuan ji*, 29.769).

76   Here I am paraphrasing and expanding comments and observations in Spring, "A Stylistic Study of Tang 'Guwen,'" 283.

77   See his "Created Nature in T'ang Literature." In reference to the "Fashioner-Creator," the descriptive term "supernatural entity" is Professor Schafer's (154).

78   Liu Zongyuan , *Liu Zongyuan ji*, 29.772.

79   Cf. the comments in Spring, "T'ang Landscapes of Exile," 320: "Liu Zongyuan similarly restructured his environment so that it conformed more concretely to his personal vision of the natural realm."

80   Some of Yuan Jie's essays, such as "Account of Rightside Creek," also voice this same idea of "neglect" or "abandonment" of attractive scenes ("And yet, ever since this county was established, no one has appreciated and admired it."). It is unclear if Yuan Jie is talking about himself and posting to Dao county in Hunan, where he was dispatched three times but never exiled.

81   Liu Zongyuan, *Liu Zongyuan ji*, 29.763.

82   Nienhauser was first to make this observation. See *Liu Ts'ung-yüan*, 74.

83   Although literary historians usually identify Li Ao as a practitioner and supporter of *guwen* prose, his approach to writing about landscape was quite different from that of Liu Zongyuan. For additional information, see the comments in Emmerich, *Li Ao*, 90ff.

84   Complete and annotated translations of Li Ao's diary can be found in my *On the Road in Twelfth Century China*, 26–29, and in Strassberg, 128–31.

85   Zhang Jiuling (678–740), a native of Shao county (Shaozhou; in northern Guangdong), was an important author and statesman who flourished in the 730s. The tomb mentioned here, located at the foot of Mount Luoyuan (Luoyuan Shan) in the northwestern suburbs of modern Shaozhou, was excavated in 1960. For more information, see Paul W. Kroll's entry on Zhang Jiuling in Nienhauser et al., *Indiana Companion*, 207–09.

86   The examples presented here from Li Ao's diary are based on the text in his collected works, *Li Wengong ji*, 18.78–79.

3. Maturity in the Song

Epigraph: Yang Wanli Fan Chengda juan, 147.

1   In my essay "Some Preliminary Remarks on the Travel Records of the Song Dynasty (960–1279)," I identified the first variety of Song *youji* as "daytrip essays." For reasons

that will become evident in the discussion that follows, I now prefer to call these works "sightseeing accounts."

2   The "approximately fifty million" figure is based on census numbers for the 740s and 750s summarized in Durand, "The Population Statistics of China, A.D. 2–1953," 209–56 (see especially table 2 on p. 223). On the Song figure "about one hundred million," see Ping-ti Ho (He Bingdi), "An Estimate of the Total Population in Sung-Chin China," especially 52.

3   There is a rich body of scholarship on the Tang-Song transition. A useful introduction, dealing mainly with political history, can be found in Twitchett and Smith, *The Cambridge History of China*. For more details, especially regarding the methodological models by which Western, Chinese, and Japanese historians have studied the transition, see Luo Yinan, "A Study of the Changes in the Tang-Song Transition Model." Still useful sources on the growth of large cities and commerce under the Song are Shiba, *Commerce and Society in Sung China*, and Ma, *Commercial Development and Urban Change in Sung China*. The most comprehensive study of the Song economy in any language is Liang Keng-yao's (Liang Genggyao) two-volume *Songdai shehui jingji shi lunji*.

4   On the expansion of the examination system and government bureaucracy under the Song, see Lee, *Government Education and Examinations in Sung China*, and Chaffee's *The Thorny Gates of Learning in Sung China*. Chaffee (25–26) mentions that the Song bureaucracy was so "oversized" that "there were too many officials for the available posts."

5   Wu Yating's 2007 doctoral dissertation and Cong Ellen Zhang's monograph on travel and culture in the Song, *Transformative Journeys*, both demonstrate in convincing fashion that travel/movement was central to elite life in the Song dynasty.

6   See Zhang, *Transformative Journeys*, especially 6–8 (the section on "Literati and Non-literati Travelers in the Song"), and especially Wu Ya-Ting, "Bu'an de xiehou—Songren yu lüsu changsuo de hudong yu qi kongjian yinxiang," 134–42. While such investigations are useful in providing information on mobility and travel, few of these non-literati travelers left written accounts of their experiences.

7   I refer here to Wang Fuxin's study *Songdai lüyou yanjiu*. The idea of a "tourist industry" existing during the Song will be addressed at the end of this chapter.

8   I use the verb "sightseeing" in the sense of visiting an identifiable place to observe and appreciate its appealing visual qualities and/or its historical and literary heritage.

9   Chaffee, *The Thorney Gates of Learning in Sung China*, 27.

10   See, for instance, the comments on this in Zhang, *Transformative Journeys*, especially 43–68.

11   On the various leisure activities and amusements popular during the Song, the best source in a Western language is still Jacques Gernet's *Daily Life in China on the Eve of the Mongol Invasion 1250-1276*, especially 219–43.

12   On the importance of *shidafu* contributions to and participation in various social and entertainment activities and how such experiences contributed to a changing sense of elite self-identification during the Song, see Cong Ellen Zhang, "Things Heard in the Past."

13   *Zhongguo youji wenxue shi,* especially 119–26.

14   Wang, *Zhongguo gudai shanshui youji yanjiu,* 131ff.

15   The organizational schemes described here appear in the three histories of *youji* by Mei and Yu, Wang Liquan, and Zhu Yaoting discussed in the introduction.

16   These works are translated in Strassberg, 173–77 and 219–23, respectively.

17   For an informative discussion of the Jade Splendor Palace and its history, and especially the famous poem written by Du Fu (712–770) that immortalized it, see Chan, "Wall Carvings, Elixirs, and the Celestial King."

18   "Serried Clouds" (Paiyun) and "Felicitous Clouds" (Qingyun) may also be audience halls, though the original text is not clear about this.

19   In other words, it is a natural rock formation.

20   "Method master" is a literal translation of the Chinese term *fangshi,* which refers to a person skilled in esoteric practices such as divination and alchemy.

21   That is, imperial palaces, monastic complexes, and so on.

22   Here I follow the gloss in Ni, *Zhongguo gudai youji xuan,* 1:237n47, and read *yilao* (literally, "deceased elders") as a general reference to the "elders of yesteryear" or "wise men of the past."

23   *Youzhi xubian,* 26–29.

24   Zhang Min makes this declaration presumably because he thought it was "grand" that he and his friends were among the first visitors to the site.

25   See, for instance, Chen Xiaojie, "Tang Yuhua gong jianzhu kao."

26   Translations of Su's Red Cliff compositions are available in Strassberg, 185–88.

27   *Quan Tangshi,* 217.2276.

28   Another important Northern Song text that describes, in travel diary format, physical antiquities surviving from the Tang dynasty is Zhang Li (eleventh century), "Account of a Sightseeing Trip South of the City" (You Chengnan ji). This work, which describes a one-week investigative trip to the suburbs of Chang'an in 1086, is like Zhang Min's account in that it reads like the field notes prepared by an archeologist. Zhang Li's report, however, differs in significant ways from that of Zhang Min. In addition to its dated, travel-diary format, Zhang Li's text also includes his own notes and annotations on what he observed. He also cites documentary sources related to Tang history. What most distinguishes Zhang Li's account, however, is that his primary interest is to provide readers with a thorough archeological accounting, based on a rigorous scholarly method, of the surviving Tang ruins and relics in the southern suburbs of the former Tang capital. Zhang's text certainly falls within the definition of *youji* employed in this study, but should probably be viewed as a distinct form of the Northern Song travel diary tradition (discussed below). For a useful introduction and analysis of the *You Chengnan ji,* see Rudolph, "The Power of Places."

29   Zhang Min's call for more scrutiny and care concerning matters historical and their preservation is an early reflection of the later Song ideal of research and investigation of natural and historical landscape to gain knowledge. As Strassberg has noted, some influential thinker-philosophers of the Song "emphasized both the search for knowledge in the external world and the application of that knowledge in generating

enlightenment of the moral mind of the individual. Conceiving of reality as a texture of principles (*li*) on the metaphysical, concrete, and mental levels, these thinkers were concerned with how to realize the Confucian ideal of sagehood by active engagement with events and objects in the world" (*Inscribed Landscapes*, 46). One concept critical to the process of self-cultivation was *gewu*, which is usually translated as "classifying things." The central idea here is that empirical inquiry—through a process of observing and recording the world—was a key element in this process, and such activity finds some (but not common) expression in Northern Song dynasty *youji*. A good Northern Song textual example of this approach is Su Shi's "Account of Stone Bells Mountain," which is discussed below.

30 Chao Buzhi, *Jibei Chao xiansheng Jile ji*, 31.1a–2b. The English version here of Chao Buzhi's account, with some minor changes, follows the translation in my *On the Road in Twelfth Century China*, 49–50.

31 Bei and Ye, *Lidai youji xuan*, 53.

32 Another good example is the popular anthology piece written in 995 by the early Song *guwen* proponent Liu Kai (947–1000) and titled "Account of a Sightseeing Trip to Heavenly Peace Mountain" (You Tianping Shan ji). For an English translation, see Strassberg, 151–55.

33 Just one such example from among Su Shi's travel writings is his "Account of a Sightseeing Trip on the Pine River" (Jiyou Songjiang), in Su Shi, *Dongpo zhilin*, 1.3.

34 For an expanded discussion of Su Shi's key role in the development of the Northern Song sightseeing account, see my "What Need is there to Go Home"?

35 This standard anthology selection is translated in Strassberg, 190–91. In "Literary Innovation," Rudolph spends much of her chapter "The Travel Diary and Travel Essay" (34–65) discussing how Su Shi's "Record of the Stone Bells Mountain" serves as a "model of the [*youji*] genre" (34).

36 The line attributed by Su Shi to Li Daoyuan appears nowhere in modern editions of the *Commentary on the Waterways Treatise*. In fact, in both instances, Su Shi is quoting from Li Bo's "Discerning 'Account of Stone Bells Mountain'" (Bian Shizhong ji). See *Quan Tangwen*, 712.7310.

37 Wang Liqun, "Su Shi de *youji* wen," 39. The imprecise "seventeen or eighteen" number is explained by the fact that Wang Liqun is not sure if one of Su Shi's compositions, "You Huanshan ji," qualifies as *youji*, because it "lacks description of attractive landscape." Su Shi wrote about his travel experiences in different literary forms, including letters and prefaces. Since Wang Liqun focuses solely on works in the *ji* form, his number of "seventeen or eighteen" is conservative at best.

38 Other examples that chronicle the author's pleasure trips include his "An Idle Man Sightseeing in Zhedong" (Yiren you Zhedong), "Account of a Sightseeing Trip at Night to the Chengtian Monastery" (Ji Chengtian yeyou), and "Account of a Sightseeing Trip to Mount Lu" (Jiyou Lushan). These works are anthologized in Su Shi, *Dongpo zhilin*, 1.1–2, 1.2, and 1.4, respectively, and are translated and discussed in my essay "What Need is there to Go Home?" (191–94). Mei and Yu, *Zhongguo youji wenxue shi*, 190–95, distinguish these and similar works by other authors as *biji ti youji*, or "notation book travel writing," mainly because of their

preservation in notation book collections such as *Dongpo zhilin* and their terse, informal nature. One prominent textual example they cite to illustrate such works as a distinct form (*tishi*) of travel writing is Shen Gua's (1031–95) "Account of the Yandang Mountains" (Yandang shan ji), which is drawn from Shen's well-known *biji* collection *Notes and Talks from Dream Creek* (Mengxi bitan). A translation of Shen's text is included in Strassberg, 180–81. Such works, I would argue, do not qualify as *youji* because they lack a travel component and lyrical content. Song dynasty notation books (*biji*) are an important source of shorter, informal descriptions of places, but not all these works qualify as travel writing, at least as I have defined it in this study.

39 Yishao was the courtesy name (*zi*) of Wang Xizhi, the famous fourth-century calligrapher.

40 Su Shi, *Dongpo zhilin*, 1.2.

41 Incidentally, although Wang's famous preface includes no travel narrative whatsoever, it is nevertheless included in virtually every *youji* anthology ever published, including *Inscribed Landscapes*, 65–66. Strassberg defends its inclusion by saying it "articulates an archetypal response to being in Nature after arriving at a scenic place" (64).

42 In the first of Su's two famous *youji* works on the Red Cliff, which were also written during his exile years in Huangzhou, he likewise assuages the sadness of one of his guests who laments what happened to the famous general Cao Cao in a famous battle at the Red Cliff fought many centuries earlier. And in the second of his Red Cliff compositions, Su ends his account on a light note, recounting a dream about how two Daoist immortals visited him after an enjoyable midnight excursion with friends.

43 "Shihu jixing sanlu ba" (*Zhibuzu zhai congshu* ed.), 23 *ji*, 389.

44 On the development of distinct types of diaries in ancient China, see Wu Pei-yi, *The Confucian's Progress*, especially 93–141. One fascinating observation by Wu concerns the liberation of autobiography from traditional Confucian biographical forms, which he says began in the late thirteenth century and flourished in the Ming period. Some of these new "spiritual autobiographers," he further says, presented their stories in journey format, and so "they naturally turned to travel literature for cues in selecting a suitable style or format for their life stories" (93). Wu also identifies a new type of writing in the Ming he calls "spiritual autobiography." See my comments on this in chapter 4, n. 13.

45 On the diaries of Wang Anshi, Sima Guang, and several other Song government officials, see Chen Zuogao, *Zhongguo riji shilue*, 7–14, and Deborah Marie Rudolph, "Literary Innovation and Aesthetic Tradition," especially 145–54.

46 Huang Tingjian's *Household Activities in Yi County* (Yizhou jiasheng) records his various quotidian activities over a period of eight months just before his death in 1105.

47 Despite the brevity of the *Chronicle of Going into Service* and its predecessor, Li Ao's *Register of Coming South*, they are important for establishing much of the formulaic, travel-related terminology ("on such-and-such cyclical date reached place-x, spent

the night in such-and-such town," and so on) that became common in later travel diaries. See the remarks on this in my *On the Road in Twelfth Century China*, 51–52.

48   Most extant diaries of the Song period are collected in Gu Hongyi and Li Wen's *Compendium of Song Era Diaries* (Songdai riji congbian). I agree with the assessment by Mei and Yu, *Zhonggguo youji wenxue shi*, 211, that these works are for the most part "simple and plain" with "emphasis on making records of natural landscapes," which are usually confined to a single mountain or county. Mei and Yu (211) also note that the journey described in these works is usually of short duration (usually a week or two), and that these trips were undertaken by two or more people together, with one or two of them writing the *youji* after the trip was concluded.

49   For the original text, see http://ctext.org/wiki.pl?if=gb&chapter=510371.

50   On the importance of the *Chenxing lu* as a precursor to Fan Chengda and Lu You's river diaries, see Mei Xinlin and Cui Xiaojing, "Zhang Shunmin 'Chenxing lu' kaolun," 151–58.

51   According to the modern geographer Chen Cheng-siang (Chen Zhengxiang), the *Wuchuan lu* comprises 16,700 Chinese characters (*Zhongguo youji xuanzhu*, 1.11). As for Lu You's diary, it is divided into six chapters (*juan*) and, according to one internet source, comprises over 40,000 Chinese characters (https://zh.wikipedia .org/wiki/入蜀記).

52   Chang and Smythe, *South China in the Twelfth Century*, 3.

53   Hargett, *Riding the River Home*, 58. The river diaries, like the sightseeing accounts, are always written in the first person, but Fan and Lu never traveled alone. As government officials, they were always accompanied by logistical and support staff. Even low-ranking officials rarely traveled by themselves. According to Zhang: "They [that is, Song government officials] typically took to the road with great fanfare and in the company of many" (*Transformative Journeys*, 83).

54   Strassberg, 49.

55   This is the translation of Chang and Smythe, *South China in the Twelfth Century*, 161.

56   Li Bai's famous poem on the Yellow Crane Tower is preserved in *Quan Tangshi*, 174.1785, and *Li Bai ji jiaozhu*, 15.935-36; for Cui Hao's verse, see *Quan Tangshi*, 130.1329.

57   *Ru Shu ji*, in Lu You, *Lu Fangweng quanji*, 43.264–48.298. This is my translation, but I have benefitted from consulting the Chang and Smythe rendition in *South China in the Twelfth Century*, 134.

58   Cong Ellen Zhang argues convincingly that Lu's and Fan's reports about historical sites and how they relate to the literary past in a way provided a means by which the river diarist could become part of the historical and literary legacy, or cultural memory, of a famous place. By so doing in a diary written for public consumption, Lu and Fan were in effect building their own literary identities and legacies. Zhang's chapter "Sightseeing and Site Making" provides great insight into the ways in which Fan Chengda and other traveling Song literati participated in what she calls "site making." See Zhang, *Transformative Journeys*, 154–79.

59 Hargett, *Riding the River Home*, 41. "Plum rains" refers to the rainy season along the Great River, Xiang River, and Huai River regions that falls just before the summer solstice.

60 Yanyu Heap (Yanyu Dui) refers to a rocky promontory in the middle of the Great River just east of Kui county in eastern Sichuan.

61 Hargett, *Riding the River Home*, 134–35.

62 Tūla (Chinese: *douluo* 兜羅) is the Sanskrit word for "cotton."

63 Ibid., 66–67.

64 Chang and Smythe, *South China in the Twelfth Century*, 165. "Shu" is an old name for Sichuan.

65 Hargett, *Riding the River Home*, 43. Fan was so appalled by the sheep slaughter that he wrote a poem titled "Song of the Partition Mound" (Lidui xing) to criticize it. See Fan Chengda, *Fan Shihu ji*, 18.247–48. For an English translation of the verse, see my *On the Road in Twelfth Century China*, 89.

66 Hargett, *Riding the River Home*, 70–73.

67 Levine, "Welcome to the Occupation," 383.

68 This reign period lasted from 25 January 1126 until 2 June 1127.

69 The Jīn (or "Jurchen") invasion of China in 1126–27 also resulted in the capture of the Song emperor and heir apparent. The Song exile capital in Lin'an was established by another son of the emperor who fled south, along with members of the Song government who had the opportunity and means to do so.

70 It is certain that all Song ambassadors submitted some form of written intelligence reports after their return home from the north. It seems highly likely that the four travel accounts listed here are related in some way to those official documents, but it is unclear whether the diaries drew on information in the official reports or the other way around. It is also possible that official and private accounts were written separately. Cf. the comments by David Curtis Wright in his study of the reports of Song ambassadors to the state of Liao in the eleventh century; Wright notes that they submitted "records of conversations" (*yulu*) on their return to Kaifeng. Wright also points out that these reports of "conversations" with Liao officials were transcribed by interpreter-clerks (*yiyu tongshi*). See his *From War to Diplomatic Parity in Eleventh-Century China: Sung's Foreign Relations with the Kitan Liao*, 175. See also Fu Lehuan, "Songren shi Liao yulu xingcheng kao," 3–5. There is consensus among experts in the field that the four surviving embassy accounts were written as documents intended for contemporary readers and posterity. In other words, they were "non-official" in terms of production. See also the remarks and references on this issue in Levine, "Welcome to the Occupation," 383n3.

71 On Lou Yue's and Fan Chengda's diaries, see Linda Walton, "Diary of a Journey North," and Hargett, "*Lan-p'ei lu*," respectively. Zhou Hui's account has been studied and translated by Édouard Chavannes, "Pei Yuan Lou, Récit d'un voyage dans le Nord," 163–92. As for Cheng Zhuo's diary, see Franke, "A Sung Embassy Diary of 1211–12," 171–207.

72   Some modern scholars interested in diasporic memory and pre-invasion textual representations of the north have profitably mined the embassy accounts. See especially Levine's "Welcome to the Occupation."

73   For instance, see Wright, *From War to Diplomatic Parity in Eleventh-Century China*, 177.

74   As an example of the intelligence documents prepared by Northern Song envoys to the Liao, see Wright's discussion of Lu Zhen's (957–1014) embassy report *Register of a Ride in a One-Horse Carriage* (Chengyao lu) in *From War to Diplomatic Parity*, 183–86.

75   These themes are discussed at length in Levine, "Welcome to the Occupation," and in West, "Discarded Treasure."

76   Levine, "Welcome to the Occupation," 393. Keep in mind that Fan Chengda, like other Song envoys, had no diplomatic experience in the modern sense, had never traveled in the north, and whatever knowledge he had about the lands now occupied by the Jin came from written texts and perhaps oral accounts or stories passed down by family members or friends and colleagues.

77   That is, the huge area between the outer- and inner-city walls.

78   Hargett, "Fan Ch'eng-ta's *Lan-p'ei lu*," 148–49 (with minor changes).

79   "Grand Preceptor, [the Duke of] Zheng" refers to Fu Bi (1004–83), a Northern Song prime minister.

80   Levine, "Welcome to the Occupation," 401. "Xuanhe" refers to the "Promulgated Accord" reign of 1119–26, just before the 1126–27 siege and capture of Kaifeng.

81   For a study of how Lu You's poems relate to the prose descriptions in his river diary, see Egan, "When There is a Parallel Text in Prose."

82   Levine convincingly argues that the four surviving envoy accounts of Kaifeng under Jin rule "were not unmediated textual translations of visual experiences, presenting accurate and realistic pictures of what they experienced. Instead, these texts were the products of a much more complex and chaotic epistemic process, as subjective representations of individual memory that drew upon a collective body of geographical knowledge and historical experience ("Welcome to the Occupation," 441).

83   Fan Chengda, *Fan Shihu ji*, 12.147. My translation follows Levine, "Welcome to the Occupation," 419, with minor alterations.

84   Walton, "Diary of a Journey to the North," 21.

85   Ibid., 22.

86   Hargett, "Fan Ch'eng-ta's *Lan-p'ei lu*," 170–71.

87   Walton, "Diary of a Journey to the North," 25.

88   West, "Discarded Treasure," 189.

89   For a brief description of the contents of Xu's diary, see Chen Zuogao, *Zhongguo riji shilue*, 25. The circumstances of Xu Mingshan's embassy to a tributary state (Annan) were, of course, quite different in purpose from the missions of Song envoys to the Liao and Jin.

90   For a convenient listing of these works with brief descriptions of their contents, see Chen Zuogao, *Zhongguo riji shilue*, 25ff.

91 The various points raised here, and some others as well, are all articulated well in Strassberg, 45–56.

92 Wang, *Songdai lüyou yanjiu*, especially chapters 3 and 4 (232–342).

4. Transition and Innovation in the Jīn, Yuan, and Early to Mid-Ming

Epigraph: Qian Qianyi, *Muzhai Chuxue ji*, 32.927.

1 Strassberg, *Inscribed Landscapes*, 269.

2 The rise of the Mongol empire, its destruction of the Song and alien border states Liao and Jīn, and the history of Mongol rule in China are all well documented in Franke and Twitchett, *The Cambridge History of China*. On the Song-Yuan transition and the subsequent fall of the Mongols to the Ming, see Smith and von Glahn, *The Song-Yuan-Ming Transition in Chinese History*.

3 Yuan Haowen's text is translated in Strassberg, 236–43. A year after composing this account (that is, in 1136), Yuan visited Mount Tai in Shandong and commemorated the trip by writing "Brief Account of a Sightseeing Trip East" (Dongyou lueji). See Yuan Haowen, *Yuan Haowen wen biannian jiaozhu*, 1:4.386–87. Yuan's main concern in this text is to provide a scholarly inventory of ancient sites and structures on the mountain and their history. On this account, Yuan Haowen's "Brief Account" is at once reminiscent of the prose format we saw in Li Daoyuan's *Commentary on the Waterways Treatise* and later in Su Shi's "Account of a Sightseeing Trip to Stone Bells Mountain," and it is one that will become a major style of late Ming *youji* composition.

4 The most complete study and translation available of Yelü Chucai's account is still Igor Rachewiltz, "The Hsi-Yu Lu," 1–128. Strassberg translates the travel itinerary portion of Yelü Chucai's account in *Inscribed Landscapes*, 229–33.

5 My translation of Yang Weizhen's account is based on the text in *Youzhi xubian*, 147–49.

6 The comment about "grasping at the moon" (*zhuo yue*) alludes to a popular tale concerning the poet Li Bai, which says that one night while drunk and traveling by boat on the Great River, he reached down to "grasp" the reflection of the moon on the water but accidently fell in and drowned.

7 Following the text in Ni et al., *Zhongguo gudai youji xuan*, 2:65, and reading *yao yu* 邀余 ("invited me").

8 Yu Jin resided on Gan's Hill during the Yuan dynasty.

9 *Youzhi xubian*, 149. The various Daoist adepts mentioned in this passage are otherwise unknown.

10 Extended Ming travel accounts to distant destinations are discussed in chapter 5.

11 Rachewiltz's *Monumenta Serica* article provides a detailed outline and explanation of the controversy between Yelü Chucai and Qiu Chuji. Similarly, one of Qiu's followers, Li Zhichang (1193–1256), wrote a text titled *Account of a Journey to the West by Changchun, the Realized One* (Changchun zhenren Xiyou ji) to chronicle Qiu Chuji's journey from Shandong to Afghanistan (1220–24), where he visited Genghis Khan. As with Yelü Chucai's account, the first part of Li Zhichang's text presents his

travel itinerary, written in the style of Xuanzang's *Accounts of the Western Regions*; the second part describes the advice that Qiu Chuji gave to Genghis Khan. For an English translation of Li Zhichang's account, see Bretschneider, *Si You Ki*.

12 Sadula's text is titled "Account of Dragon Gate" (Longmen ji). It is translated in Strassberg, *Inscribed Landscapes*, 266.

13 Wu Pei-yi, in his *The Confucian's Progress*, identifies a new type of writing during the Ming he calls "spiritual autobiography." Wu argues that the authors of these introspective accounts did not have earlier forms of self-biography on which to model their texts and so turned to other genres for structural formats. The most important of these, Wu says (see especially the remarks on 95–99), is *youji*. In these Ming dynasty works concerning individual self-consciousness, the travel metaphor was utilized to represent one's life journey, the ongoing process of learning, and so on. Some of the spiritual-autobiography authors Wu describes, such as Luo Hongxian (1504–64), do combine scenic description and commentary about self-cultivation. In most of the other "spiritual biographies" the author discusses, however, the journey functions only as a metaphor. For this reason, I would argue that these works do not represent any major new trend in *youji* writing.

14 Mei and Yu, *Zhongguo youji wenxue shi*, 214. Similar assessments can be found in Ni et al., *Zhongguo gudai youji xuan*, 1:21–22, and Ward, *Xu Xiake*, 14.

15 Mei and Yu, *Zhongguo youji wenxue shi*, 221–28. Just some of the authors they cite as examples include Wang Yun (1227–1304), Yu Ji (1272–1348), Sadula, Li Dong (1274–1332), and Li Xiaoguang (1285–1348). Among these writers, one of the most important is Li Xiaoguang.

16 A *gui*, also called *yugui*, is a tablet or flat scepter held by nobles or rulers on ceremonial occasions. The point here is that the rock face of the peak is very flat.

17 "Sightseer" or "visitor" (*ke*) in this line seems to be a self-reference to Li Xiaoguang himself, though travel writers in traditional China rarely referred to themselves in this way. I suspect this line in the original text is corrupt.

18 The reference here is impossible to identify with precision because any of the three main subspecies of gibbon (*yuan*) in China can be "golden yellow" in color. See the remarks in van Gulik, *The Gibbon in China*, 2–3.

19 This Buddhist temple, built in 991, was one of the most prestigious monasteries on Yandang.

20 Li Xiaoguang, *Li Xiaoguang ji jiaozhu*, 20–21.

21 In other words, during the Han dynasty, Bell Mountain served as a barrier or bulwark that protected Yangdu (modern Yangzhou), located northeast of Nanjing.

22 The famous military strategist Zhuge Liang was once dispatched to Jinling (or modern Nanjing). Upon first gazing at the topography around the city, he remarked, "Bell Mountain, where dragons coil and tigers squat upon boulders—this is the abode of emperors and kings." Cited in *Taiping yulan*, 1:193.931.

23 "Master Xie" refers to Xie An (320–85), an important political and literary figure of the Eastern Jin period. Xie and Wang Xizhi supposedly often climbed the knoll together.

24 Wang Anshi, also known as the "Prince of Shu" (Shuwang), resided in the temple in 1084. Standing water had long been a problem in the general area around the temple, and so he had the water diverted to a nearby river. See *Wang Anshi nianpu sanzhong*, 120.

25 "Abbot Qin" refers to Yuanwu Keqin (1063–1135), a well-known Chan (or Zen) monk of the Northern Song. The Grand Tranquility and Ascendant Nation Monastery, mentioned in the next line, takes its name from a Song reign period (976–84) of the same designation.

26 Song Lian, *Song Lian quanji*, 1:4.89; also in Ni et al., *Zhongguo gudai youji xuan*, 2: 69–81. For a complete English translation of Song Lian's account, see Wu Wei, *Mingdai youji xuanyi*, 8–21.

27 Many scholars have studied and written about the intense interest in geographical knowledge and historical geography during the Ming, which resulted in the production of numerous gazetteers and geographical reference works. For a good overview of this process, see Tang Xiaofeng, *From Dynastic Geography to Historical Geography*. Yongtao Du sees the massive increase in production of comprehensive gazetteers during the last century of Ming rule, many of which were compiled by private individuals, as a theme in late Ming society that indicates concern for "spatial order" and "ordering the world"; see his "Literati and Spatial Order." Scholars are still debating the reasons that led to this Ming concern with spatial order, but these issues need not concern us. What is relevant, however, is this: commercial interest in publishing works related to geography and place, including *youji*, was certainly sparked by the growing number of people from all walks of society who were traveling and sightseeing on a regular basis. This explains why widely circulated Ming reference texts like Lu Yingyang's (1567–1644) *Accounts of the Grand Realm* (Guangyu ji; 24 *juan*) focus on famous sightseeing locations and historical figures as they relate to place. Works like this provided reader-travelers with comprehensive geographical, historical, and sightseeing-related information, including relevant *youji* accounts, about scenic sites throughout China. Song Lian and his contemporaries, concerned with historical and geographical matters as they relate to sightseeing destinations, consulted them often.

28 Several scholars have studied the concentration of tourist activity and *youji* production in Jiangnan and the Great River Delta region during the Ming and Qing periods. An especially useful source in this regard is Chen Jianqin, *Ming Qing lüyou huodong yanjiu: yi Changjiang sanjiaozhou wei zhongxin*. See especially 158–97, where the author lists 467 *youji* authors/titles surviving from the Ming and Qing periods concerning sightseeing destinations in the Lower Delta region alone. Chen (214–16) also points out that among the 181 authors he surveyed, most were natives of Jiangnan. Moreover, among this pool of Jiangnan writers, 61 were natives of Suzhou alone.

29 Du, *The Order of Places*, 201. The title of Michael Marmé's monograph *Suzhou: Where Goods of All the Provinces Converse* summarizes well the importance of the city as a commercial hub during the Ming.

30   Timothy Brook has discussed the difficulty of travel in the early Ming in his "Guides for Vexed Travelers: A Second Supplement," 98–99, and the section on "Travel" in his "Communication and Commerce" essay, 619–20. Land routes were usually not marked, and inclement weather usually made overland travel difficult or impossible. Travel by water, when available, was much preferred and cheaper. But whether traveling by land or by water, bandits always posed a great danger. On his last and most challenging journey, which lasted almost four years (1640–43), Xu Xiake was robbed no less than three times. See Ward, *Xu Xiake*, 43.

31   On the various government regulations restricting travel by common people throughout the various dynasties, see Zheng and Guan, "Zhongguo gudai chuxing de falü zhidu tanxi," 38–43.

32   The seven articles in the Ming Code concerning transgressions at guard posts or fords are translated in Jiang Yonglin, *The Great Ming Code*, 138–41.

33   Langlois, "The Hung-wu reign, 1368–1398," 123.

34   Quoted in Liscomb, *Learning from Mount Hua*, 11.

35   Xue Xuan, *Jingxuan wenji*, 18.1a–3a.

36   Shi Jian's travel accounts are remarkably similar in content and style to Xue Xuan's "Account of a Sightseeing Trip to Dragon Gate." See, for instance, the ten accounts (*ji*) that comprise *juan* 7 of Shi's collected works *Xicun ji*, several of which describe sightseeing outings to Hangzhou.

37   I refer specifically to Li's description of the Three Gorges. See chapter 1, "The Account."

38   Although collections of individual works on a single theme written by one author may not seem extraordinary to the modern reader, keep in mind that *youji* collections of this type did not appear in China until the Ming dynasty. The main reason for this development is that Ming authors traveled more and produced many more *youji* than their predecessors, especially in the later years of the dynasty.

39   Other prominent examples of the album format include Qiao Yu's (1457–1524) *Sightseeing Accounts from Jinyang* (Jinyang youji); Li Lian's (dates uncertain) *Sightseeing Accounts from Ji'nan* (Ji'nan youji); Zheng Dongbai's (dates uncertain) *Miscellaneous Accounts from Jinhua* (Jinhua zaji); and Li Yuanyang's (1497–1579), *Sightseeing Accounts from Southern Yunnan* (Diannan youji).

40   According to a recent article by Meir Shahar, Du Mu visited Mount Song to examine ancient inscriptions because he "was interested in the Shaolin inscriptions both as masterpieces of ancient calligraphy and as sources of the monastery's history," especially as it related to the warrior tradition associated with Shaolin monks (see Sharhar's "Epigraphy, Buddhist Historiography, and Fighting Monks"). The contents of Du Mu's album are drawn from writings he produced during an official trip to Gansu. Matters concerning the official side of his long journey were kept by Du in a separate text titled *Diary of an Ambassadorial Mission to the West* (Shixi riji).

41   China's most famous grouping of mountains, which are often identified as "sacred sites," are the Wuyue, or "Five Marchmounts." They are generally aligned according to the four main points on a compass, with a "Central Marchmount" in the middle. In ancient times, emperors sometimes journeyed to these mountains to perform sacrifices.

42   "Crown Prince Luling" refers to Li Xian (756–10), known posthumously as Emperor Zhongzong of the Tang, who reigned twice as emperor, once in 684 and then again from 705 to 710. He held the title Prince of Luling from 684 until 699.

43   This famous passageway on Mount Song was drilled under the supervision of Ma Zhongfu (dates uncertain), who, during the Song dynasty, served as administrator of Yanshi. The passageway is also known as Huanyuan guan, or Huanyuan Pass.

44   The Shaolin Buddhist Monastery near the base of Mount Song is regarded as the birthplace of Chan Buddhism in China. The Tang emperor Gaozong (628–84; r. 649–84) visited the monastery sometime between 670 and 674, but specific details related to his visit(s) and patronage of the monastery, as well as that of his wife, the later empress Wu Zetian, 624–705; r. 690–705), are mired in legend and myth.

45   Du Mu, *You Mingshan ji*, 3254.

46   Ward, *Xu Xiake*, 27.

47   Du Mu, *You Mingshan ji*, 3293.

48   Ibid., 3275.

49   Du, *The Order of Places*, 202–03.

50   James Cahill's essay "Huang Shan Paintings as Pilgrimage Pictures" provides a useful overview of topographical paintings concerning the Yellow Mountains produced in the late Ming and early Qing.

51   Liscomb, *Learning from Mount Hua*, 119. She speculates that Wang "may also been influenced by woodblock gazetteer illustrations."

52   Translated in Ganza, "The Artist as Traveler," 27–28. As noted by Cahill (260), a "problem of authenticity hangs over this work, as indeed over the whole persona of Leng Qian."

53   For instance, see Shen Zhou's *Album of Twelve Views of Tiger Hill* (Huqiu shier jing tuce), which is available for viewing at www.360doc.com/content/15/ 1029/11/6433232 _509172700.shtml.

54   For instance, see Wen Zhengming's *Album of Paintings and Poems on the Humble Administrator's Garden* (Zhuozheng yuan tuyong ce), available at http://slide.collec tion.sina.com.cn/slide_26_17348_27197.html#p=4.

55   As noted by Liscomb, *Learning from Mount Hua*, 117, most Chinese landscape paintings do not show scholar-figures (as Wang Lü does) facing great danger as they scaled perilous mountains.

56   Cahill, "Huang Shan Paintings as Pilgrimage Pictures," 256.

5. The Golden Age of Travel Writing in the Late Ming

Epigraph: Du Yongtao, *The Order of Places*, 23.

1   The description of late Ming travel literature just described essentially repeats that in Mei and Yu, *Zhongguo youji wenxue shi*, 238–39.

2   Timothy Brook, *The Confucians of Pleasure*, 180.

3   There are numerous published secondary sources in Chinese on the rise of tourism in the late Ming. Among the most detailed and informative of these works are Wu and Di Biase, *Youdao—Ming Qing lüyou wenhua*; and Chen Jianqin, *Ming Qing*

lüyou huodong yanjiu. Wu Jen-shu's 2003 article on tourism in the Jiangnan region, "Wan Ming de lüyou huodong yu xiaofei wenhua," is also insightful.

4   On Zhang Dai's fascinating life and writings, see Jonathan Spence, *Return to Dragon Mountain*.

5   The source for these numbers is Zhang Dai's "Daizhi," in *Langhuan wenji*, 2.66. For additional details on Zhang Dai's description of the tourist industry on Mount Tai, see Pei-yi Wu, "The Ambivalent Pilgrim," especially 73–76. For Zhang's comments on tourist accommodations at Mount Tai, see his *Taoan mengyi*, 73–74, and Spence, *Return to Dragon Mountain*, 114–19.

6   In imperial China, ten candareens (*fen*) equaled 1 mace (*qian*), which was $\frac{1}{10}$ of a tael (*liang*) of silver. During the Ming, a tael was around 36 grams, so $\frac{1}{10}$ would be approximately 3.6 grams. Today (2018), 3.6 grams of pure silver is worth about $17.50. Although it seems impossible to determine the precise equivalency in Ming dynasty coinage, still the price of admission to Mount Tai in the late Ming was probably a hefty sum for most tourists.

7   Spence, *Return to Dragon Mountain*, 119.

8   Huang Shiang-Mei (Huang Xiangmei), in her 2015 Master's thesis "Wan Ming Jiangnan diqu funü de chuyou huodong," outlines the various roles that women from elite families played in Jiangnan tourism. Many of the women who participated in the late Ming travel boom were courtesans, who either accompanied their male patrons on sightseeing trips or else took up residence with those patrons at scenic places such as West Lake. Courtesans also traveled extensively in the Ming. The most famous sojourner among them is probably Wang Wei (1597–1647), who was an accomplished poet. She is also credited with compiling a collection titled *Accounts of Famous Mountains* (Mingshan ji). Dorothy Ko calls Wang Wei "the courtesan who more than any other women contributed to the traveling boom [during the late Ming]." See her *Teachers of the Inner Chamber*, 285.

9   An excellent survey of these studies can be found in Lü Lifen's 2011 doctoral dissertation "Wan Ming youji wenxue yanjiu." As observed by Lü (13), most of these works approach late Ming *youji* as it relates to tourism.

10   Zhou, "Cong Mingren wenji kan wan Ming lüyou fengqi ji qi dilixue de guanxi," 73.

11   Jiang, a close friend of Yuan Hongdao, once remarked that "contemporary sightseeing accounts probably number into the thousands." See Jiang's preface to Yuan's *Jietuo ji*, cited in A Ying, *Wan Ming ershijia xiaopin*, 45.

12   Best known among these collections are He Tang's *Gujin you mingshan ji*; Shen Meng's (*jinshi* 1553) *General View of Various Accounts of Famous Mountains* (Mingshan zhusheng yilan ji); and Wang Shizhen's *Accounts of Famous Mountains: An Expanded Version* (Mingshan ji guangbian). It should also be mentioned that *youji* texts were included in local and regional gazetteers in the late Ming, as well as in individual treatises on famous sightseeing spots.

13   Most late Ming critical comments concerning *youji* as a literary form are brief, and these appear in prefaces to individual works and collections. To cite one example, in his preface to Hong Ruhan's (dates unknown) "Account of a Sightseeing Trip to Drum

Mountain" (Gushan youji), Cao Xuequan praises his friend's travel account because rather than being full of passages of information dug out of "histories and gazetteers" (*shizhuan fangzhi*), it instead expresses Hong's "true feelings about sightseeing" (*youqing*). Cao's preface is quoted in Shi Zhecun, *Wan Ming ershijia xiaopin*, 151.

14   Zhang Dai, *Langhuan wenji*, 5.244.

15   Wu, "An Ambivalent Pilgrim," 72.

16   That is, around 8:00 p.m.

17   Zhang Dai is referring here to himself and the boatman as "specks" in the snow scene.

18   "Huxin ting kan xue," in Zhang Dai, *Taoan mengyi*, 56.

19   McDowall raises this point in his *Qian Qianyi's Reflections on Yellow Mountain*, 20.

20   Brook, "Communication and Commerce," 624.

21   This statement is based on a survey of vignette *youji* anthologized in the following collections: Shidai Shuju, ed., *Mingren xiaopin*; Zhu Jianxin, *Wan Ming xiaopin xuanzhu*; Wu Chengxue, *Wan Ming xiaopin yanjiu*; A Ying, *Wan Ming ershi jia xiaopin*; and Shi Zhecun, *Wan Ming ershijia xiaopin*.

22   Strassberg, 305–6. The other Yuan Hongdao selection included by Strassberg, concerning Heavenly Eyes Mountain (Tianmu shan), does include some narrative of Yuan ascending the mountain, but the focus of the piece is clearly on praising the beauty of the mountain's landscape.

23   Also translated in Strassberg, 342–44.

24   During his own lifetime, Yuan Hongdao was not known mainly as a prose stylist but as a poet. His talent as a vignette author is undeniable, but his fame as a "master of *xiaopin wen*" was essentially created by the twentieth-century literary historians Zhou Zuoren (1885–1968) and Lin Yutang (1895–1976) to serve their own literary agendas. For additional information on this, see Chou Chih-p'ing's informative article "The Landscape Essays of Yuan Hung-tao."

25   This traditional festival usually fell in March, when flowers were planted, admired, and celebrated in verse.

26   "Account of a Sightseeing Trip to Brimming Well" (Manjing youji), in *Yuan Hongdao ji jianjiao*, 17.681. An English translation of this text is included in Wu Wei, *Mingdai youji xuanyi*, 181–83. In several places, my reading and translation of the original text differs from that of Wu Wei.

27   I refer to Chaves's journal article "The Yellow Mountain Poems of Ch'ien Ch'ien-i (1582–1664)" and to McDowall's monograph *Qian Qianyi's Reflections on Yellow Mountain*.

28   The topography of Nine Bends Stream and related matters are discussed in Delphine Ziegler, "The Cult of the Wuyi Mountains and Its Cultivation of the Past."

29   The Seventh Night (Qixi) Festival fell on the seventh day of the seventh month on the lunar calendar, which traditionally celebrated the annual meeting of the Herdboy (Niulang) and Weaving Maid (Zhinü), who legend says were once banished to opposite sides of the Milky Way.

30   Built during the Tang dynasty and alternately known as Myriad Years Abbey (Wannian Guan), this structure was one of the main Daoist worship sites on Wuyi.

31 The Jade Emperor is the supreme deity in religious Daoism. The Supreme Dame is also a Daoist divinity who supposedly took up residence on Wuyi during the Qin dynasty. As for the Thirteen Immortals, tradition says that at the end of the Warring States period, a man from the state of Wei named Wang Ziqian came to Wuyi in search of the Way (that is, the secret to immortality). His residence on the mountain attracted several others, who eventually selected him to be their master (or leader, *zhu*). This group later became known as the "Thirteen Immortals." Cao Xuequan is here describing statues he viewed in the Myriad Years Palace.

32 The Wuyi Mountains were appropriated by Chinese rule during the Han dynasty, and the Martial Emperor of the Han performed sacrifices there sometime after 110 BCE. While at the mountain, the emperor also sacrificed to an indigenous deity named the Lord of Wuyi (Wuyi Jun), whose food preference was dried fish (*ganyu*). *Shiji*, 28.1386.

33 This peak marks the main entranceway to the Wuyi Mountains.

34 *"Annals"* refers to the *Annals of the Religious Rites for Wuyi*.

35 According to Daoist tradition, the Lord of Wuyi once convened a meeting of mortals and immortals on the summit of Canopy Pavilion Peak. The story goes that the Lord somehow fashioned a rainbow bridge over the summit, which allowed the mortal residents of Wuyi (that is, the Lord's "great grandsons") to ascend the peak and enjoy a banquet with the Daoist gods who had invited them. There are many versions of what happened at this event, which supposedly took place in 245 BCE. Lyrics to a tune titled "Sorrowful is the Human World" are reprinted in *Wuyi shan zhi*, 7.2a.

36 Chen Youding was a native of Fujian and a loyalist Yuan dynasty military commander. The references here to the "ancient city" and "tiger" are unclear.

37 Bai Yuchan was a Daoist adept who lived during the Southern Song. He supposedly once killed an evil snake in one of Wuyi's caverns, after which the local people performed sacrifices in Bai's honor.

38 "Master Zhu" refers to Zhu Xi, who was a native of Fujian.

39 "Cloud Nest" is the name of a cavern. Chen Danshu once served as an official in the Ming government, but later in life retired to Wuyi, where he pursued the Way and brewed elixirs.

40 "Yellow caps" (*huangguan*) is another name for *daoshi*, or Daoist adepts. Elixirs were brewed in "cinnabar chambers."

41 "Wuling" refers to the utopian land described in Tao Yuanming's famous poem and prose account "Account of the Peach Blossom Spring."

42 This cavern is named after a Daoist adept who once practiced asceticism there.

43 As far as I have been able to determine, this work is not extant.

44 "Scholarly *youji*" during the Qing dynasty is discussed in Mei and Yu, *Zhongguo youji wenxue shi*, 330–38. Even though it lacks a travel narrative, Gu Yanwu's "Account of Five Terrace Mountain" (Wutai shan ji) is often cited as a representative example of "scholarly travel writing." For an English translation, see Strassberg, 357–60.

45 V. K. Ting, "On Hsü Hsia-k'o," 331.

46 Although there is a substantial body of scholarship on Wang Shixing in Chinese, there is very little in English, except for a brief biography in Goodrich and Fang, *Dictionary of Ming Biography*, 2:1405–6. This is surprising because Wang's fame among his contemporaries as a writer-traveler rivaled that of Xu Xiake.

47 Chun-shu Chang, "Appendix: Hsü Hsia-k'o (1586–1641)," in Li, *The Travel Diaries of Hsü Hsia-k'o*, 231. The Qing dynasty bibliophile and printer Ye Tingjia (1754–1832), in his preface to the 1808 edition of Xu Xiake's travel accounts, says this number "represents only about one-sixth of the first edition of the diaries." Ye's preface is reprinted in *Xu Xiake youji*, 2:1266. Most of Xu's travel writings, then, have been lost. A longer and more detailed edition of Xu Xiake's diaries was discovered in Beijing in the 1970s. For details on this and various other editions of Xu's diaries, see Tang and Yang, *Xu Xiake ji qi youji yanjiu*, 215–44, and Ward, *Xu Xiake*, 69–76.

48 Xu Xiake, *Xu Xiake youji*, 1:6.

49 Ibid., 2:1195.

50 This is an ancient name for a mountain, the precise location of which is unknown.

51 Modern editions of the *Commentary* provide additional and different information: "The source of the Lu River is the Capital of the Three Emperors. It passes north of Pengze town and from the north flows into the Great River" (Chen, *Shuijing zhu jiaozheng*, 39.923).

52 In other words, the word for hermitage or cottage (*lu*) was adopted as the mountain's name.

53 "Lushan youji," in Wang, *Wuyue you cao*, 104. "Li, the Middle Ruler of Southern the Tang" (Nan Tang Li Zhongzhu) refers to Li Jing (r. 943–61), the second of three rulers of the Kingdom of the Southern Tang (937–75).

54 The reference here is to Ouyang Xiu's poem "Mount Lu on High: Presented to Fellow Student Liu Zhongyun on His Return Home to Nankang" (Lushan gao: zeng tongnian Liu Zhongyun gui Nankang), in Ouyang Xiu, *Ouyang Xiu shiwen ji jiaojian*, 8.142 For an English translation of the verse, see Hawes, *The Social Circulation of Poetry in the Mid-Northern Song*, 86–88.

55 As an example, see Cong Ellen Zhang's case study of the "Cave of the Three Sightseers" as a literary-historical heritage site, in *Transformative Journeys*, 167–75.

56 Dennis, *Writing, Publishing, and Reading Local Gazetteers in Imperial China, 1100–1700*, 303 and 307–8.

57 I follow my usual practice of translating *you* as "to sightsee" in this line, but here Xu is also using it in the sense of "climb to the summit."

58 The comment about "as before" refers to Xu Xiake's earlier visit to the Yellow Mountains in 1616.

59 Xu was not alone in his ascent but was accompanied by Chengyuan and perhaps his servant as well. Chinese travel writers typically did not count servants and guides as members of their traveling parties.

60 Xu Xiake, *Xu Xiake youji*, 1:30–31. I have benefitted greatly from consulting Li Chi's English translation of this passage in *The Travel Diaries of Hsü Hsia-k'o*, 80–81.

61 Wang Shixing, *Wuyue you cao*, preface, 24.

62 Yongtao Du, *The Order of Places*, 209–10.

63   Ibid., 233–34.

64   "Central Counties" (Zhongzhou) is another name for the Central Plains, referring generally to the area along the lower reaches of the Yellow River, the traditional cradle of Chinese civilization.

65   Su 蘇 probably refers to *zisu* 紫蘇, *Perilla frutescens*, a purple-leaved plant of the mint family indigenous to south China.

66   The precise referent of *lei* 蠃 is unclear.

67   Tentative translation for *rongshan* 狨氈.

68   Wang Shixing, *Wuyue you cao*, 191.

69   Zhou Zhenhe, "Wang Shixing de dilixue sixiang ji qi yingxiang," 48.

70   Gu Yanwu's monumental *Advantages and Disadvantages of the Commanderies and States in the Empire* (Tianxia junguo libing shu; begun in 1639, preface written in 1662), in its focus on the advantages and disadvantages of various physical environments is clearly indebted to Wang Shixing's commentaries. See Zhou Zhenhe comments on this in "Wang Shixing de dilixue sixiang ji qi yingxiang," 23. Gu Yanwu, however, was the consummate scientific-investigative scholar, geographer, and *youji* author. His main interest was not so much on interpretation as it was on the accumulation of historical, literary, and geographical sources that could supplement his own writings and support his arguments. Gu's idea of some environments being advantageous (*li*) and others having shortcomings (*bing*), evident in the title of his *Advantages and Disadvantages of the Commanderies and States in the Empire*, in fact came from Wang Shixing.

71   See note 45.

72   Historical perspectives on the source of the Changjiang and Xu Xiake's contribution to locating that source are summarized in Xu Xueshu, "Dui 'Jiangyuan Minshan' xiang 'Jiangyuan Jinsha' guandian zhuanbian de wenhua fansi," 58–64.

73   The expedition that made the discovery was led by the Hong Kong-based explorer and photojournalist Wong Hao Man, president and founder of the China Exploration and Research Society. On the 2005 expedition, see his *Voyage of Discovery*.

74   Xu Xiake wrote a detailed essay on the origins of the Great River, but unfortunately this text has been lost. A brief abstract, however, preserved in a local gazetteer, survives. It is translated in V. K. Ting's essay "On Hsü Hsia-k'o," 335.

75   Nataša Ravbari, "The Earliest Chinese Karstologist Xu Xiake," 243. Ravbari also mentions that, as pioneer of Chinese speleology, Xu "visited over 300 caves, more than any of his predecessors or contemporaries worldwide" (248); 288 of them were karst caverns in Yunnan and Guangxi.

76   Needham and Ling, *Science and Civilisation in China*, 3:524.

77   "Hill" (*shan*), mentioned here and again below, refers to Seven Stars Spire; that is, the aboveground portion of the Seven Stars karst formation. The underground cave situated below the spire is Seven Stars Cavern.

78   The "small rock" (*xiaoshi*) mentioned in this line is a popular tourist attraction in Guilin known as "Hibiscus Rock" (Furong Shi).

79   Cao Nengshi is Cao Xuequan. He served as an official in Guangxi in 1623.

80   Literally, "rocky bamboo shoots" (*shisun*).

81 Limestone contains pores that are large enough to serve as storage areas for gas or oil, so I suspect the concern here is that lit torches might trigger an explosion.

82 Sudhana is a famous young Buddhist pilgrim who sought enlightenment by traveling extensively to study with various master-teachers and bodhisattvas.

83 Zeng Bu (1036–1107) was a Northern Song official who, in 1178, was appointed to serve as the administrative and military commissioner of the region now known as Guangxi. During one of his sightseeing tours in Guilin, he explored Seven Stars Cavern and later sponsored construction of the stone bridge mentioned here by Xu Xiake.

84 Fazang (643–712) was an important and influential patriarch of the Huayan school of Buddhism. Prayer wheels were used to help one accumulate wisdom and gain good karma.

85 Xu Xiake, *Xu Xiake youji*, 1:293–95.

86 Bangbo Hu, "Xu Xiake, a Chinese Traveller of the Seventeenth Century," 154.

87 Qian's biography says that Xu, near the time of his death, remarked that he would "die contently" if he could become China's fourth great explorer. See *Xu Xiake youji jiaozhu*, 2:1244.

88 Tang and Yang, *Xu Xiake ji qi youji yanjiu*, 53, mention that Xu Xiake used the "sun shadow" technique (*riying*; in English, this is known as the "shadow-tip" method) to determine the direction toward which the *entrances* to caverns faced but say nothing about his determining compass direction underground, where sunlight and stars were unavailable for reference. Regarding the accuracy of his directional references, in addition to the remarks in Tang and Yang, 53, see also the comments in Chen Shupeng, "Guilin Qixing yan kesite dongxue dimao tu," 159–77.

89 Liu Zongyuan, *Liu Zongyuan ji*, 29.765–66.

90 Zheng, "Xu Xiake's Travel Notes: Motion, Records and Genre Change," 33.

91 Needham and Ronan, *The Shorter Science and Civilisation in China*, 252.

92 This is the observation of Qian Qianyi. See Xu Xiake, *Xu Xiake youji jiaozhu*, 2:1242.

93 Research on China's "foreign travel writing" in the late Qing and early Republican period is still limited. Some important work has been published in Chinese by Zhong Shuhe (see bibliography), but much more needs to be done. Even less work has been produced in Western languages, although some Qing travelogues have been studied and translated into English. For instance, see Charles Desnoyers, *A Journey to the East*; and R. David Arkush and Leo Ou-fan Lee, *Land Without Ghosts*. For Liang Qichao's fascinating assessment about "The Power and Threat of America" in the early twentieth century, see *Land Without Ghosts*, 81–95. The most complete study available in English of Qing dynasty travel literature, especially foreign travel writing, is Tsui Wai's doctoral dissertation, "A Study of Wang Tao's (1828–1897) *Manyou suilu* and *Fusang youji*."

Postface

Epigraph: Hester Lynch Piozzi (1741–1821), *Letters to and from the Late Dr. Samuel Johnson, LL.D., To Which Are Added Some Poems Never Before Printed* (Dublin, 1788): 1.101.

1   *Su Shi shi ji*, 23.1219.

2   This phrase functions as a key concept in Wang's well-known work on poetic criticism *Talks on Ci Poems in the Human World* (Renjian cihua), published in 1908.

3   Shao Yong's "Chapter Observing the Physical World" (Guanwu pian) is included in his treatise *August Principles of Governing the World* (Huangji jingshi). For Shao Yong, the act of "observing the human world" is a key manifestation of human experience, and that experience has the potential to take on artistic and aesthetic significance.

4   *Shiji*, 130.3294.

BIBLIOGRAPHY

Note: An asterisk before the English title of a non-English-language work indicates that the English title was included with the original publication.

Primary Sources in Chinese (Including Modern Editions)

Bao Zhao 鮑照 (414?–66). *Bao Canjun jizhu* 包參軍集注 (Bao Canjun's collected works, with commentary). Edited by Qian Zhonglian 錢仲聯. Shanghai: Shanghai Gudian Wenxue Chubanshe, 1957.

Cao Cao 曹操 (155–220). *Cao Cao ji* 曹操集 (Cao Cao's collected works). Beijing: Zhonghua Shuju, 1962.

Cao Pi 曹丕. *Cao Pi ji jiaozhu* 曹丕集校注 (Cao Pi's collected works, with collations and commentary). Edited by Wei Hongcan 魏宏燦. Hefei: Anhui Daxue Chubanshe, 2009.

Chao Buzhi 晁補之 (1053–1110). *Jibei Chao xiansheng Jile ji* 濟北晁先生雞肋集 (Master Chao of Jibei's Chicken Bone Collection). *Sibu congkan* edition.

Da Tang Xiyu ji jiaozhu 大唐西域記校注 (Accounts of the Western Regions during the Great Tang, with collations and commentary). Edited by Ji Xianlin 季羨林 et al. Beijing: Zhonghua Shuju, 1985. Reprinted in 1994.

Du Mu 都穆 (1459–1525). *You mingshan ji* 游名山記 (Accounts of sightseeing trips to famous mountains). Preface dated 1515. *Biji xiaoshuo daguan* edition.

Fan Chengda 范成大 (1126–93). *Fan Shihu ji* 范石湖集 (Fan Shihu's collected works). Beijing: Zhonghua Shuju, 1962.

Fan Chengda biji liuzhong 范成大筆記六種 (Six informal prose works by Fan Chengda). Edited by Kong Fanli 孔凡禮. Beijing: Zhonghua Shuju, 2002.

Faxian zhuan jiaozhu 法顯傳校注 (Biography of Faxian, with collations and commentary). Edited by Zhang Xun 章巽 (1914–94). Beijing: Zhonghua Shuju, 1985.

Guwen yuan 古文苑 (Garden of ancient literature). Compiled by Zhang Qiao 章譙 (*jinshi* 1213). *Sibu congkan* edition.

Hanshu 漢書 (Documents on the Han). Compiled by Ban Gu 班固 (32–92 CE). Beijing: Zhonghua Shuju, 1962.

Hou Hanshu 後漢書 (Documents on the Later Han). Compiled by Fan Ye 范曄 (398–445). Beijing: Zhonghua Shuju, 1966.

Jinshu 晉書 (Documents on the Jin). Compiled by Fang Xuanling 房玄齡 (579–648) et al. Beijing: Zhonghua Shuju, 1974.

Li Ao 李翱 (d. 838). *Li Wengong ji* 李文公集 (Li Wengong's collected works). *Sibu congkan* edition.

Li Bai 李白 (701–62). *Li Bai ji jiaozhu* 李白集校注 (Li Bai's collected works, with collations and commentary). Edited by Qu Shuiyuan 瞿蛻園 and Zhu Jincheng 朱金城. Shanghai: Shanghai Guji Chubanshe, 1980.

Li Xiaoguang 李孝光 (1285–1350). *Li Xiaoguang ji jiaozhu* 李孝光集校注 (Li Xiaoguang's collected works, with collations and commentary). Edited by Chen Zengjie 陳增傑. Shanghai: Shanghai Shehui Kexueyuan Chubanshe, 2005.

Liu Zongyuan 柳宗元 (773–819). *Liu Zongyuan ji* 柳宗元集 (Liu Zongyuan's collected works). Beijing: Zhonghua Shuju, 1979.

Lu You 陸游 (1125–1210). *Lu Fangweng quanji* 陸放翁全集 (Complete collected works of Lu Fangweng). Taibei: Heluo Tushu Chubanshe, 1975.

Lushan lueji 廬山略記 (Brief accounts of Mount Lu). *Siku quanshu* edition.

Ouyang Xiu 歐陽修. (1007–72). *Ouyang Xiu shiwen ji jiaojian* 歐陽修詩文集校箋 (Ouyang Xiu's collected poetry and prose, with collations and notes). Shanghai: Shanghai Guji Chubanshe, 2009.

Qian Qianyi 錢謙益 (1582–1664). *Muzhai Chuxue ji* 牧齋初學集 (The beginning learner's collected works from the Shepherd's Studio). Shanghai: Shanghai Guji Chubanshe, 1985.

Quan Shangu Sandai Qin Han Sanguo Liuchao wen 全上古三代秦漢三國六朝文 (Complete prose of High Antiquity, the Three Dynasties, Qin, Han, the Three Kingdoms, and Six Dynasties). Edited by Yan Kejun 嚴可均 (1762–1843). Beijing: Zhonghua Shuju, 1958.

Quan Tangshi 全唐詩 (Complete Tang poetry). Edited by Cao Yin 曹寅 (1658–1712) et al. Beijing: Zhonghua Shuju, 1960.

Quan Tangwen 全唐文 (Complete Tang prose). Edited by Dong Hao 董浩 (1740–1818) et al. Beijing: Zhonghua Shuju, 1983.

Shi Jian 史鑒 (1434–96). *Xicun ji* 西村集 (Xicun's collected works). *Siku quanshu* edition.

Shiji 史記 (Historical records). Compiled by Sima Qian 司馬遷 (*ca.* 145–*ca.* 86 BCE). Second edition, Beijing: Zhonghua Shuju, 1982.

Shuijing zhu 水經注 (Commentary on the Waterways Treatise). Collations by Wang Guowei 王國維 (1877–1927). Shanghai: Shanghai Renmin Chubanshe, 1984.

Shuijing zhu jiaozheng 水經注校證 (Commentary on the Waterways Treatise with collations and verifications). Edited by Chen Qiaoyi 陳橋驛. Beijing: Zhonghua Shuju, 2007.

Shuowen jiezi 說文解字 (Interpreting ancient pictographs, analyzing semantic-phonetic characters). Compiled by Xu Shen 許慎 (30–124). Beijing: Zhonghua Shuju, 1963.

Shuowen jiezi zhu 說文解字注 (Commentary on interpreting ancient pictographs, analyzing semantic-phonetic characters). Commentary by Duan Yucai 段玉裁 (1735–1815). Shanghai: Shanghai Guji Chubanshe, 1981.

Siku quanshu 四庫全書 (Complete books of the Imperial Library). Wenyuan ge 文淵閣 edition. Electronic version, Shanghai: Renmin Chubanshe, n.d.

Siku quanshu zongmu tiyao 四庫全書總目提要 (Abstracts of titles in the general catalog of the Complete Books of the Imperial Library). In *Heyin Siku quanshu zongmu tiyao ji Siku weishou shumu jinmie shumu* 合印四庫全書總目提要及四庫未收書目禁燬書目. Edited by Wang Yunwu 王雲五. Taibei: Shangwu Yinshuguan, 1978.

Song Lian 宋濂 (1310–81). *Song Lian quanji* 宋濂全集 (Complete collected works of Song Lian). Beijing: Renmin Wenxue Chubanshe, 2014.

Songdai riji congbian 宋代日記叢編 (Compendium of Song era diaries). Compiled by Gu Hongyi 顧宏義 and Li Wen 李文. Shanghai: Shanghai Shudian, 2013.

Su Shi 蘇軾 (1037–1101). *Dongpo zhilin* 東坡志林 (East Slope's forest of notes). Beijing: Zhonghua Shuju, 1981. Reprinted in 1997.

———. *Su Shi shiji* 蘇軾詩集 (Su Shi's collected poetry). Edited by Wang Wenhao 王文浩 (1764–?). Beijing: Zhonghua Shuju, 1982.

Suishu 隋書 (Documents on the Sui). Compiled by Wei Zheng 魏徵 (580–643). Beijing: Zhonghua Shuju, 1973.

Taiping yulan 太平御覽 (Imperial reader of the Great Peace reign). Compiled by Li Fang 李昉 (925–96) et al. Beijing: Zhonghua Shuju, 1960.

Tao Yuanming shiwen huiping 陶淵明詩文彙評 (Assembled criticism on Tao Yuanming's poetry and prose). Edited by Taiwan Zhonghua shuju. Taiwan Zhonghua Shuju, 1969.

Wang Anshi nianpu sanzhong 王安石年譜三種 (Chronological biographies of Wang Anshi, three versions). Edited by Zhan Dahe 詹大和 (twelfth century) et al. Beijing: Zhonghua Shuju, 1994.

Wang Shixing 王士性 (1547–98). *Wuyue you cao*; *Guangyou yi* 五嶽游草; 廣游繹 (Drafts of sightseeing trips to the Five Marchmounts; Sorting out my extensive jottings). Edited by Zhou Zhenhe 周振鶴. Beijing: Zhonghua Shuju, 2006.

Wenxuan 文選 (Literary selections). Compiled by Xiao Tong 蕭統 (501–31). Commentary by Li Shan 李善 (?–689). Hong Kong: Shangwu Yinshuguan, 1973.

Wenyuan yinghua 文苑英華 (Choice flowers from the garden of literature). Compiled by Li Fang 李昉 (925–96) et al. Beijing: Zhonghua Shuju, 1966.

Wuyi shan zhi 武夷山志 (Gazetteer on the Wuyi Mountains). Edited by Dong Tiangong 董天工 (1703–71). 1754. Reprinted in 1846.

Xie Lingyuan 謝靈運. *Xie Lingyun ji jiaozhu* 謝靈運集校注 (Xie Lingyun's collected works, with collations and commentary). Edited by Gu Shaobo 顧紹柏. Zhengzhou: Zhongzhou Guji Chubanshe, 1987.

Xin Tangshu 新唐書 (New documents on the Tang). Compiled by Song Qi 宋祁 (998–1061). Beijing: Zhonghua Shuju, 1975.

Xu Xiake. *Xu Xiake youji* 徐霞客遊記 (Travel accounts of Xu Xiake). Edited by Chu Shaotang 褚紹唐 and Liu Siyuan 劉思源. Shanghai: Shanghai Guji Chubanshe, 1980.

———. *Xu Xiake youji jiaozhu* 徐霞客遊記校注 (Travel accounts of Xia Xiake, with collations and commentary). Edited by Zhu Huirong 朱惠榮. Kunming: Yunnan Renmin Chubanshe, 1985.

Xue Xuan 薛瑄 (1389–1464). *Jingxuan wenji* 敬軒文集 (Jingxuan's collected prose writings). *Siku quanshu* edition.

Yang Wanli Fan Chengda juan 楊萬里范成大卷 (Critical documents on Yang Wanli and Fan Chengda). Edited by Zhan Zhi 湛之 (Fu Xuanzong 傅璇琮). Beijing: Zhonghua Shuju, 1964.

Youzhi xubian 遊志續編 (Compendium of travels: The continuation volume). Compiled by Tao Zongyi 陶宗儀 (fl. 1360–68). *Wanwei biecang* 宛委別藏 edition (compiled between 1796 and 1820). Reprint, Taibei: Shangwu Yinshuguan, 1974.

Yuan Haowen 元好問 (1190–1257). *Yuan Haowen wen biannian jiaozhu* 元好問文編年校注 (Chronology of Yuan Haowen's prose, with collations and commentary). Edited by Di Baoxin 狄寶心. Beijing: Zhonghua Shuju, 2012.

Yuan Hongdao 袁宏道 (1568–1610). *Yuan Hongdao ji jianjiao* 袁宏道集箋校 (Yuan Hongdao's collected works, with collations and commentary). Shanghai: Shanghai Guji Chubanshe, 1981.

Yuan Jie 元結 (719–72). *Yuan Cishan ji* 元次山集 (Yuan Cishan's collected works). *Sibu beiyao* edition.

Zhang Dai 張岱 (*ca.* 1597–*ca.* 1679). *Taoan mengyi; Xihu mengxun* 陶庵夢憶; 西湖夢尋 (Taoan's dreamy recollections; Searching for West Lake in my dreams). Edited by Xia Xianchun 夏咸淳 and Cheng Weirong 程維榮. Shanghai: Shanghai Gudian Chubanshe, 2001.

———. *Langhuan wenji* 琅環文集 (Writings from the magic book repository). Beijing: Gugong Chubanshe, 2012.

Zhibuzu zhai congshu 知不足齋叢書 (Collectaneum of the Knowledge-is-Insufficient Studio). Edited by Bao Tingbo 鮑廷博 (1728–97). Beijing: Zhonghua Shuju, 1999.

Secondary Sources

A Ying 阿英, ed. *Wan Ming ershijia xiaopin* 晚明二十家小品 (Vignettes by twenty late Ming authors). Kaifeng: Henan Renmin Chubanshe, 1989.

Adams, Percy G. *Travel Literature and the Evolution of the Novel.* Lexington: University of Kentucky Press, 1983.

Aoyama, Sadao 青山定雄. *Tō Sō no jidai kōtsū to chishi chizu no kenkyū* 唐宋の時代交通と地誌地圖の研究 (*Study of the Communications Systems of the [*sic*] T'ang and Sung China and the Development of Their Topographies and Maps*). Tokyo: Yoshikawa Kōbun Kan, 1963.

Arkush, R. David, and Leo Ou-fan Lee. *Land Without Ghosts: Chinese Impressions of America from the Mid-Nineteenth Century to the Present.* Berkeley: University of California Press, 1989.

Bao Yuanhang 鮑遠航. "Yuan Shansong yu Zhongguo shanshui sanwen de kaichuang" 袁山松與中國山水散文的開創 (Yuan Shansong and the beginning of landscape prose in China). *Huaiyin shifan xueyuan xuebao* 淮陰師範學院學報 (*Zhexue shehui kexue ban*) 26, no. 5 (2004): 674–80.

———. "Nanbeichao shanshui sanwen luelun: yi *Shuijing zhu* he Nanchao shanshui xiaopin wei li" 南北朝山水散文略論: 以水經注和南朝山水小品為例 (A brief essay on the landscape prose of the Northern and Southern Dynasties: Focusing on the *Commentary on the Waterways Treatise* and landscape vignettes from the Southern Dynasties as examples). *Huzhou shifan xueyuan xuebao* 湖州師範學院學報 27, no. 6 (December 2005): 13–17.

————. "Nanbeichao shanshui sanwen de wenhua yizhi—yi *Shuijing zhu* he Nanbeichao shanshui shuzha wei li" 南北朝山水散文的文化異質—以水經注和南北朝山水書札為例 (Cultural heterogeneity in the landscape prose of the Northern and Southern Dynasties: Focusing on the *Commentary on the Waterways Treatise* and landscape letters of the Northern and Southern Dynasties as examples). *Beifang luncong* 北方論叢 5 (2007): 14–17.

Barthélemy-Sanit-Hilaire, J. *Hiouen Thsang in India*. Translated by Laura Ensor. Calcutta: Susil Gupta, 1952.

Bei Yuanchen 貝遠辰 and Ye Youming 葉幼明, eds. *Lidai youji xuan* 歷代遊記選 (Selections of travel accounts from the successive eras). Changsha: Hunan Renmin Chubanshe, 1980.

Birch, Cyril, ed. *Anthology of Chinese Literature*, Vol. 1, *From Early Times to the Fourteenth Century*. New York: Grove Press, 1965.

Boulton, Nancy Elizabeth. "Early Chinese Buddhist Travel Records as a Literary Genre." PhD diss., Georgetown University, 1982.

Bretschneider, Emil, trans. *Si You Ki, Travels to the West of Kiu Ch'ang Ch'un*. London: Trubner & Co., 1888.

Brook, Timothy. "Guides for Vexed Travelers: Route Books in the Ming and Ch'ing." *Ch'ing-shih wen-t'i* 4, no. 5 (June 1981): 32–76.

————. "Guides for Vexed Travelers: A Second Supplement." *Ching-shih wen-t'i* 4, no. 8 (December 1982): 96–109.

————. "Communication and Commerce." In *Cambridge History of China*, Vol. 7, *The Ming Dynasty, 1368–1644, Part 2*, edited by Denis Twitchett and Frederick W. Mote, 579–707. Cambridge: Cambridge University Press, 1998.

————. *The Confucians of Pleasure*: *Commerce and Culture in Ming China*. Berkeley and Los Angeles: University of California Press, 1999.

————. *Geographical Sources of Ming-Qing History, Second Edition*. Ann Arbor: University of Michigan Press, 2002.

Cahill, James. "Huang Shan Paintings as Pilgrimage Pictures." In *Pilgrimage and Sacred Sites in China*, edited by Susan Naquin and Chün-fang Yü, 246–92. Berkeley and Los Angeles: University of California Press, 1992.

Cao Daoheng 曹道衡. "Guanyu Wei Jin Nanbeichao de pianwen he sanwen" 關於魏晉南北朝的駢文和散文 (On parallel prose and free prose during the Wei, Jin, and Northern and Southern Dynasties). In *Zhonggu wenxue shi lunwen ji* 中古文學史論文集, 29–58. Beijing: Zhonghua Shuju, 1986; 2002.

Chaffee, John W. *The Thorny Gates of Learning in Sung China: A Social History of Examinations*. Albany: State University of New York Press, 1985. New edition, 1995.

Chan, Timothy Wai Keung (Chen Weiqiang). "Wall Carvings, Elixirs, and the Celestial King: An Exegetic Exercise on Du Fu's Poems on Two Palaces." *Journal of the American Oriental Society* 127, no. 4 (2007): 471–89.

————. "Dedication and Identification in Wang Bo's Compositions on the Gallery of Prince Teng." *Monumenta Serica* 50 (2002), 215–55.

Chang Chun-shu (Zhang Chunshu 張春樹) and Joan Smythe, trans. *South China in the Twelfth Century*: *A Translation of Lu Yu's Travel Diaries, July 3–December 6, 1170*. Hong Kong: The Chinese University Press, 1981.

Chang Kang-i Sun (Sun Kangyi 孫康宜). "Description of Landscape in Early Six Dynasties Poetry." In *The Vitality of the Lyric Voice*: *Shih Poetry from the Late Han to the T'ang*, edited by Shuen-fu Lin and Stephen Owen, 105–29. Princeton: Princeton University Press, 1986.

———. *Six Dynasties Poetry*. Princeton: Princeton University Press, 1986.

Chapman, Beryl. "Travel Diaries of the Southern Sung Dynasty with Particular Reference to Fan Chengda's *Wuchuan lu*." PhD diss., University of Sydney, 1983.

Chavannes, Édouard. "Pei Yuan Lou, Récit d'un voyage dans le Nord." *T'oung Pao* 5, no. 2 (1904): 163–92.

Chaves, Jonathan. "Not the Way of Poetry: The Poetics of Experience in the Sung Dynasty." *Chinese Literature: Essays, Articles, and Reviews* 4, no. 2 (July 1982): 199–212.

———. "The Yellow Mountain Poems of Ch'ien Ch'ien-i (1582–1664): Poetry as *Yu-chi*." *Harvard Journal of Asiatic Studies* 48, no. 2 (December 1988): 465–92.

———. *Every Rock a Universe*: *The Yellow Mountains and Chinese Travel Writing*. Warren, Connecticut: Floating World Editions, 2013.

Chen Cheng-siang (Chen Zhengxiang 陳正祥). *Zhongguo youji xuanzhu* 中國遊記選註 (Selected and annotated Chinese sightseeing accounts). Taibei: Nantian, 1979. Reprinted in 1994.

Chen Fei 陳飛. *Zhongguo gudai sanwen yanjiu* 中國古代散文研究 (A study of prose in ancient China). Fuzhou: Fujian Renmin Chubanshe, 2005.

Chen Jianqin 陳建勤. *Ming Qing lüyou huodong yanjiu*: *yi Changjiang sanjiaozhou wei zhongxin* 明清旅遊活動研究: 以長江三角洲為中心 (A study of tourist activity during the Ming and Qing, focusing on the Great River Delta). Beijing: Zhongguo Shehui Kexue Chubanshe, 2008.

Chen Shupeng 陳述彭. "Guilin Qixing yan kesite dongxue dimao tu" 桂林七星岩喀斯特洞穴地貌圖 (Geomorphologic illustrations of the karst caverns and caves in Guilin's Seven Stars Spire). In *Dixue de tansuo* 地學的探索 1, Beijing: Kexue Chubanshe, 1990: 159–77.

Chen Suzhen 陳素貞. "Songdai shanshui youji yanjiu" 宋代山水遊記研究 (A study of landscape travel accounts during the Song era). *Shida guowen yanjiusuo jikan* 師大國文研究所季刊 31 (June 1987): 623–740.

Chen Xiaojie 陳曉捷. "Tang Yuhua gong jianzhu kao" 唐玉華宮建築考 (*Architecture of Tang Dynasty Yuhua Palace). *Kaoguxue yanjiu* 考古學研究 153, no. 4 (2016): 65–75.

Chen Xin 陳新, ed. *Lidai youji xuanyi*: *Songdai bufen* 歷代遊記選譯: 宋代部分 (Selected translations of travel accounts from successive eras: The Song era). Beijing: Baowentang Shudian, 1987.

———. *Songren Changjiang youji* 宋人長江遊記 (Travel accounts about the Great River by Song authors). Shenyang: Chunfeng Wenyi Chubanshe, 1987.

Chen Yu-shih. *Images and Ideas in Chinese Classical Prose*: *Studies of Four Masters*. Stanford: Stanford University Press, 1988.

Chen Zuogao 陳左高. *Zhongguo riji shilue* 中國日記史略 (Short history of the diary in China). Shanghai: Shanghai Fanyi Chubanshe, 1990.

Chou Chih-p'ing (Zhou Zhiping 周質平). "The Landscape Essays of Yuan Hung-tao." *Tamkang Review* 13, no. 3 (1983): 297–312.

———. *Yuan Hung-tao and the Kung-an School*. Cambridge: Cambridge University Press, 1987.

Chu Binjie 褚彬傑. *Zhongguo gudai wenti gailun* 中國古代文體概論 (A general discussion of prose genres in ancient China). Taibei: Xuesheng Shuju, 1984. Revised and expanded edition, 1991.

Cihai 辭海 (Sea of words). Shanghai: Shanghai Cishu Chubanshe, 1979.

Cohen, Alvin P. *Grammar Notes for Introductory Classical Chinese*. San Francisco: Chinese Materials Center, Inc., 1980.

Cohen, Ralph. "History and Genre." *New Literary History* 17, no. 2 (Winter 1986): 203–18.

Cresswell, Tim. *Place: An Introduction*. 2nd edition. West Sussex, UK: John Wiley & Sons, Ltd., 2015.

Cui Xiaojing 崔小敬 and Mei Xinlin 梅新林. "Zouxiang chengshu de Tangdai youji wenxue" 走向成熟的唐代遊記文學 (The move toward maturity in travel accounts of the Tang era). *Guangxi minzu xueyuan bao* 廣西民族學院報 (*Zhexue shehui kexue ban*) 23, no. 3 (May 2001): 101–6.

De Geest, Dirk, and Hendrik van Gorp. "Literary Genres from a Systemic-Functionalist Perspective." *European Journal of English Studies* 3, no.1 (1999): 33–50.

Deeg, Max, trans. *Das Gaoseng-Faxian-Zhuan als religionsgeschichtliche Quelle*. Wiesbaden: Harrassowitz Verlag, 2005.

Dennis, Joseph R. *Writing, Publishing, and Reading Local Gazetteers in Imperial China, 1100–1700*. Cambridge, MA: Harvard University Asia Center, 2015.

Derrida, Jacques. "La Loi du genre." In *Parages*, 249–87. Paris: Galilée, 1986.

Desnoyers, Charles, trans. *A Journey to the East: Li Gui's A New Account of a Trip Around the Globe*. Ann Arbor: University of Michigan Press, 2004.

Du Yongtao. *The Order of Places: Translocal Practices of the Huizhou Merchants in Late Imperial China*. Leiden: Brill, 2015.

———. "Literati and Spatial Order: A Preliminary Study of Late Ming Comprehensive Gazetteers." *Journal of Ming Studies* 66 (September 2012): 16–43.

Durand, John R. "The Population Statistics of China, A.D. 2–1953." *Population Studies* 13, no. 3 (March 1960): 209–56.

Durrant, Stephan, Wai-yee Lee, Michael Nylan, and Hans van Ess. *The Letter to Ren An and Sima Qian's Legacy*. Seattle: University of Washington Press, 2016.

Egan, Ronald. "When There is a Parallel Text in Prose: Lu You's 1170 Yangzi River Journey in Poetry and Prose." In *Reading Medieval Chinese Poetry: Text, Context, and Culture*, edited by Paul W. Kroll, 221–50. Leiden: Brill, 2014.

———. *Qian Zhongshu, Limited Views: Essays on Ideas and Letters*. Cambridge, MA, and London, UK: Harvard University Asia Center, Harvard University Press, 1998.

Eggert, Marion. "Art and Politics: The Political Dimension in Ming-Qing *Youji* Writing." In *Crossings: Travel, Art, Literature, Politics*, edited by Rudolphus Teeuwen and Shu-li Chang, 167–87. Taipei: Bookman Books, 2001.

———. "Der Reisebericht (*youji*)." In *Die klassische chinesische Prosa. Reisebericht, Essay, Skizzen. Geschichte der chinesischen Literatur*, edited by Wolfgang Kubin et al., 95–165. München: K. G. Saur, 2003.

Elsner, Jaś, and Joan-Pau Rubiés. *Voyages and Visions: Towards a Cultural History of Travel*. London: Reaktion Books, 1996.

Emmerich, Reinhard. *Li Ao (ca. 772–ca. 841), ein chinesisches Gelehrtenleben*. Wiesbaden: Otto Haricots, 1987.

Fowler, Alastair. *Kinds of Literature: An Introduction to the Theory of Genres and Modes*. Cambridge, MA: Harvard University Press, 1982.

Franke, Herbert. "A Sung Embassy Diary of 1211–12: The *Shih-Chin Lu* of Ch'eng Cho." *Bulletin de l'École Française d'Éxtreme-Orient* 69 (1981).

Franke, Herbert, and Denis Twitchett, eds. *The Cambridge History of China: Alien Regimes and Border States, 907–1368*. Cambridge: Cambridge University Press, 1994.

Frodsham, J. D. "The Origins of Chinese Nature Poetry." *Asia Major* 8, no. 1 (1960): 72–73.

———. *The Murmuring Stream: The Life and Works of the Chinese Nature Poet Hsieh Ling-yün (385–433), Duke of K'ang-lo*. Kuala Lumpur: University of Malaya Press, 1967.

Frye, Northrup. *Anatomy of Criticism: Four Essays*. New York: Atheneum, 1966.

Fu Lehuan 傅樂煥. "Songren shi Liao yulu xingcheng kao" 宋人使遼語錄形成考 (Investigation into the formation of the conversation transcripts of Song ambassadors to the Liao). In *Liaoshi congkao* 遼史叢考, 1–29. Beijing: Zhonghua Shuju, 1984.

Fu, Li-tsui Flora. *Framing Famous Mountains: Grand Tour and Mingshan Paintings in Sixteenth-Century China*. Hong Kong: The Chinese University Press, 2009.

Ganza, Kenneth S. "The Artist as Traveler: The Origin and Development of Travel as a Theme in Chinese Landscape Painting of the Fourteenth to Seventeenth Centuries." PhD diss., Indiana University, 1990.

Gernet, Jacques. *Daily Life in China on the Eve of the Mongol Invasion 1250–1276*. Translated by H. M. Wright. Stanford: Stanford University Press, 1962.

Goodrich, L. Carrington, and Chaoying Fang, eds. *Dictionary of Ming Biography, 1368–1644*. New York and London: Columbia University Press, 1976.

Hargett, James M. "Fan Ch'eng-ta's *Lan p'ei lu*: A Southern Sung Embassy Account." *Tsing Hua Journal of Chinese Studies, New Series* 16, nos. 1–2 (December 1984): 119–77.

———. "Some Preliminary Remarks on the Travel Records of the Song Dynasty (960–1279)." *Chinese Literature: Essays, Articles, Reviews* 7, nos. 1–2 (July 1985): 67–93.

———. *On the Road in Twelfth Century China: The Travel Diaries of Fan Chengda (1126–1193)*. Stuttgart: Franz Steiner Verlag, 1989.

———. "The Travel Records (*Yu-chi*) of Su Shih (1037–1101)." *Han-hsüeh yen-chiu* 漢學研究 8, no. 2 (December 1990): 369–96.

———. *Riding the River Home: A Complete and Annotated Translation of Fan Chengda's* 范成大 (1126–1193) *Diary of a Boat Trip to Wu (Wuchuan lu* 呉船録). Hong Kong: The Chinese University Press, 2008.

———. "What Need Is There to Go Home? Travel as a Leisure Activity in the *Youji* 游記 of Su Shi 蘇軾 (1037–1101)." *Chinese Historical Review* 23, no. 2 (2016): 1–19.

Harrist, Robert E., Jr. *The Landscape of Words: Stone Inscriptions from Early and Medieval China*. Seattle: University of Washington Press, 2008.

Hawes, Colin C. *The Social Circulation of Poetry in the Mid-Northern Song*: *Emotional Energy and Literati Self-Cultivation*. Albany: SUNY Press, 2011.

He Li 何李. "Tangdai jiti wen yanjiu" 唐代記體文研究 (Study of the *ji* prose form during the Tang era). PhD diss., East China Normal University, 2010.

He Peixiong 何沛雄 (aka Kenneth Ho). *Yongzhou baji daodu* 永洲八記導讀 (Reader's guide to "Eight Accounts of Yong County"). Hong Kong: Zhonghua Shuju, 1990.

He Zhan 何瞻 (James M. Hargett). "Chongxin pinggu Xu Xiake zai Zhongguo gudai wenxue shi shang de diwei" 重新評估徐霞客在中國古代文學史上的地位 (Xu Xiake and his place in the history of traditional Chinese travel literature: A reassessment). *Xu Xiake yanjiu* 徐霞客研究 28 (2014): 23–35.

Hightower, James Robert. "Some Characteristics of Parallel Prose." In *Studies in Chinese Literature*, edited by John L. Bishop, 108–39. Cambridge: Harvard University Press, 1966.

Ho Ping-ti (He Bingdi 何炳棣). "An Estimate of the Total Population in Sung-Chin China." In *Études Sung: Song Studies: In Memoriam Étienne Balázs*, vol. I, especially 52. The Hague, Netherlands: Mouton & Co., 1970.

Holzman, Donald. *Landscape Appreciation in Ancient and Early Medieval China*: *The Birth of Landscape Poetry*. Six Lectures Given at National Tsing Hua University, February–March 1995. Hsin-chu, Taiwan: National Tsing Hua University, Program for Research of Intellectual-Cultural History, 1996.

Hostetler, Laura. *Qing Colonial Enterprise*: *Ethnography and Cartography in Early Modern China*. Chicago: University of Chicago Press, 2001.

Hsieh Chiao-min. "Hsia-Ke Hsu—Pioneer of Modern Geography in China." *Annals of the Association of American Geographers* 48, no. 1 (March 1958): 73–82.

Hu Bangbo. "Xu Xiake, a Chinese Traveller of the Seventeenth Century, and His Contribution to Karst Studies." *Cave Science* 18, no. 3 (December 1991): 153–57.

Hu Yicheng 胡義成, ed. *Ming xiaopin sanbai pian* 明小品三百篇 (Ming vignettes: three hundred selections). Xi'an: Xibei Daxue Chubanshe, 1992.

Huang Hua'nan 黃華南. "Qianlun *Shuijing zhu* de wenxue jiazhi" 淺論水經注的文學價值 (A brief discussion of the literary value of the *Commentary on the Waterways Treatise*). *Jingji yu shehui fazhan* 經濟與社會發展 3, no. 11 (November 2005): 161–63.

Huang Meiling 黃美玲. *Ming Qing shiqi Taiwan youji yanjiu* 明清時期臺灣遊記研究 (A study of travel accounts about Taiwan during the Ming and Qing periods). Taibei: Wenjin Chubanshe Youxian Gongsi, 2012.

Huang Shiang-Mei (Huang Xiangmei) 黃湘娟. "Wan Ming Jiangnan diqu funü de chuyou huodong" 晚明江南地區婦女的出遊活動 (*Women's excursions in Jiangnan region during late Ming period). Master's thesis, National Cheng Kung University (Taiwan), 2014.

Hulme, Peter, and Tim Youngs, eds. *The Cambridge Companion to Travel Writing*. Cambridge: Cambridge University Press, 2002.

Hulsewé, A. F. P. "The Problem of the Authenticity of *Shih-chi*, ch. 123, the Memoir on Ta-yüan." *T'oung Pao* 61, nos. 1–3 (1975): 83–147.

Jenner, W. J. F., trans. *Memories of Loyang: Yang Hsüan-chih and the Lost Capital, 493–534*. Oxford: Oxford University Press, 1981.

Jiang Yonglin. *The Great Ming Code / Da Ming lü*. Seattle: University of Washington Press, 2005.

Kam Pun Pun 金彬彬 (Jin Binbin). "Wan Ming xiaopin chutan" 晚明小品初探 (*A preliminary study of the xiao pin in the late Ming period, ca.1573–1644). Master's thesis, University of Hong Kong, 2012.

Kirkova, Zornica. "Distant Roaming and Visionary Ascent: Sun Chuo's 'You Tiantai shan fu' Reconsidered." *Oriens Extremus* 47 (2008): 192–214.

———. *Roaming into the Beyond: Representations of* Xian *Immortality in Early Medieval Verse*. Leiden and Boston: Brill, 2016.

Knechtges, David R., trans. Wen xuan *or Selections of Refined Literature, Volume 1: Rhapsodies on Metropolises and Capitals*. Princeton: Princeton University Press, 1983.

———. Wen Xuan *or Selections of Refined Literature, Volume II: Rhapsodies on Sacrifices, Hunting, Travel, Sightseeing, Palaces and Halls, Rivers and Seas*. Princeton: Princeton University Press, 1987.

———. "Poetic Travelogue in the Han Fu." In *Proceedings of the Second International Conference on Sinology*, vol. 1, 127–52. Taibei: Academia Sinica, 1989.

———. Wen Xuan *or Selections of Refined Literature, Volume III: Rhapsodies on Natural Phenomena, Birds and Animals, Aspirations and Feelings, Sorrowful Laments, Literature, Music, and Passions*. Princeton: Princeton University Press, 1996.

Knechtges, David R., and Taiping Chang, eds. *Ancient and Early Medieval Chinese Literature: A Reference Guide, Part 3 & 4*. Leiden: Brill, 2014.

Ko, Dorothy. *Teachers of the Inner Chamber: Women and Culture in Seventeenth-Century China*. Stanford: Stanford University Press, 1995.

Kroll, Paul W., ed. *A Student's Dictionary of Classical and Medieval Chinese*. Leiden: Brill, 2015.

Langlois, John D., Jr. "The Hung-wu reign, 1368–1398," in *Cambridge History of China*, Vol. 7, *The Ming Dynasty, 1368–1644, Part 1*, edited by Frederick W. Mote and Denis Twitchett, 107–81. Cambridge: Cambridge University Press, 1988.

Lee, Thomas H. C. *Government Education and Examinations in Sung China*. Hong Kong: The Chinese University of Hong Kong, 1985.

Legge, James, trans. *A Record of Buddhistic Kingdoms: Being an Account by the Chinese Monk Fâ-Hien of His Travels in India and Ceylon (A.D. 399–414) in Search of the Buddhist Books of Discipline*. 1886. Reprint, New York: Paragon Book Reprint Corporation / Dover Publications, Inc., 1965.

Levine, Ari Daniel. "Welcome to the Occupation: Collective Memory, Displaced Nostalgia, and Dislocated Knowledge in Southern Song Ambassadors' Travel Records of Jin-Dynasty Kaifeng." *T'oung Pao* 99, nos. 4–5 (2013): 379–444.

Li Boqi 李伯齊. *Zhongguo gudai jiyou wenxue shi* 中國古代紀游文學史 (History of travel literature in ancient China). Ji'nan: Shandong Youyi Shushe, 1989.

Li Chi, trans. *The Travel Diaries of Hsü Hsia-k'o*. Hong Kong: The Chinese University Press of Hong Kong, 1974.

Liang Keng-yao 梁庚堯 (Liang Genggyao). *Songdai shehui jingji shi lunji* 宋代社會經濟史論集 (Collected essays on the history of society and the economy during the Song era). Taibei: Yunchen Wenhua Shiye Gufen Youxian Gongsi, 1997.

Liscomb, Kathlyn Maurean. *Learning from Mount Hua: A Chinese Physician's Illustrated Travel Record and Painting Theory*. Cambridge: Cambridge University Press, 1993.

Lü Lifen 呂麗粉. "Wan Ming youji wenxue yanjiu" 晚明遊記文學研究 (* "Study on travel literature in Late Ming Dynasty"). PhD diss., Chinese Culture University (Taiwan), 2011.

Lu Zongli (Lü Zongli). "Problems Concerning the Authenticity of *Shih-chi* 123 Reconsidered." *Chinese Literature: Essays, Articles, Reviews* 17 (1995): 51–68.

Luca, Dinu. "Zong Bing, Xie Lingyuan and the Invention of Landscape." Unpublished manuscript. Adobe PDF File.

Luo Yinan. "A Study of the Changes in the Tang-Song Transition Model." *Journal of Sung-Yuan Studies* 35 (2005): 99–127.

Luo Yuming, ed. *A Concise History of Chinese Literature*. Leiden: Brill, 2011.

Lusthaus, Dan. *Buddhist Phenomenology: A Philosophical Investigation of Yogācāra Buddhism and the* Ch'eng Wei-shih lu. London and New York: RoutledgeCurzon, 2002.

Ma, Lawrence. *Commercial Development and Urban Change in Sung China: 960–1279*. Ann Arbor: University of Michigan, Department of Geography, 1971.

Mair, Victor H., ed. *The Columbia History of Chinese Literature*. New York: Columbia University Press, 2001.

Marmé, Michael. *Suzhou: Where Goods of All the Provinces Converse*. Stanford: Stanford University Press, 2007.

Mather, Richard. "The Landscape Buddhism of the Fifth Century Poet Hsieh Ling-yün." *The Journal of Asian Studies* 18, no. 1 (November 1958): 67–79.

———. "The Mystical Ascent of the T'ian-tai Mountains." *Monumenta Serica* 20 (1961): 226–45.

———, trans. "Preface to the Golden Valley Poems." In *Classical Chinese Literature: From Antiquity to the Tang*, edited by John Minford and Joseph S. M. Lau, 475–76. New York: Columbia University Press, 2000.

McDowall, Stephen. *Qian Qianyi's Reflections on Yellow Mountain: Traces of a Late Ming Hatchet and Chisel*. Hong Kong: Hong Kong University Press, 2009.

Mei Xinlin 梅新林 and Cui Xiaojing 崔小敬. "Zhang Shunmin 'Chenxing lu' kaolun" 張舜民《郴行錄》考論 (Critical essays on Zhang Shunming's *Register of a Trip to Chen County*). *Wenxian* 文獻 1 (2001): 151–58.

Mei Xinlin 梅新林 and Yu Zhanghua 俞樟華. *Zhongguo youji wenxue shi* 中國游記文學史 (History of travel-account literature in China). Shanghai: Xuelin Chubanshe, 2004.

Mirsky, Jeannette, ed. *The Great Chinese Travelers: An Anthology*. London: Allen & Unwin, 1965.

Moessner, Lilo. "Genre, Text Type, Style, Register: A Terminological Maze?" *European Journal of English Studies* 5, no. 2 (2001): 131–38.

Murayama Yoshihiro 村山吉廣. "Ri Kō no 'Rainan roku' ni tsuite" 李翱の來南錄について (On Li Ao and his *Register of Coming South*). *Chūgoku koten kenkyū* 中国古典研究 18 (1971): 43–63.

Needham, Joseph, and Ronan, Colin A. *The Shorter Science and Civilisation in China*, vol. 2, *History of Scientific Thought*. Reprint, Cambridge: Cambridge University Press, 1985.

Needham, Joseph, and Wang Ling. *Science and Civilisation in China*, Vol. 3, *Mathematics and the Sciences of the Heavens and the Earth*. Reprinted edition, Cambridge: Cambridge University Press, 1992.

Ni Qixin 倪其心 et al., eds. *Zhongguo gudai youji xuan* 中國古代游記選 (Selected travel accounts from ancient China). Beijing: Zhongguo Lüyou Chubanshe, 1985.

Nienhauser, William H., Jr., et al. *Liu Tsung-yüan*. New York: Twayne Publishers, 1973.

Nienhauser, William H., Jr., et al., eds. *The Indiana Companion to Traditional Chinese Literature*. Bloomington: Indiana University Press, 1986.

Nugent, Christopher M. B. *Manifest in Words, Written on Paper: Producing and Circulating Poetry in Tang Dynasty China*. Cambridge: Harvard University Asia Center, 2011.

Nylan, Michael. "Wandering the Ruins: The *Shuijing zhu* Reconsidered." In *Interpretation and Literature in Early Medieval China*, edited by Alan K. L. Chan and Yuet Keung Lo, 63–102. Albany: State University of New York Press, 2010.

Obi Kōichi 小尾郊一. "Rokuchō ni okeru yūki" 六朝に於ける遊記 (On travel accounts from the Six Dynasties). *Shinagaku kenkyū* 支那學研究 16 (February 1957): 12–32.

———. *Zhongguo wenxue zhong suo biaoxian de ziran yu ziran guan* 中國文學中所表現的自然與自然觀 (Nature and the views of nature expressed in Chinese literature). Translated by Shao Yiping 邵毅平. Shanghai: Shanghai Guji Chubanshe, 1989. This is a Modern Chinese translation of Obi's *Chūgoku bungaku ni arawareta shizen to shizenkan, chūsei bungaku o chūshin to shite* 中国文学に現われた自然と自然観—中世文学を中心として, Tokyo: Iwanami, 1963.

Qian Zhongshu 錢鍾書. *The Limited Views Collection* (Guanzhui bian 管錐編). Beijing, Zhonghua Shuju, 1979.

Rachewiltz, Igor. "The Hsi-Yu Lu 西遊錄 by Yeh-Lü Ch'u-ts'ai 耶律楚材." *Monumenta Serica* 21 (1962): 1–128.

Ravbari, Nataša. "The Earliest Chinese Karstologist Xu Xiake." *Acta carsologica* 32, no. 1 (2003): 243–54.

Ren Fangqiu 任訪秋. "*Shuijing zhu* yu youji wenxue" 水經注與遊記文學 (*Commentary on the Waterways Treatise* and travel account literature). *Wenshi zhishi* 文史知識 9 (1984): 20–25.

Ren Huanlin 任唤麟. *Mingdai lüyou dili yanjiu* 明代旅游地理研究 (*A Study on the Tourism Geography of Ming Dynasty*). Hefei: Zhongguo Kexue Jishu Daxue Chubanshe, 2013.

Ren Huanlin 任唤麟, Gong Shengsheng 龔勝生, and Zhou Jun 周軍. "Wan Ming lüyou ziyuan leixing jiegou yu diyu fenbu, yi *Sancai tuhui* yu *Mingshan shengji* wei shuju laiyuan" 晚明旅遊資源類型結構與地域分佈, 以《三才圖會》與《名山勝記》為數據來源 (*Study on the composition of types and geographical distribution of tourism resources in the late Ming dynasty*). *Dili yanjiu* 地理研究 30, no. 3 (2011): 477–85.

Richter, Antje. *Letters and Epistolary Culture in Early Medieval China*. Seattle: University of Washington Press, 2013.

Rickett, Adele Austin, trans. *Wang Kuo-wei's Jen-chien Tz'u-hua: A Study in Chinese Literary Criticism*. Hong Kong: Hong Kong University Press, 1977.

Rudolph, Deborah Marie. "Literary Innovation and Aesthetic Tradition in Travel Writing of the Southern Sung: A Study of Fan Ch'eng-ta's *Wu-ch'uan lu*. PhD diss., University of California, Berkeley, 1996.

———. "The Power of Places: A Northern Sung Literatus Tours the Southern Suburbs of Ch'ang-an." *Journal of the American Oriental Society* 114, no. 1 (January-March 1994): 11–22.

Schafer, Edward H. "Created Nature in T'ang Literature." *Philosophy East and West* 15 (1965): 155.

———. *Vermilion Bird*: *T'ang Images of the South*. Berkeley and Los Angeles: University of California Press, 1967.

Sharhar, Meir. "Epigraphy, Buddhist Historiography, and Fighting Monks: The Case of The Shaolin Monastery." *Asia Major, Third Series* 13, no. 2 (2000): 15–36.

Shi Zhecun 施蟄存, ed. *Wan Ming ershijia xiaopin* 晚明二十家小品 (Vignettes from twenty late Ming authors). Taibei: Xinwen Feng Chuban Gongsi, 1977.

Shiba, Yoshinobu. *Commerce and Society in Sung China*. Translated by Mark Elvin. Ann Arbor: University of Michigan Press, 1970.

Shidai shuju 時代書局, ed. *Mingren xiaopin* 明人小品 (Vignettes by Ming authors). Taibei: Shidai Shuju, 1975.

Smith, Paul Jakov, and Richard von Glahn, eds. *The Song-Yuan-Ming Transition in Chinese History*. Cambridge, MA: Harvard University Asia Center, 2003.

Soper, Alexander C. "Early Chinese Landscape Painting." *The Art Bulletin* 23, no. 2 (June, 1941): 141–64.

Speake, Jennifer, ed. *Literature of Travel and Exploration*: *An Encyclopedia*. New York: Fitzroy Dearborn, 2003.

Spence, Jonathan D. *Return to Dragon Mountain*: *Memories of a Late Ming Man*. New York: Viking, 1988.

Spring, Madeline K. "A Stylistic Study of Tang 'Guwen': The Rhetoric of Han Yu and Liu Zongyuan." PhD diss., University of Washington, 1983.

———. "T'ang Landscapes of Exile." *Journal of the American Oriental Society* 117, no. 2 (April–June 1997): 312–23.

Strassberg, Richard E., trans. *Inscribed Landscapes*: *Travel Writing from Imperial China*. Berkeley and Los Angeles: University of California Press, 1994.

Su Jui-lung (Su Ruilong 蘇瑞隆), trans. "An Annotated English Translation of Bao Zhao's 'Letter to My Younger Sister upon Ascending the Bank of Thunder Lake' 登大雷岸與妹書." *Renditions* 41–42 (1994): 18–24.

Sullivan, Michael. "Notes on Early Chinese Landscape Painting." *Harvard Journal of Asiatic Studies* 18, nos. 3–4 (December 1955): 422–46.

———. *The Birth of Landscape Painting in China*. Berkeley: University of California Press, 1962.

Sun Changwu 孫昌武. *Liu Zongyuan zhuan lun* 柳宗元傳論 (Essays on the biography of Liu Zongyuan). Beijing: Renmin Wenxue Chubanshe, 1982.

Swartz, Wendy. "Naturalness in Xie Lingyun's Poetic Works." *Harvard Journal of Asiatic Studies* 70, no. 2 (December 2010): 355–86.

Sweeting, Marjorie M. *Karst in China: Its Geomorphology and Environment*. Berlin and Heidelberg: Springer-Verlag, 1995.

Tang Xiaofeng, *From Dynastic Geography to Historical Geography: A Change in Perspective towards the Geographic Past of China*. Beijing: The Commercial Press, 2000.

Tang Xiren 唐錫仁 and Yang Wenheng 楊文衡. *Xu Xiake ji qi youji yanjiu* 徐霞客及其遊記研究 (Study of Xu Xiake and his travel accounts). Beijing: Zhongguo Shehui Kexue Yuan, 1987.

Teng, Emma J. *Taiwan's Imagined Geographies: Chinese Colonial Travel Writing and Pictures*. Cambridge: Harvard University Press, 2004.

Thompson, Carl, ed. *The Routledge Companion to Travel Writing*. London and New York: Routledge, Taylor & Francis Group, 2016.

Tian Xiaofei 田曉菲. *Visionary Journeys: Travel Writings from Early Medieval and Nineteenth-Century China*. Cambridge: Harvard University Asia Center, 2012.

———. *Tao Yuanming & Manuscript Culture: The Record of a Dusty Table*. Seattle: University of Washington Press, 2005.

Ting, V. K. (Ding Wenjiang 丁文江). "On Hsü Hsia-k'o 徐霞客, Explorer and Geographer." *The New China Review* (Shanghai) 3, no. 5 (October 1921): 325–37.

Tsui Wai (Xu Wei 徐瑋). "A Study of Wang Tao's (1828–1897) *Manyou suilu* and *Fusang youji* with Reference to Late Qing Chinese Foreign Travels." PhD diss., University of Edinburgh, 2009.

Tuan Yi-fu (Duan Yifu 段義孚). *Space and Place: The Perspective of Experience*. Minneapolis: University of Minnesota Press, 1977.

Twitchett, Denis, and Paul Jakov Smith, eds. *The Cambridge History of China*, Vol. 5, Part 1, *The Sung Dynasty and Its Precursors*. Cambridge: Cambridge University Press, 2009.

van Gulik, Robert H. *The Gibbon in China: An Essay in Chinese Animal Lore*. Leiden: E. J. Brill, 1967.

Walton, Linda. "*Diary of a Journey to the North*: Lou Yue's *Beixing rilu*." *Journal of Song-Yuan Studies* 32 (2002): 1–38.

Wang Fengyang 王鳳陽. *Guci bian* 古辭辨 (Differentiating ancient terminology). Changchun: Jilin Wenshi Chubanshe, 1993.

Wang Fuxin 王福鑫. *Songdai lüyou yanjiu* 宋代旅遊研究 (A study of tourism during the Song era). Baoding: Hebei Daxue Chubanshe, 2007.

Wang Liping. "Paradise for Sale: Urban Space and Tourism in the Social Transformation of Hangzhou, 1589–1937." PhD diss., University of California-San Diego, 1997.

Wang Liqun 王立群. "Su Shi de *youji* wen" 蘇軾的游記文 (Su Shi's prose travel accounts). *Henan daxue xuebao* 河南大學學報 (*Shehui kexue ban*) 2 (1986): 39–41.

———. *Zhongguo gudai shanshui youji yanjiu* 中國古代山水游記研究 (A study of landscape travel accounts from China's ancient eras). Beijing: Zhongguo Shehui Kexue Chubanshe, 2008.

Wang Yi-t'ung, trans. *An Account of Buddhist Monasteries in Lo-yang*. Princeton: Princeton University Press, 1984.

Wang Yuyi 王雨翌. "Wan Ming youji wenxue yanjiu" 晚明游記文學研究 (A study of late Ming travel account literature). Master's thesis, Zhejiang University, 2013.

Ward, Julian. *Xu Xiake (1587–1641): The Art of Travel Writing*. Richmond (London): Curzon, 2001.

Watson, Burton. "Cao Pi: Two Letters to Wu Zhi, Magistrate of Zhaoge." *Renditions* 41–42 (Spring and Autumn 1994): 7–11.

———. *Chinese Rhyme-Prose: Poems in the Fu Form from the Han and Six Dynasties Period*. New York and London: Columbia University Press, 1971.

———. *Records of the Grand Historian of China, Han Dynasty II*. New York: Columbia University Press, 1961. Revised edition, 1993.

West, Stephen H. "Discarded Treasure: The Wondrous Rocks of Lingbi." In *Space and Cultural Fields: The Cultural Interpretation of Mobility*, 187–248. Taipei: Center for Chinese Studies, 2009.

Whitfield, Peter. *Travel: A Literary History*. Oxford: The Bodleian Library, 2011.

Wilhelm, Hellmut. "Shih Ch'ung 石崇 and His Chin-ku-yüan 金谷園." *Monumenta Serica* 18 (1959): 314–27.

Wong Hao Man. *Voyage of Discovery*. Taibei: Commonwealth Publishing Group, 2007.

Wriggins, Sally Hovey. *The Silk Road Journey with Xuanzang*. Revised edition, Boulder: Westview Press, 2004.

Wright, David Curtis. *From War to Diplomatic Parity in Eleventh-Century China: Sung's Foreign Relations with the Kitan Liao*. Leiden and Boston: Brill, 2005.

Wu Chengxue 吳承學, ed. *Wan Ming xiaopin yanjiu* 晚明小品研究 (Study of late Ming vignettes). Nanjing: Jiangsu Guji Chubanshe, 1998.

Wu Jen-shu 巫仁恕 (Wu Renshu). "Wan Ming de lüyou huodong yu xiaofei wenhua— yi Jiangnan wei taolun zhongxin" 晚明的旅遊活動與消費文化:以江南為討論中心 (*Travel and consumption culture in late Ming China: A case study of the Jiangnan Region*"). Nan'gang, Taiwan: *Zhongyang yanjiuyuan: Jindai shi yanjiusuo jikan* 中央研究院: 近代史研究所集刊 41 (September 2003): 87–143.

Wu Jen-shu 巫仁恕 (Wu Renshu) and Imma Di Biase (狄雅斯). *Youdao—Ming Qing lüyou wenhua* 遊道—明清旅遊文化 (*Serious sightseers: Travel culture during the Ming and Qing*). Taibei: Sanmin Shuju, 2010.

Wu Pei-yi 吳佩宜 *The Confucian's Progress: Autobiographical Writings in Traditional China*. Princeton: Princeton University Press, 1990.

———. "An Ambivalent Pilgrim to T'ai Shan in the Seventeenth Century." In *Pilgrimage and Sacred Sites in China*, edited by Susan Naquin and Chün-fang Yü (Yu Junfang 于君方), 65–88. Berkeley: University of California, 1992.

Wu Wei 吳衛, trans. *Mingdai youji xuanyi* 明代遊記選譯 (*Classical travel sketches of the Ming dynasty*). Beijing: Shangwu Yinshuguan, 2015.

Wu Ya-Ting (Wu Yating) 吳雅婷. "Yidong de fengmao: Songdai lüxing huodong de shehui wenhua neihan" 移動的風貌: 宋代旅行活動的社會文化內涵 (*Movement Matters: Sociocultural Connotations of Travel Activity During the Song Era*). PhD diss., National Taiwan University, 2007.

———. "Bu'an de xiehou—Songren yu lüsu changsuo de hudong yu qi kongjian yinxiang" 不安的邂逅—宋人於旅宿場所的互動與其空間印象 (*Anxious Encounters: Travel Accommodations and Impressions of Space during the Song Dynasty*). *Xin Shixue* 新史學 (*New History*) 21, no. 4 (December 2010): 141–202.

Xu Xueshu 徐學書. "Dui 'Jiangyuan Minshan' xiang 'Jiangyuan Jinsha' guandian zhuanbian de wenhua fansi" 對 "江源岷山" 向 "江源金沙" 觀點轉變的文化反思 (*"Cultural reflection on the change of 'River Source in Minshan' to 'River Source in Jinsha'"). *Zhonghua wenhua luntan* 中華文化論壇 5 (2013): 58–64.

Xuanzang 玄奘. *The Great Tang Dynasty Record of the Western Regions*. Translated by Li Rongxi. Berkeley: Numata Center for Buddhist Translation and Research, 1996.

Xue Zhongshan 薛仲三 and Ouyang Yi 歐陽頤, eds. *A Sino-Western Calendar for Two Thousand Years* (Liangqian nian Zhong-Xi li duizhao biao 兩千年中西曆對照表). Shanghai: Shangwu Yinshuguan, 1940.

Yang, Xiaoshan 楊曉山. "Naming and Meaning in the Landscape Essays of Yuan Jie and Liu Zongyuan." *Journal of the American Oriental Society* 120, no. 1 (January-March 2000): 82–96.

Yu Kwang-chung (Yu Guangzhong 余光中). "The Sensuous Art of the Chinese Landscape Journal." Translated by Yang Qinghua. *Renditions* 19–20 (Spring-Autumn 1983): 23–40.

———. "Zhongguo shanshui youji de zhixing" 中國山水遊記的知性 (The intellectual art of the Chinese landscape account). *Mingbao yuekan* 明報月刊 17, no. 12 (December 1982): 69–72.

Zhang, Ellen Cong 張聰. *Transformative Journeys: Travel and Culture in Song China*. Honolulu: University of Hawai'i Press, 2011.

———. "Things Heard in the Past, Material for Future Use: A Study of Song *biji* Prefaces." *East Asian Publishing and Society* 6 (2016): 22–53.

Zhang Hanxun 張翰勛. "*Shuijing zhu* de xiejing yuyan" 水經注的寫景語言 (Language describing scenery in the *Commentary on the Waterways Treatise*). *Lanzhou daxue xuebao* 蘭州大學學報 3 (1981): 86–96.

Zhang Jiaxin 張嘉昕. *Mingren de lüyou shenghuo* 明人的旅遊生活 (The travel lifestyle of people during the Ming). Yilan xian (Taiwan): Mingshi Yanjiu Xiaozu, 2004.

Zhao Shugong 趙樹功. "Xie Lingyun *You mingshan zhi* bianming ji yiwen" 謝靈運《游名山志》辨名及逸文 (Distinguishing names and lost text from Xie Lingyun's *Notes on Sightseeing Trips to Famous Mountains*). *Wenxian* 文獻 2 (April 2009): 175–77.

Zheng, Yi. "Xu Xiake's Travel Notes: Motion, Records and Genre Change." In *Motion and Knowledge in the Changing Early Model World*, edited by Ofer Gal and Yi Zheng, 31–46. Dordrecht: Springer, 2014.

Zheng Xianwen 鄭顯文 and Guan Xiaoli 管曉立. "Zhongguo gudai chuxing de falü zhidu tanxi" 中國古代出行的法律制度探析 (*The study of the traffic law system in ancient China), *Beijing hangkong hangtian daxue xuebao* 北京航空航天大學學報 (*Journal of Beijing University of Aeronautics and Astronautics, Social Sciences Edition*) 27, no. 1 (January 2014): 38–43.

Zhong Shuhe 鍾叔河. *Zouxiang shijie: jindai zhishi fenzi kaocha Xifang de lishi* 走向世界: 近代知識分子考察西方的歷史 (Going out to the world: A history of modern intellectuals' investigation of the West). Beijing: Xinhua Shudian, 1985.

Zhong Xiaoyan 鍾小燕. "Liu Zongyuan yu Ouyang Xiu shanshui ji bijiao" 柳宗元與歐陽修山水記比較 (A comparison of Liu Zongyuan and Ouyang Xiu's landscape accounts). *Wenshizhe* 文史哲 3 (Shandong daxue 山東大學) (1986): 12–21.

Zhou Luanshu 周鑾書 and Zhao Ming, 趙明, eds. *Lushan youji xuan* 廬山游記選 (Selections of travel accounts on Mount Lu). Nanchang: Jiangxi Renmin Chubanshe, 1996.

Zhou Zhenhe 周振鶴. "Wang Shixing de dilixue sixiang ji qi yingxiang" 王士性的地理學思想及其影響 (*Wang Shixing's geographical ideas and its impact). *Dili xuebao* 地理學報 (*Acta Geographica Sinica*) 48, no. 1 (1993): 19–23.

———. "Cong Mingren wenji kan wan Ming lüyou fengqi ji qi dilixue de guanxi" 從明人文集看晚明旅游風氣及其地理學的關係 (*The traveling fashion in late Ming dynasty and its relationship with geography: A research on the anthologies of literators in Ming). *Fudan xuebao* 復旦學報 (*Shehui kexue ban*) 1 (2005): 72–78.

Zhu Defa 朱德發. "Shilun Zhongguo youji sanwen de wenti tezheng" 式論中國游記散文的文體特徵 (A tentative discussion of the generic features of China's prose travel accounts). *Heze shizhuan xuebao* 荷澤師專學報 2 (2001): 1–7, 89.

Zhu Jianxin 朱劍心, ed. *Wan Ming xiaopin xuanzhu* 晚明小品選注 (Selections of vignettes from the late Ming with annotations), Taibei: Shangwu Yinshuguan, 1964.

Zhu Yaoting 朱耀廷 and Gong Bin 巩濱, eds. *Zhongguo gudai youji* 中國古代遊記 (Travel accounts from China's ancient eras). Beijing: Beijing Daxue Chubanshe, 2007.

Ziegler, Delphine. "The Cult of the Wuyi Mountains and Its Cultivation of the Past: A Topo-cultural Perspective." *Cahiers d'Extrême-Asie* 10 (1998): 255–86.

GLOSSARY/INDEX

Chinese language sources appear first by their translated titles, e.g., *Accounts of Rites* (Liji 禮記), "Account of Five Terrace Mountain" (Wutai Shan ji 五臺山記). **Chinese government organ names and office titles** are listed by their English translations, e.g., Department of State Affairs (Shangshu Sheng 尚書省), Court Gentleman (Langguan 郎官). **Chinese terms** appear first according to Hanyu Pinyin spelling and Chinese characters, followed by an English translation in parentheses, e.g., *nan* 楠 (camphor trees), *changran* 悵然 (chagrined; dissatisfied), *ma han xue* 馬汗血 (horses that sweat blood). **Chinese place-names** appear in one of two ways: either in Hanyu Pinyin (examples would include larger geographic units such Hunan 湖南, Guiji 會稽, and Hangzhou 杭州) or, in cases where a more local toponym merits translation, an English version is provided first, as in Big Thunder Garrison (Dalei Shu 大雷戍), Stone Chamber Mountain (Shishi Shan 石室山), Purple Creek (Zixi 紫溪).